ADVENTURE TOURISM

ADVENTURE TOURISM

By

Thomas Walsh

DISCOVERY PUBLISHING HOUSE PVT. LTD.

NEW DELHI-110 002

Published by:

Namit Wasan

DISCOVERY PUBLISHING HOUSE PVT. LTD.

4383/4B, Ansari Road, Darya Ganj

New Delhi-110 002 (India)

Phone : +91-11-23279245, 23253475, 43596065

E-mail : discoverybooksindia@gmail.com

discoverypublishinghouse@gmail.com

web : www.discoverypublishinggroup.com

***Reprinted:* 2019**

***First Published:* 2011**

ISBN: 978-81-8356-892-0

Adventure Tourism

Printed at:

Infinity Imaging Systems

Delhi

PREFACE

Adventure recreation refers to active and outdoor activities such as backpacking (wilderness), rafting, climbing, and outdoor survival. A few universities give degrees in adventure recreation, which aim to teach graduates how to run a business in the field of adventure recreation. Along with hands-on training on activities included in adventure recreation, basic courses needed for any business, such as accounting, are required to obtain a degree. Some adventure recreation businesses cater to tourists, while others, such as indoor rock climbing, appeal to people wanting to be active on a regular basis.

Mountain biking has become increasingly more specialized for travel over technical dirt (hiking width) trails called single track, while road cycling focuses increasingly on maximizing travel over pavement. Traditional bicycle touring is typically considered road biking with travel primarily on paved roads, often carrying heavy loads of camping gear. Rough riding, in contrast, incorporates travel on both dirt and pavement; it stresses efficient travel on any surface or topography, a greater freedom of travel, and self-reliance.

Hiking is one of the fundamental outdoor activities on which many others are based. Many beautiful places can only be reached overland by hiking, and enthusiasts regard hiking as the best way to see nature. Hikers see it as better than a tour in a vehicle of any kind (or on an animal; see horseback riding) because the hiker's senses are not intruded upon by distractions such as windows, engine noise, airborne dust and fellow passengers. Hiking over long distances or over difficult terrain requires both the physical ability to do the hike and the knowledge of the route and its pitfalls.

Adventure tourism gains much of its excitement by allowing its participants to step outside of their comfort zone. This may be from experiencing culture shock or through the performance of acts, that require significant effort and involve some degree of risk (real or perceived) and/or physical danger. This may include activities such as mountaineering, trekking, bungee jumping, mountain biking, rafting, zip-lining and rock climbing. Some obscure forms of adventure travel include disaster and ghetto tourism. Other rising forms of adventure travel include social and jungle tourism.

Contents

CHAPTER 1

ADVENTURE TRAVEL

Adventure travel is a type of tourism, involving exploration or travel to remote, exotic and possibly hostile areas. Adventure tourism is rapidly growing in popularity, as tourists seek different kinds of vacations. According to the U.S. based Adventure Travel Trade Association, adventure travel may be any tourist activity, including two of the following three components: a physical activity, a cultural exchange or interaction and engagement with nature.

Adventure tourism gains much of its excitement by allowing its participants to step outside of their comfort zone. This may be from experiencing culture shock or through the performance of acts, that require significant effort and involve some degree of risk (real or perceived) and/or physical danger. This may include activities such as mountaineering, trekking, bungee jumping, mountain biking, rafting, zip-lining and rock climbing. Some obscure forms of adventure travel include disaster and ghetto tourism. Other rising forms of adventure travel include social and jungle tourism.

Access to inexpensive consumer technology, with respect to Global Positioning Systems, flashpacking, social networking and photography, have increased the worldwide interest in adventure travel. The interest in independent adventure travel has also increased as more specialist travel websites emerge offering previously niche locations and sports.

Types of Adventure Travel

Accessible Tourism

There is a trend for developing tourism specifically for the disabled. Adventure travel for the disabled has become a $13 billion USD a year industry in North America. Some adventure travel destinations offer diverse programs and job opportunities developed specifically for the disabled.

Disaster Tourism

Disaster tourism is the act of traveling to a disaster area as a matter of curiosity. The behavior can be a nuisance if it hinders rescue, relief, and recovery operations. If not done because of pure curiosity, it can be cataloged as disaster learning.

Ethno Tourism

Ethno tourism refers to visiting a foreign location for the sake of observing the indigenous members of its society for the sake of non-scientific gain. Some extreme forms of this include attempting to make first contact with tribes that are protected from outside visitors.

Two controversial issues associated with ethno tourism include bringing natives into contact with diseases they do not have immunities for, and the possible degradation or destruction of a unique culture and/or language.

Ghetto Tourism

Ghetto tourism refers to the growing popularity of tourism in ghettos.

Jungle Tourism

Jungle tourism is a rising subcategory of adventure travel defined by active multifaceted physical means of travel in the jungle regions of the earth. Although similar in many respects to adventure travel, jungle tourism pertains specifically to the context of region, culture and activity. According to the Glossary of Tourism Terms, jungle tours have become a major component of green tourism in tropical destinations and are a relatively recent phenomenon of western international tourism.

Overland Travel

Overland travel or overlanding refers to an "overland journey" - perhaps originating with Marco Polo's first overland expedition in the 13th century from Venice to the Chinese court of Kublai Khan. Today overlanding is a form of extended adventure holiday, embarking on a long journey, often in a group. Overland companies provide a converted truck or a bus plus a tour leader, and the group travels together overland for a period of weeks or months.

Since the 1960s overlanding has been a popular means of travel between destinations across Africa, Europe, Asia (particularly India), the Americas and Australia. The "Hippie trail" of the 60s and 70s saw thousands of young westerners travelling through the Middle East to India and Nepal.

Urban Exploration

Urban exploration (often shortened as urbex or UE) is the examination of the normally unseen or off-limits parts of urban areas or industrial facilities. Urban exploration is also commonly referred to as infiltration, although some people consider infiltration to be more closely associated with the exploration of active or inhabited sites. It may also be referred to as "draining" (when exploring drains) "urban spelunking", "urban caving", or "building hacking".

The nature of this activity presents various risks, including both physical danger and the possibility of arrest and punishment. Many, but not all, of the activities associated with urban exploration could be considered trespassing or other violations of local or regional laws.

Adventure

An adventure is an activity that is perceived to involve risk, danger or exciting experiences.

The term is often used to refer to activities with some potential for physical danger, such as skydiving, mountain climbing, breaking and entering, committing misdemeanors, and participating in extreme sports. The term also broadly refers to any enterprise that is potentially fraught with physical, financial or psychological risk, such as a business venture, a love affair, or other major life undertakings.

Adventurous experiences create psychological and physiological arousal, which can be interpreted as negative or positive and which can be detrimental as stated by the Yerkes-Dodson law. For some people, adventure becomes a major pursuit in and of itself. According to adventurer André Malraux, in his La Condition Humaine (1933), "If a man is not ready to risk his life, where is his dignity?". Similarly, Helen Keller famously stated that "Life is either a daring adventure or nothing."

Outdoor adventurous activities are typically undertaken for the purposes of recreation or excitement: examples are adventure racing and adventure tourism. Adventurous activities can also lead to gains in knowledge, such as those undertaken by explorers and pioneers. Adventure education intentionally uses challenging experiences for learning.

Adventure in Mythology

The oldest and most widespread stories in the world are stories of adventure. Mythologist Joseph Campbell discussed his notion of the monomyth in his book, The Hero with a Thousand Faces. Campbell proposed that the heroic mythological stories from culture to culture followed a similar underlying pattern, starting with the "call to adventure", followed by a hazardous journey, and eventual triumph. The adventure novel exhibits these "protagonist on adventurous journey" characteristics as do many popular feature films, such as Star Wars.

Adventurers

An adventurer is a person who bases his lifestyle or their fortunes on adventurous acts. An adventurer or adventuress is a term that usually takes one of three meanings:

- One whose travels are unusual and often exotic, though not so unique as to qualify as exploration.
- One who lives by their wits.
- One who takes part in a risky or speculative course of action for profit or position.

In fiction, the adventurer figure or Picaro may be regarded as a descendant of the knight-errant of Medieval romance. Like the knight, the adventurer roams through episodic encounters, usually involving wealth, romance, or fighting. Unlike the knight, the adventurer was a realistic figure, often lower class or otherwise impoverished, who is forced to make his way to fortune, often by deceit. Also, an adventurer is a roguish hero of low social class who lives by his or her wits in a corrupt society. The picaresque novel originated in Spain in the middle of the fifteenth century. Novels such as Lazarillo de Tormes were influential across Europe. Throughout the eighteenth century, a great number of novels featured bold, amoral, adventuring protagonists, who made their way into wealth and happiness, sometimes with and sometimes without the moral conversion that generally accompanies the Spanish model.

Under Victorian morality the term, used without qualifiers, came to imply a person of low moral character, often someone trying to marry for money.

In comic books such as Official Handbook of the Marvel Universe and Who's Who: The Definitive Directory of the DC Universe, the term "adventurer" is used as a synonym for "super-hero" when listing a character's occupation.

In role-playing games, the player characters are often professional adventurers, who earn wealth and fame by adventure, such as undertaking hazardous missions, exploring ruins, and slaying monsters. This stereotype is strong enough that the adventurers can often be used as a synonym for the player characters. Non-player character groups of adventurers can also exist, and can be an interesting encounter for the players.

Adventure Recreation

Adventure recreation refers to active and outdoor activities such as backpacking (wilderness), rafting, climbing, and outdoor survival. A few universities give degrees in adventure recreation, which aim to teach graduates how to run a business in the field of adventure recreation. Along with hands-on training on activities included in adventure recreation, basic courses needed for any business, such as accounting, are required to obtain a degree. Some adventure recreation businesses cater to tourists, while others, such as indoor rock climbing, appeal to people wanting to be active on a regular basis.

In contemporary society, the term outdoor adventure generally implies an educational or recreational activity that is exciting and physically challenging. Adventure recreation can be any number of leisure pursuits which provide exposure to physical danger.

University Outdoor Recreation programs are becoming more popular in the United States. Universities often offer indoor rock climbing walls, equipment rental, ropes courses and trip programming.

Accessible Tourism

Accessible tourism is the ongoing endeavour to ensure tourist destinations, products and services are accessible to all people, regardless of their physical limitations, disabilities or age. It encompasses publicly and privately owned tourist locations. The term has been defined by Darcy and Dickson (2009, p34) as:

Accessible tourism enables people with access requirements, including mobility, vision, hearing and cognitive dimensions of access, to function independently and with equity and dignity through the delivery of universally designed tourism products, services and environments. This definition is inclusive of all people including those travelling with children in prams, people with disabilities and seniors .

Modern society is increasingly aware of concept of integration of people with disabilities. Issues such accessibility, design for all and universal design are featured in the international symposia of bodies such as the European Commission. Steps have been taken to promote guidelines and best practices, and major resources are now dedicated to this field.

A greater understanding of the accessible tourism market has been promoted through research commissioned by the European Commission where a stakeholder analysis has provided an insight into the complexities of accessible tourism. Similarly, the Australian Sustainable Tourism Cooperative Research Centre funded an Accessible Tourism Research Agenda that sought to outline a research base on which to develop the supply, demand and coordination/regulation information required to develop the market segment. The research agenda has now seen three other funded projects contribute towards a sound research base on which the tourism industry and government marketing authorities can now make more informed decisions.

As of 2008, there were more than 50 million persons with disabilities in Europe, and more than 600 million around the world. When expanded to include all beneficiaries of accessible tourism, as defined above, the number grows to some 130 million people affected in Europe alone. In addition to the social benefits, the market represents an opportunity for new investment and new service requirements, rarely provided by key players in the tourism sector.

According to ENAT, the European Network for Accessible Tourism, accessible tourism includes:

- Barrier-free destinations: infrastructure and facilities
- Transport: by air, land and sea, suitable for all users
- High quality services: delivered by trained staff
- Activities, exhibits, attractions: allowing participation in tourism by everyone
- Marketing, booking systems, web sites & services: information accessible to all

Specific Needs and Requirements

Specific problems found by travellers or tourists with disabilities include:

- Inaccessible, or only partly accessible, web sites
- Lack of accessible airport transfer
- Lack of wheelchair accessible vehicles
- Lack of well-adapted hotel rooms
- Lack of professional staff capable of dealing with accessibility issues
- Lack of reliable information about a specific attraction's level of accessibility
- Lack of accessible restaurants, bars, and other facilities
- Lack of adapted toilets in restaurants and public places
- Inaccessible streets and sidewalks
- Lack of technical aids and disability equipment such as wheelchairs, bath chairs and toilet raisers

Brief history

Europe and United States of America are home to the majority of the existing companies in this niche. However, around the world many companies are starting to appear as the result of a growing need, largely driven by senior tourism, due to increasing life expectancy in developed countries. Australian researchers

Portugal, Spain, the United Kingdom, Germany, France and other northern European countries are increasingly prepared to receive tourists in wheelchairs, and to provide disability equipment and wheelchair accessible transport.

BACKPACKING (TRAVEL)

Backpacking is a term that has historically been used to denote a form of low-cost, independent international travel. Terms such as independent travel and/or budget travel are often used interchangeably with backpacking. The factors that traditionally differentiate backpacking from other forms of tourism include but are not limited to the following: use of public transport as a means of travel, preference of youth hostels to traditional hotels, length of the trip vs. conventional vacations, use of a backpack, an interest in meeting the locals as well as seeing the sights.

The definition of a backpacker has evolved as travelers from different cultures and regions participate and will continue to do so, preventing an air-tight definition. Recent research has found that, "...backpackers constituted a heterogeneous group with respect to the diversity of rationales and meanings attached to their travel experiences. They also displayed a common commitment to a non-institutionalised form of travel, which was central to their self-identification as backpackers." Backpacking as a lifestyle and as a business has grown considerably in the 2000s as the commonplace of low-cost airlines, hostels or budget accommodation in many parts of the world, and digital communication and resources make planning, executing, and continuing a long-term backpacking trip easier than ever before.

History

While there is no definitive answer as to the precise origin of backpacking, its roots can be traced, at least partially, to the Hippie trail of the 1960s and 70s, which in turn followed sections of the old Silk Road. In fact, some backpackers today seek to re-create that journey, albeit in a more comfortable manner, while capitalizing on the current popularity of the green movement. Looking further into history, Giovanni Francesco Gemelli Careri has been cited by some as one of the world's first backpackers.

While travel along the old Hippie Trail has been rendered complicated since the early 80s due to unrest in Afghanistan, Iraq and Iran that continues today, backpacking has expanded to most regions of the world. In recent years, the increase of budget airlines and low-cost flights has contributed to this expansion. At present, new "hippie trails" are being formed towards Northern Africa in places such as Morocco and Tunisia and other destinations being reached by low-cost airlines.

Technological changes and improvements have also contributed to changes in backpacking. Traditionally backpackers did not travel with expensive electronic equipment such as laptop computers, digital cameras and PDAs due to concerns about theft, damage, and additional luggage weight. However, the desire to stay connected coupled with trends in lightweight electronics have given rise to the flashpacking trend, which has been in a state of continuous evolution in recent years. Simultaneous with a change in "what" they're carrying, backpacking is also becoming less and less reliant on the physical backpack in its initial form although the backpack can still be considered the primary luggage of backpackers.

Culture

Of importance in backpacking is a sense of authenticity. Backpacking is perceived as being more than a vacation, but a means of education. Backpackers want to experience the "real" destination rather than the packaged version often associated with mass tourism, which has led to the assertion that backpackers are anti-tourist. There is also the feeling of "sneaking backstage" and witnessing real life with more involvement with local people.

Criticism

Backpacking, like other forms of travel, remains controversial. Some of these criticisms date back to travelers' actions along the Hippie Trail. Criticism comes from many sides, including the host countries and other travelers who disagree with the actions of backpackers although the perception of backpackers seems to have improved as backpacking has become more mainstream. Erik Cohen notes that even though one of the primary aims of backpacking is to seek the authentic, the majority of backpackers spend most of their time interacting with other backpackers and interactions with locals are of "secondary importance".

Variants

Flashpacking

Flashpacking is a neologism used to refer to an affluent backpacker. Whereas backpacking is traditionally associated with budget travel and destinations that are relatively cheap, flashpacking has an association of more disposable income while traveling and has been defined simply as backpacking with a bigger budget.

A simple definition of the term Flashpacker can be thought of as backpacking with flash, or style. One school of thought defines the flashpacker as a rapidly growing segment of travelers who adhere to a modest accommodation and meal budget, while spending freely, even excessively, for activities at their chosen destination. Another school of thought defines flashpacking as an incongruous mix of 'slumming it' and luxury; of adventurous travel with those on a budget by day and sedate dining and comfortable accommodation by night. Flashpackers have been further defined as tech-savvy adventurers who often prefer to travel with a cell phone, digital camera, mp3 player and a laptop, although none of these is required in order to be a flashpacker. As with other forms of travel, the term flashpacker is mainly one of self-identification. The origin of the term itself is obscure.

The term also reflects a growing demographic of travelers who are forsaking traditional organized travel, venturing to destinations once the reserve of more adventurous backpackers, and the increasing number of individuals who leave well paid jobs or take career breaks, using the time to travel independently, but with greater comfort and many of the gadgets they are accustomed to at home. As a result, hostels are evolving and offering more up-market accommodation and facilities to those still traveling on a budget in order to obtain their business. Hostels have realized a need to evolve in order to meet the changing demands of travelers.

Gap-packing

"Gap-packing" is a neologism used typically to refer to people who backpack to several countries in a short period of time whilst on their gap year between school and university, or between university and their first job.

Backpacking (Wilderness)

Backpacking (in US; tramping, trekking, or bushwalking in other countries) combines hiking and camping in a single trip. A backpacker hikes into the backcountry to spend one or more nights there, and carries supplies and equipment to satisfy sleeping and eating needs.

Definition

An outdoor activity wherein a backpacker packs all of his or her gear into a backpack. This gear must include food, water, and shelter, or the means to obtain them, but very little else, and often in a more compact and simpler form than one would use for stationary camping. A backpacking trip must include at least one overnight stay in the wilderness (otherwise it is a day hike). Many backpacking trips last just a weekend (one or two nights), but long-distance expeditions may last weeks or months, sometimes aided by planned food and supply drops.

Backpacking camps are more spartan than ordinary camps. In areas that experience a regular traffic of backpackers, a hike-in camp might have a fire ring and a small wooden bulletin board with a map and some warning or information signs. Many hike-in camps are no more than level patches of ground without scrub or underbrush. In very remote areas, established camps do not exist at all, and travelers must choose appropriate camps themselves.

In some places, backpackers have access to lodging that is more substantial than a tent. In the more remote parts of Great Britain, bothies exist to provide simple (free) accommodation for backpackers. Another example is the High Sierra Camps in Yosemite National Park. Mountain huts provide similar accommodation in other countries, so being a member of a mountain hut organization is advantageous (perhaps required) to make use of their facilities. On other trails (e.g. the Appalachian Trail) there are somewhat more established shelters of a sort that offer a place for weary hikers to spend the night without needing to set up a tent.

Most backpackers purposely try to avoid impacting on the land through which they travel. This includes following established trails as much as possible, not removing anything, and not leaving residue in the backcountry. The Leave No Trace movement offers a set of guidelines for low-impact backpacking.

Professional Backpacking

For some people, backpacking is a necessary and integral part of their job.

In the US military a framed backpack is referred to as a "rucksack" or simply a "ruck". Soldiers who serve in the militaries of most nation-states usually receive at least some rudimentary backpacking training while infantrymen are often trained to a more advanced backpacking skill level. They share many common attributes with amateur backpackers: being self-contained, use of land-navigation skills and actively minimizing their environmental foot-print. There are, however, a few differences—such as the need to carry weapons, ammunition, and communication equipment, and sometimes the need to maintain "noise and light discipline", which means remaining silent and in darkness to avoid detection.

Other professional backpackers include scientific and academic researchers, professional guides, photographers, park-rangers and "search & rescue" personnel.

Motivation

People are drawn to backpacking primarily for recreation, to explore places that they consider beautiful and fascinating, many of which cannot be accessed in any other way. A backpacker can travel deeper into remote areas, away from people and their effects, than a day-hiker can. However, backpacking presents more advantages besides distance of travel. Many weekend trips cover routes that could be hiked in a single day, but people choose to backpack them anyway, for the experience of staying overnight.

These possibilities come with disadvantages. The weight of a pack, laden with supplies and gear, forces traditional backpackers to travel more slowly than day-hikers would, and it can become a nuisance and a distraction from enjoying the scenery. In addition, camp chores (such as pitching camp, breaking camp, and cooking) can easily consume several hours every day. However, with practice, much of this downtime can be removed from the day.

Backpackers face many risks, including adverse weather, difficult terrain, treacherous river crossings, and hungry or unpredictable animals (although the perceived danger from wild animals usually greatly exceeds the true risk). They are subject to illnesses, which run the gamut from simple dehydration to heat exhaustion, hypothermia, altitude sickness, physical injury, and giardiasis. The remoteness of backpacking locations exacerbates any mishap. However, these hazards do not deter backpackers who are properly prepared. Some simply accept danger as a risk that they must endure if they want to backpack; for others, the potential dangers actually enhance the allure of the wilderness.

Equipment

Almost all backpackers seek to minimize the weight and bulk of gear carried. A lighter pack causes less fatigue, injury and soreness, and allows the backpacker to travel longer distances. Every piece of equipment is evaluated for a balance of utility versus weight. Significant reductions in weight can usually be achieved with little sacrifice in equipment utility, though very lightweight equipment can be significantly more costly.

A large industry has developed to provide lightweight gear and food for backpackers. The gear includes the backpacks themselves, as well as ordinary camping equipment modified to reduce the weight, by either reducing the size, reducing the durability, or using lighter materials such as special plastics, alloys of aluminium, titanium, composite materials, impregnated fabrics and carbon fiber. Designers of portable stoves and tents have been particularly ingenious. Homemade gear is common too, such as the beverage-can stove.

Some backpackers use lighter and more compact gear than do others. The most radical measures taken in this regard are sometimes called ultralight backpacking.

Due to the emphasis on weight reduction, a practical joke common in some circles is to secretly pack a small but relatively heavy luxury item, such as a soft drink, into another backpacker's pack. Then, once the group stops for a rest, the perpetrator retrieves the item, thanks the bearer for carrying it, and consumes it.

Water

Backpackers often carry some water from the trailhead, to drink while walking. For short trips, they may carry enough to last the whole trip, but for long trips this is not practical. A backpacker needs anywhere from 2 to 8 litres (roughly 1/2 to 2 U.S. gallons), or more, per day, depending on conditions, making a water supply for more than a few days prohibitively heavy. 1 litre (1.1 US qt) of water weighs 1 kilogram (2.2 lb).

Backpackers may carry one to four litres of water, depending on conditions and availability. Although some backpacking camps in heavily-used areas provide potable water, it must usually be obtained from lakes and streams or preferably springs.

Many backpackers believe that drinking water needs treatment before consumption to protect against bacteria and protozoa. Some treatment methods include:

- boiling
- treatment with chemical tablets (such as chlorine and iodine)
- passing through ceramic or pressed solid chemical filters (in conjunction with chemical treatments)
- ultraviolet light-based systems

Recent research on the topic of consuming untreated water found in backcountry settings in the United States and Canada is beginning to suggest treatment is unnecessary. Cited in this report is a study of a collection of wilderness areas in the Western United States which found infiltrate levels to be well within safe drinking tolerances. Further research in this topic may eventually shift common opinion away from requiring treatment for most water sources.

Ultimately, it is important to research water conditions and sources in prospective backpacking locations in order to prepare appropriate gear. If water is unavailable, or if the water available will be unfit for treatment, backpackers may need to carry large amounts of water for long distances.

Water may be stored in bottles or in soft, collapsible hydration packs (bladders). Some backpackers store water in ordinary plastic beverage bottles, while others use special Lexan bottles or metal canteens.The most popular form of water transportation is the use of a Nalgene Bottle due to water measurements and being indestructible, For accessibility they may be carried by a shoulder strap or attached to the outside of a pack. Bladders are typically made of plastic, rubber, and/or fabric. They generally weigh little and are collapsible. Water bladders may be equipped with drinking hoses to allow use without requiring the bladder be removed from the pack. In spite of this convenience, bladders are more prone to leaking than bottles, particularly at the hose connections. Hoses also allow the hiker to lose track of the water supply in the bladder and to deplete it prematurely.

Food

Some backpackers enjoy cooking elaborate meals with fresh ingredients, particularly on short trips, and others carry the gear and take the time to catch fish or hunt small game for food. However, especially for long expeditions, most backpackers' food criteria are roughly the same: high food energy content, with long shelf life and low mass and volume. An additional concern is the mass and volume of any equipment required to cook the food; while Dutch oven and campfire cookery are historically popular, small liquid-fuel campstoves and ultralight cooking pots ("billycans") made of aluminum or titanium are more common in modern usage due to weight limitations and fire restrictions in many locales.

Ordinary household foods used on backpacking trips include cheese, crackers, bread, sausage, fruit, peanut butter, and pasta.

Popular snack foods include trail mix, easily prepared at home; nuts, convenient and nutritious energy bars, chocolate, and other forms of candy, which provide quick energy and flavor. Traditional outdoor food includes dried foodstuffs such as jerky or pemmican, and also products like oatmeal (which can also be consumed raw in emergency situations). Household food items are typically repackaged in zippered plastic bags.

Most backpackers avoid canned food, except for meats or small delicacies. Metal cans and glass jars and their contents are usually heavy, and like all trash the empties must be carried back out.

For dinners, many hikers use specially manufactured, pre-cooked food that can be eaten hot. It is often sold in large, stiff bags that double as eating vessels. One common variety of special backpacking food is freeze-dried food, which can be quickly reconstituted by adding hot water. One can also purchase a commercial food dehydrator which removes the majority of water from a pre-cooked meal. To eat, water is mixed in with the meal several minutes before eating and allowed to rehydrate before heating. Some various distributors of this are Backpackers Pantry and Mountain House. Another kind of special backpacking food is UHT-packaged without dehydration, and can be reheated with a special, water-activated chemical heater. This technology originated with the U.S. military's Meal Ready-to-Eat ("MRE"), but is now produced also for the commercial market. The small chemical heater obviates the need for a portable stove and fuel, however the added weight of the MRE's and their packaging reduce the weight advantage. MRE's can be useful to backpackers for several reasons:

- They do not need to be rehydrated or heated which is useful in areas where flame is not allowed, and water is scarce (Most of Australia)
- They are very durably packaged
- A single MRE contains a full meal complete with snack and dessert

- They offer a great deal of variety in each meal, including condiments
- They are individually packaged inside the "brown plastic wrapper", so you can place individual components in various pockets and "eat on the move".

As more and more "big box" retail stores carry pre-packaged dehydrated foods (such as Mountain House Brand) however, it is becoming increasingly easier to buy packaged meals retail versus mail order, whereas MRE's are rarely carried in retail stores.

There is a genre of cookbooks specializing in trailside food and the special challenges inherent in backcountry cooking. Most such cookbooks espouse one of two philosophies; the first, generally used on short trips, involves planning out meals and preparing many ingredients in one's home kitchen before departure. The second method, bulk rationing, simply supplies the hiker with ingredients, allowing on-trail cooking with minimal prior planning, and is sometimes used for extended outings. A third form of the genre deals in Dutch oven cookery, which has considerable historical cachet (especially in countries such as the United States with a long pioneer tradition), but is dependent on suitable locations for a campfire.

Winter Backpacking

Although backpacking in the winter is rewarding, it can be dangerous and generally requires more gear. Backpackers may need skis or snowshoes to traverse deep snow, or crampons and an ice axe to cross ice in colder climates. Cotton clothing, which absorbs moisture and chills the body, is particularly dangerous in cold weather, so backpackers stick to synthetic materials or materials that won't hold moisture. Special low-temperature sleeping bags and tents can be expensive, but will be more comfortable than many layers of warm clothing. However when hiking in cold weather it is always better to hike with varying layers of clothing so that as the body heats up layers can be taken off without causing the wearer to sweat or become very chilled.

Skills and Safety

- Survival skills are handy for peace of mind: In case the weather, terrain or environment is more challenging than prepared for.
- Navigation and orienteering are useful to find the trailhead, then find and follow a route to a desired sequence of destinations, and then an exit. In case of disorientation, orienteering skills are important to determine where you are and formulate a route to somewhere more desirable. At their most basic, navigation skills allow you to choose the correct sequence of trails to follow.
- First aid: effectively dealing with minor injuries (splinters, punctures, sprains) is considered by many a fundamental backcountry skill. More subtle, but maybe even more important, is recognizing and promptly treating hypothermia, heat stroke, dehydration and hypoxia, as these are rarely encountered in daily life.
- Leave No Trace is the backpacker's version of the golden rule: To have beautiful and pristine places to enjoy, help make them. At a minimum, don't make them worse.
- Distress signaling is a skill of last resort.

Backpacking with Animals

Some backpackers bring along a pack animal, such as a horse, llama, or dog to help carry the weight of the gear. These animals need special considerations when accompanying backpackers on a trip. Some areas restrict the use of horses and other pack animals. The Great Basin National Park does not allow pets at all in the back country areas. Like their human counterparts, pack animals require special backpacking gear like a variety of leads, harnesses, and packs. Dog packs are widely available at outdoor sporting goods stores. Wild animals can be attracted to pack animals so extreme caution is necessary when bringing domesticated animals into the back country areas. Some trails like the Libby Creek Quartet have pre-made corrals which specifically cater to large pack animals. Other animals, like dogs, need few special arrangements while backpacking overnight.

Chapter 2

Various Type of Adventure Tourism

Disaster tourism

Disaster tourism is the act of traveling to a disaster area as a matter of curiosity. The behavior can be a nuisance if it hinders rescue, relief, and recovery operations.

If not done because of pure curiosity, it can be cataloged as disaster learning.

Hurricane Katrina

Disaster tourism took hold in the Greater New Orleans Area in the aftermath of Hurricane Katrina. There are now guided bus tours to neighborhoods that were severely damaged by storm-related flooding. Some local residents have criticized these tours as unethical, because the tour companies are profiting from the misery of their communities and families. The Army Corps of Engineers has noted that traffic from tour buses and other tourist vehicles have interfered with the movement of trucks and other cleanup equipment on single-lane residential roads. Furthermore, during the first six months after the storm, most of these neighborhoods lacked electricity, phone access, street signs, or access to emergency medical or police assistance. Simply traveling to these neighborhoods was hazardous. For these reasons, organized disaster tours are now banned from two of the most severely damaged areas in the city, the Lower 9th and St. Bernard Parish near the Industrial Canal.

On the other hand, such communities as Gentilly and Lakeview, along the 17th Street Canal, have welcomed organized tour groups as a means to publicize the scale of the destruction and attract more aid to the city. Much of the recovery effort in the New Orleans relies on out-of-state volunteers and donations. Numerous non-profit organization, including Habitat for Humanity International and Catholic Charities, have converged on the city to gut and rebuild homes. There is also a movement by local residents to bring congressmen and other national leaders to the city and view the damage in person, since recovery efforts have been hampered by the failure of many homeowners and businesses to receive claims from their insurance providers.

2010 Eruption of Eyjafjallajökull

Eyjafjallajökull, on Iceland, began erupting on 20 March 2010. At this time, about 500 farmers and their families from the areas of Fljótshlíð, Eyjafjöll, and Landeyjar were evacuated overnight, but allowed to return to their farms and homes after Civil Protection Department risk assessment. On 14 April, 2010, Eyjafjallajökull erupted for the second time, requiring 800 people to be evacuated.

Disaster tourism quickly sprang up in the wake of the first eruption, with tour companies offering trips to see the volcano. However, the ash cloud from the second eruption disrupted air traffic over Great Britain and most of northern and western Europe, making it difficult to travel to Iceland even though Iceland's airspace itself remained open throughout.

ACCESSIBLE TOURISM

Accessible tourism is the ongoing endeavour to ensure tourist destinations, products and services are accessible to all people, regardless of their physical limitations, disabilities or age. It encompasses publicly and privately owned tourist locations. The term has been defined by Darcy and Dickson as:

Accessible tourism enables people with access requirements, including mobility, vision, hearing and cognitive dimensions of access, to function independently and with equity and dignity through the delivery of universally designed tourism products, services and environments. This definition is inclusive of all people including those travelling with children in prams, people with disabilities and seniors .

Overview

Modern society is increasingly aware of concept of integration of people with disabilities. Issues such accessibility, design for all and universal design are featured in the international symposia of bodies such as the European Commission. Steps have been taken to promote guidelines and best practices, and major resources are now dedicated to this field.

A greater understanding of the accessible tourism market has been promoted through research commissioned by the European Commission where a stakeholder analysis has provided an insight into the complexities of accessible tourism. Similarly, the Australian Sustainable Tourism Cooperative Research Centre funded an Accessible Tourism Research Agenda that sought to outline a research base on which to develop the supply, demand and coordination/regulation information required to develop the market segment. The research agenda has now seen three other funded projects contribute towards a sound research base on which the tourism industry and government marketing authorities can now make more informed decisions.

As of 2008, there were more than 50 million persons with disabilities in Europe, and more than 600 million around the world. When expanded to include all beneficiaries of accessible tourism, as defined above, the number grows to some 130 million people affected in Europe alone. In addition to the social benefits, the market represents an opportunity for new investment and new service requirements, rarely provided by key players in the tourism sector.

According to ENAT, the European Network for Accessible Tourism, accessible tourism includes:

- Barrier-free destinations: infrastructure and facilities
- Transport: by air, land and sea, suitable for all users
- High quality services: delivered by trained staff
- Activities, exhibits, attractions: allowing participation in tourism by everyone
- Marketing, booking systems, web sites & services: information accessible to all

Specific Needs and Requirements

Specific problems found by travellers or tourists with disabilities include:

- Inaccessible, or only partly accessible, web sites
- Lack of accessible airport transfer
- Lack of wheelchair accessible vehicles
- Lack of well-adapted hotel rooms
- Lack of professional staff capable of dealing with accessibility issues
- Lack of reliable information about a specific attraction's level of accessibility
- Lack of accessible restaurants, bars, and other facilities
- Lack of adapted toilets in restaurants and public places
- Inaccessible streets and sidewalks

- Lack of technical aids and disability equipment such as wheelchairs, bath chairs and toilet raisers

Brief History

Europe and United States of America are home to the majority of the existing companies in this niche. However, around the world many companies are starting to appear as the result of a growing need, largely driven by senior tourism, due to increasing life expectancy in developed countries. Australian researchers

Portugal, Spain, the United Kingdom, Germany, France and other northern European countries are increasingly prepared to receive tourists in wheelchairs, and to provide disability equipment and wheelchair accessible transport.

GHETTO TOURISM

Ghetto tourism refers to the growing popularity of tourism in ghettos.

Studies

Ghetto tourism was first studied in 2005 by Michael Stephens in the cultural-criticism journal, PopMatters. Ghetto tourism includes all forms of entertainment — "gangsta rap," video games, movies, TV, and other forms that allow consumers to traffic in the inner city without leaving home.

As Stevens says, "digital media achieves more detailed simulations of reality. The quest for thrills mutates into a desire, not just to see bigger and better explosions, but to cross class and racial boundaries and experience other lifestyles." International tourists to New York City in the 1980s led to a successful tourism boom in Harlem. By 2002, Philadelphia began offering tours of blighted inner-city neighborhoods. After Hurricane Katrina, tours were offered in flood-ravaged Lower Ninth Ward, a notoriously violent and poor section of New Orleans.

Musical Influence

With respect to the vast historic references to landmarks, neighborhoods and streetscapes within music, ghetto or "urban tourism" often encompasses travel to destinations made famous by direct or indirect mention by popular artists. Travel to certain parts of Detroit that include 8 Mile Road, known for the role the travel route played in the similarly titled 8 Mile film starring Eminem, or to Crenshaw Boulevard in South Central Los Angeles, a metropolitan area that inspired an entire generation of pioneering musical influence, could potentially be included as urban tourism. The Jane-Finch area of Toronto, Canada is gaining notoriety as another area in transition.

Graffiti Travel

Artists have been featured in The Source magazine and some individuals travel to different urban settings to adapt and learn new graffiti styles.

JUNGLE TOURISM

Jungle tourism is a rising subcategory of adventure travel defined by active multifaceted physical means of travel in the jungle regions of the earth. Although similar in many respects to adventure travel, jungle tourism pertains specifically to the context of region, culture and activity. According to the Glossary of Tourism Terms, jungle tours have become a major component of green tourism in tropical destinations and are a relatively recent phenomenon of Western international tourism.

Of the regions that take part in tourism-driven sustainable development practices and eco tourism, Mexican, Central and South American practices are the most pervasive in the industry; notably Mayan jungle excursions. Other regions include jungle territories in Africa, Australia, and the South Pacific.

Jungle Tourism in Central and South America

The majority of jungle tour operators are concentrated in what is known as the Mayan World or "Ruta Maya". The Mayan World encompasses five different countries that hosted the entirety of the Mayan Civilization: Mexico, Guatemala, Belize, Honduras and El Salvador. Most tours consist of visits to popular Mayan archaeological sites such as Tikal, Guatemala, Chichen Itza, and Copan. These day visits will usually consist of a guided tour of a heavily tourist-concentrated Mayan and archaeological site. Tikal and Chichen Itza are prime examples of popular day-visit sites. Such sites involve a tour guide, designated either by the state government or by a private company, for the tourists. These tour guides are predominantly trained professionals, certified to take large parties of fifty through heavily populated archaeological sites.

Although most of the visits to these more prominent sites involve day trips, there are also many jungle tour operators that showcase less-known, remote Mayan jungle ruins such as Nakum, Yaxha, and El Mirador. These tours involve much more preparation, time and funding to explore as they are usually in very remote and generally inaccessible regions of the Mayan jungles. These ruins and sites are reached by alternative and physically taxing means of travel such as bicycle, canoe, horseback or hiking. This is what essentially differentiates jungle tourism from any other sort of adventure travel tours. There are several tour operators that will even employ the use of machetes during tours.

Another significant and noteworthy difference is the fact that the majority of tour operators that travel deep into the Central and South American Jungle will cap the number of persons traveling in the group at ten to fifteen. This is done to minimize the impact on the jungle flora and fauna. Federal laws in some countries prohibit any given group large than fifteen people traveling through the Mayan jungle, a generally protected region, but very limited resources have kept such practices from occurring under the radar.

Overland Travel

Overland travel or overlanding refers to an "overland journey" - perhaps originating with Marco Polo's first overland expedition in the 13th century from Venice to the Chinese court of Kublai Khan. Today overlanding is a form of extended adventure holiday, embarking on a long journey, often in a group. Overland companies provide a converted truck or a bus plus a tour leader, and the group travels together overland for a period of weeks or months.

Since the 1960s overlanding has been a popular means of travel between destinations across Africa, Europe, Asia (particularly India), the Americas and Australia. The "Hippie trail" of the 60s and 70s saw thousands of young westerners travelling through the Middle East to India and Nepal.

Rail

At 9,288km the Trans-Siberian Railway is one of the longest overland journeys in existence today, taking 7 days to reach Vladivostok from Moscow, and providing an alternative to air travel for journeys between Europe and Asia.

The Indian Pacific railway, completed in 1970, links Sydney and Perth in Australia. Covering 4,343km over 4 days, the railway includes the longest stretch of straight railway line in the world.

The introduction of Japan's high speed railway To-kaido-Shinkansen in 1964 changed the face of rail travel. The railway has carried more than 4 billion passengers and its new N700 series trains are capable of 300 km/h. France's TGV holds the record for the fastest train, with a top speed of more than 500 km/h, making it faster than air travel for many journeys within the country.

The Thomas Cook Overseas Timetable is the first choice for detailed international rail information. Various online resources can also be found at websites including the excellent Man in Seat 61, and Grounded Travel.

Road

The Silk Route or Silk Road historically connects the Mediterranean with Persia and China. Today the route refers to overland journeys between Europe and China, taking either the northern route - through Russia and Kazakhstan - or the southern route - through Turkey, Iran, Pakistan and North India - to Urumqi or Xian in China. These routes are still popular today, with companies such as Oasis Overland and Odyssey Overland offering tours on the southern route.

Trans Africa Overland Routes

Some of the longest and more traditional overland routes are in Africa. The Cairo to Cape Town and v.v. route covers more than 10,000km and currently usually follows the Nile River through Egypt and Sudan, continuing to Kenya, Tanzania, Malawi, Zimbabwe, Botswana and Namibia along the way. In 1959 the pioneering American trailer manufacturer Wally Byam and a caravan of trailers travelled the route from Cape Town to Cairo via Rhodesia (now Zimbabwe and Zambia), Belgian Congo (now Democratic Republic of Congo), Uganda and north from Kenya.

From the mid 1980s, the non-operation of the Aswan to Wadi Halfa ferry between Egypt and Sudan as well instability in Sudan, northern Uganda and Ethiopia, made the journey impossible. In recent years however, the Cape to Cairo and Cairo to Cape Town route has again become possible and increasingly popular both with commercial overland trucks carrying groups of 20 or so paying passengers as well as independent travellers on motorbikes or with 4WD vehicles.

The traditional Trans Africa route is from London to Nairobi, Kenya and Cape Town, South Africa . The route started in the 1970s and became very popular with small companies using old Bedford four wheel drive trucks carrying about 24 people each, plus lots of independents, normally run by groups of friends in 4x4 Land Rovers heading out of London from

November to March every year. The usual route was from Morocco to Algeria with a Sahara desert crossing into Niger in West Africa, continuing to Nigeria. This was followed by a month long journey likened to Joseph Conrad's "Heart of Darkness" through the forests of Zaire (now Democratic Republic of Congo), surfacing into the relatively modern world in Kenya via Uganda. From Kenya the last leg was south through Tanzania to either Zimbabwe or South Africa.

This route has changed dramatically due to border closures and political instability creating no-go zones. The route has reversed itself somewhat over the last few years, with trucks now crossing from the north to the south of Africa, closely following the west coast all the way from Morocco to Cape Town with the biggest change in the route being made possible by the opening of Angola to tourism. The journey then continues through Southern and East Africa from Cape Town to Nairobi and on to Cairo.

Other Overland Routes

In Africa, commercial overland travel began with the Trans Africa and Cape to Cairo described above. From the mid 1980s East and Southern Africa became more sought after by tourists and Nairobi to Cape Town is now the most travelled overland route in Africa. As more tourists look for adventure trips that fit in to their annual holiday, shorter sections of overland routes have become available such as two to three week round trip from Nairobi taking in Kenya and Uganda.

Istanbul to Cairo, via Syria and Jordan, is a classic overland route . It is a route that has been travelled for centuries, particularly during the Ottoman empire. Historically it overlapped with the Hajj, with many people covering all or part of the route as part of their pilgrimage to Mecca. Backpackers discovered it in the '70s and '80s, with hippies searching for spiritual peace who departed to Jerusalem from Istanbul instead of going to India via Iran, Afghanistan and

Pakistan. After the peace treaty between Egypt and Israel, onward travel from Jerusalem to Cairo became a possibility. It is now well travelled by backpackers and overland companies alike although the amount of travellers journeying the route can be affected by any unrest in neighbouring countries.

Urban Exploration

Urban exploration (often shortened as urbex or UE) is the examination of the normally unseen or off-limits parts of urban areas or industrial facilities. Urban exploration is also commonly referred to as infiltration, although some people consider infiltration to be more closely associated with the exploration of active or inhabited sites. It may also be referred to as "draining" (when exploring drains) "urban spelunking", "urban caving", or "building hacking".

The nature of this activity presents various risks, including both physical danger and the possibility of arrest and punishment. Many, but not all, of the activities associated with urban exploration could be considered trespassing or other violations of local or regional laws, including—but not limited to—invasion of privacy and certain broadly-interpreted anti-terrorism laws.

Targets of Exploration

Urban explorers often attempt some or all of these subsets of urban exploration.

Abandonments

Ventures into abandoned structures are perhaps the most common example of urban exploration. At times, sites are entered first by locals, and may sport large amounts of graffiti and other acts of vandalism. Explorers face various risks in abandoned structures including collapsing roofs and floors, broken glass, guard dogs, the presence of chemicals and other harmful substances, most notably asbestos, hostile squatters and motion detectors. Some explorers wear respirators to protect their airways and proper attire to protect their bodies.

Although targets of exploration vary from one country to another, high-profile abandonments include amusement parks, grain elevators, factories, power plants, missile silos, fallout shelters, hospitals, asylums, schools, poor houses, and sanatoriums.

Many explorers find decay of uninhabited space to be profoundly beautiful and some are also proficient freelance photographers. Abandoned locations can be, at times, heavily guarded with motion sensors and active security. Others are more easily accessible and carry less risk of discovery. An important goal, overall, of exploring a location is to gain access, perform your task, and remove yourself undetected, unscathed, causing no harm to others or that which surrounds you. Abandoned sites are also popular among historians, preservationists, architects, archaeologists, industrial archaeologists, and ghost hunters.

Active Buildings

Another aspect of urban exploration is the practice of exploring active or in use buildings which includes gaining access to secured or "member-only" areas, mechanical rooms, roofs, elevator rooms, abandoned floors and other normally unseen parts of working buildings. The term "infiltration" is often associated with the exploration of active structures. People entering restricted areas may be committing trespass and civil prosecution may result.

Catacombs

Catacombs such as those found in Paris, Rome, Odessa and Naples have been investigated by urban explorers. The Mines of Paris, comprising much of the underground tunnels that are not open to public tourism like the catacombs, have been considered the "Holy Grail" by some due to their extensive nature and history. Explorers of these are known as cataphiles or Splooshers.

Sewers and Storm Drains

Entry into storm drains, or draining, is another common form of urban exploration. Groups devoted to the task have arisen, such as the Cave Clan in Australia. Draining has a specialized set of guidelines, the foremost of which is "When it rains, no drains!" The dangers of becoming entrapped, washed away, or killed increase dramatically during a heavy rainfall.

A small subset of explorers enter sanitary sewers. Sometimes they are the only connection to caves or other subterranean features. Sewers are among the most dangerous locations to explore owing to extremely high risks of poisoning by buildups of toxic gas (commonly methane and hydrogen sulfide). There have been numerous fatalities around the world where people are overcome by toxic gas from sewers.

Transit Tunnels

Exploring active and abandoned subway and underground railway tunnels, bores and stations is often considered to be trespassing and can result in civil prosecution. As a result, this type of exploration is rarely publicized. One important exception to this is the abandoned subway of Rochester, NY, the only American city to have an abandoned, formerly used, subway system.

Utility Tunnels

Universities and other large institutions, such as hospitals, often distribute steam for heating buildings and autoclaves from a central heating plant. These high pressure steam pipes are generally run through utility tunnels, which are often accessible solely for the purposes of maintenance. Many of these steam tunnels, such as those on college campuses, often also have a tradition of exploration by its students. This was once called vadding at MIT, though students there now refer to it as roof and tunnel hacking.

Steam tunnels, in general, have been secured heavily in recent years, due to their use for carrying network backbones and perceived risk of their use in terrorist activities, safety and liability.

Some steam tunnels have dirt floors, no efficient lighting and have temperatures upwards of 45 °C (113 °F). Others have concrete floors, bright light, and feature a cool low-grade temperature. Most steam tunnels have large intake fans to bring in fresh air and push the hot air out the back. Most active steam tunnels do not contain airborne asbestos but proper breathing protection may be required for other hazards. It is wise to take proper care inside active utility tunnels, since pipes can spew boiling hot water from leaky valves, puddles pool at your feet, and forceful steam may leak inward resulting in burns and slips.

Popularity

The rise in the popularity of urban exploration can be attributed to its increased media attention. Recent television shows, such as Urban Explorers on the Discovery Channel, MTV's Fear, and the Ghost Hunting exploits of The Atlantic Paranormal Society have packaged the hobby for a popular audience. Talks and exhibits on urban exploration have appeared at the 5th and 6th Hackers on Planet Earth Conference, complementing numerous newspaper articles and interviews.

With the rise in the relative popularity of the hobby due to this increased focus, there has been increasing discussion on whether the extra attention has been beneficial to urban exploration as a whole. The unspoken rule of urban exploring is "take nothing but photographs, leave nothing but footprints", but because of the rising popularity, many individuals who may have other intentions are creating a concern among many property owners.

Safety and Legality

Urban exploration is a hobby that comes with a number of inherent dangers. Storm water drains are not designed with human access as their primary use. They can be subject to flash flooding and bad air. There have been a number of deaths in storm water drains, but these are usually during floods, and are normally not Urban Explorers.

Many old abandoned structures feature hazards such as unstable structures, unsafe floors, asbestos, carbon monoxide, carbon dioxide, exposed electrical wires and entrapment hazards.

Asbestos is a long term health risk for urban explorers, along with breathing in contaminants from dried bird faeces, otherwise known as Pigeon Lung. Urban explorers may use dust masks and respirators to alleviate this danger. Some sites are occasionally used by substance abusers for either recreation or disposal, and there may be used and/or infected syringe needles en route, such as those commonly used with heroin.

The growing popularity of the activity has resulted not just in increased attention from explorers, but also from vandals and Law Enforcement. The illicit aspects of urban exploring, which may include trespassing and breaking and entering , have brought along with them critical articles in mainstream newspapers.

In Australia, the web-site of the Sydney Cave Clan was shut down by lawyers for the Roads and Traffic Authority of New South Wales, after they raised concerns that the portal could "risk human safety and threaten the security of its infrastructure." Another web-site belonging to the Bangor Explorers Guild was criticized by the Maine State Police for potentially encouraging behavior that "could get someone hurt or killed." Likewise, the Toronto Transit Commission has also used the Internet to crimp Subway Tunnel Explorations, going as far as to send Investigators to various Explorers' homes.

Jeff Chapman, who authored Infiltration, stated that genuine urban explorers "never vandalize, steal or damage anything." The thrill comes from that of "discovery and a few nice pictures." Some Explorers will also request permission for entry.

River Trekking

River trekking or river tracing is a form of hiking or outdoor adventure activity, particularly popular in Hong Kong and Taiwan, and, in some ways, similar to canyoning or canyoneering. River trekking is a combination of trekking and climbing and sometimes swimming along the river. It involves particular techniques like rock climbing, climbing on wet surfaces, understanding the geographical features of river and valleys, knotting, dealing with sudden bad weather and find out possible exits from the river.

River Trekking in Different Countries

Hong Kong

Nine Big Rivers

The Nine Big Rivers are the nine rivers that are most popular among river trekkers in Hong Kong. The Nine Big Rivers include:

Romanization	Location
Tai Shing River	in Tsuen Wan
Wan Chung River	in Tai Po
Ng Tung River	in Tai Po
Wong Lung River	on Lantau Island near Tung Chung
Sheng Luk River	in Sai Kung
Man Cheng Po	in the west of Lantau Island
Lotus River	in Tai Lam Country Park

Romanization	Hanzi	Location
Ngon Sam River		on Lantau Island near Great Buddha
Ping Nam River		close to the border between Hong Kong and mainland China

Taiwan

This sport is popular throughout Taiwan, where it is generally called river tracing.

Philippines

In the Philippines, River Trekking is just gaining its popularity especially with the introduction of Mapawa Nature Park in Cagayan de Oro in Mindanao on one of their must-do activities. There are five challenges in the river which includes swimming, rapelling, jumping and sliding among others.

The particular nature park was featured on GMA 7's now defunct reality show Extra Challenge.

South Africa

The South African version of river trekking is called kloofing and has gained a similar following from both an informal recreational and commercial point of view.

Rating of Difficulties

As river trekking has a certain level of risk, experienced river trekkers or hiking groups have developed rating systems about difficuties on different rivers. The ratings usually are various from 1 to 5 stars, even though a few rivers can be more than 5 stars because of their extreme difficulties. Such ratings are largely subjective, depends largely on river trekker's own experience. Therefore, different people or hiking groups would give different number of stars on the same river. According to Hong Kong Adventurer, an English Website about hiking and river trekking in Hong Kong, difficult scale of different rivers as:

Number of stars	Description
1	can be handled by normal healthy persons
2	not too easy
3	fairly difficult
4	difficult, absolutely not for beginners
5	very difficult, very demanding in term of strength and skill

Risk and Danger

River trekking has certain level of risk. There are occasional accidents in river trekking, including falls from steep cliffs or waterfalls, drownings, exhaustion, or getting lost. Risks that should be prepared for include the following:

First, sudden changes in weather, like rainstorms, can cause rapid rises in water levels and speed in the river. Also, the number of viable paths and climbing areas inside the river valley would be reduced suddenly in a very short period. Besides this, bad or misty weather would also cause low visibility. Low visibility may come in to quickly for trekkers to adapt to. Therefore, a torch (flashlight), preferably a head-mounted one, is a must for river trekking.

Second, steep cliffs inside river valleys require a certain level of rock climbing skills. However, because of the humid environment inside the river valley, some rock surfaces can be very wet and some rocks can be very loose despite appearing solid. To deal with such wet climbing conditions, a pair of professional river-trekking boots are strongly advised.

Volunteer Travel

Volunteer travel, volunteer vacations or voluntourism is travel which includes volunteering for a charitable cause. In recent years, "bite-sized" volunteer vacations have grown in popularity. The types of volunteer vacations are diverse, from low-skill work cleaning up local wildlife areas to providing high-skill medical aid in a foreign country. Volunteer vacations participants are diverse but typically share a desire to "do something good" while also experiencing new places and challenges in locales they might not otherwise visit.

There are also other types of travelling that engage people with scientific research and education to promote the understanding and action necessary for a sustainable environment. Participants cover a fee that would include expenses on the different sites worldwide, and engage in projects according to their interest or location.

History

Originally most volunteer vacations were undertaken by people with a direct connection to a particular cause and were considered more as short term, intense volunteer projects rather than vacations. Many of these organizations were long-standing international development assistance organizations which placed short-term volunteers on community development project sites.

1990s

During the 1990s the travel industry developed niche products and firms to provide volunteer vacations to people who had no previous experience with a cause, and to cater to the increasing number of young people taking gap years. These providers expanded the market but also drew criticism for the impact of their methods. At the same time, the first edition of "Volunteer Vacations" by Bill McMillon was published, featuring under 200 non-profit organizations which facilitated such service opportunities. According to the Travel Industry Association of America, more than 55 million Americans have participated in a volunteer vacation, and about 100 million more are considering taking one.

Controversy

While some experts on volunteering welcome the expansion of volunteer vacations as an opportunity to provide more resources to projects and to encourage a volunteer ethic in people,others have pointed out that the business methods used by tour operators, such as exclusivity deals, and catering to the needs of the volunteer rather than the volunteer project, exploit the communities the projects are intended to help. Claims by volunteer tourism organizations that these activities contribute to improving people's lives and contributing to development goals are yet to be evaluated in the vast majority of cases. It is possible that volunteer travel might excacerbate existing problems in the host community. As Dr Anna Mdee discusses contends that while there is still a lack of understanding of the direct impact volunteering overseas has on development activities that there is a much larger value that can be gained from working and living in another culture. As a founder of small international development charity Village-to-Village which works in Tanzania and has been sending volunteers to support the projects since 2006, she recognises that there is a huge difference in the types of placements on the market and urges would be volunteers to take caution when choosing placements. Dr Mdee is Senior Lecturer and Associate Dean for Learning and Teaching in the School of Social and International Studies at the University of Bradford. She is also a Deputy Director of the Centre for African Studies.

EXTREME TOURISM

Extreme tourism or shock tourism is a type of niche tourism involving travel to dangerous places (mountains, jungles, deserts, caves, etc.) or participation in dangerous events. Extreme tourism overlaps with extreme sport. The two share the main attraction, "adrenaline rush" caused by an element of risk, and differing mostly in the degree of engagement and professionalism.

Extreme tourism is a growing business in the countries of the former Soviet Union (Russia, Ukraine, Azerbaijan, etc.) and in South American countries like Peru, Chile and Argentina. The mountainous and rugged terrain of Northern Pakistan has also developed into a popular extreme tourism location.

While traditional tourism requires significant investments in hotels, roads, etc., extreme tourism requires much less to jump-start a business. In addition to traditional travel-based tourism destinations, various exotic attractions are suggested, such as flyovers in MiGs at Mach 2.5, ice diving in the White Sea, or travelling across the Chernobyl zone.

Safari

A safari (pronounced) is an overland journey, usually a trip by tourists to Africa, traditionally for a big-game hunt; today the term often refers to a trip taken not for the purposes of hunting, but to observe and photograph animals and other wildlife. There is a certain theme or style associated with the word, which includes khaki clothing, belted bush jackets, pith helmets or slouch hats, and animal skins—like leopard's skin.

Entering the English language in the late 19th century, the word safari means "long journey" in Swahili. Originally from the Arabic ???? (safar) meaning a journey The verb for "to travel" in Swahili is "kusafiri", the noun for the journey is "safari". These words are used for any type of journey, e.g. by bus from Nairobi to Mombasa. The person generally attributed to having used the word in English is Sir Richard Francis Burton, the famous explorer.

The Regimental March of the King's African Rifles was 'Funga Safari', literally 'Halt the March', or, in other words, stop work for the day.

Funga safari, funga safari. Funga safari, funga safari. Hamari ya nani? Hamari ya nani? Hamari ya Bwana Kapteni, Hamari ya keyaa.

Which is, in English:

Halt the march. Halt the march. On whose orders? On whose orders? On the order of the boss captain, On the order of the KAR.

On Kenya's independence from Britain, Funga Safari was retained as the Regimental March of the Kenya Rifles, successor to the K.A.R.

As a Cinema Genre

The safari provided countless hours of cinema entertainment in sound films from Trader Horn (1931) onwards. The safari was used in many adventure films such as the Tarzan, Jungle Jim, and Bomba the Jungle Boy film series up to The Naked Prey (1966) where Cornel Wilde, a white hunter, becomes game himself. Also, safaris and the safari genre films were parodied in the Bob Hope comedies Road to Zanzibar and Call Me Bwana. An instant 15-minute helicopter safari was shown in Africa Addio where clients are armed, flown from their hotel and landed in front of an unlucky and baffled elephant. Out of Africa has Karen Blixen and Denys Finch Hatton travelling with Denys refusing to abandon home comforts using fine china and crystal and listening to Mozart recordings over the gramophone while on safari.

Hiking

Hiking is an outdoor activity which consists of walking in natural environments, often on hiking trails. It is such a popular activity that there are numerous hiking organizations worldwide. The health benefits of different types of hiking have been confirmed in studies. The word hiking is understood in all English-speaking countries, but there are differences in usage.

Related Terms

In the United States and United Kingdom, hiking refers to cross-country walking of a longer duration than a simple walk and usually over terrain where hiking boots are required. A day hike refers to a hike that can be completed in a single day, often applied to mountain hikes to a lake or summit, but not requiring an overnight camp, in which case the term backpacking is used. Bushwhacking specifically refers to difficult walking through dense forest, undergrowth, or bushes, where forward progress requires pushing vegetation aside. In extreme cases of bushwhacking where the vegetation is so dense that human passage is impeded, a machete is used to clear a pathway. Australians use the term bushwalking for both on- and off-trail hiking. New Zealanders use tramping (particularly for overnight and longer trips), walking or bushwalking. Multi-day hiking in the mountainous regions of India, Nepal, North America, South America, and in the highlands of East Africa is also called trekking; the Dutch refer to trekking also. Hiking a long-distance trail from end-to-end is also referred to as trekking and as thru-hiking in some places, for example on the Appalachian Trail (AT) or Long Trail (LT) in Vermont. The Long Trail is the oldest long-distance hiking trail in the United States.

Comparison With Other Forms of Touring

Hiking is one of the fundamental outdoor activities on which many others are based. Many beautiful places can only be reached overland by hiking, and enthusiasts regard hiking as the best way to see nature. Hikers see it as better than a tour in a vehicle of any kind (or on an animal; see horseback riding) because the hiker's senses are not intruded upon by distractions such as windows, engine noise, airborne dust and fellow passengers. Hiking over long distances or over difficult terrain requires both the physical ability to do the hike and the knowledge of the route and its pitfalls.

Environmental Impact

Hikers often seek beautiful natural environments in which to hike. These environments are often fragile: hikers may accidentally destroy the environment that they enjoy. While the action of an individual may not strongly affect the environment, the mass effect of a large number of hikers can degrade the environment. For example, gathering wood in an alpine area to start a fire may be harmless if done once (except for wildfire risk). Years of gathering wood, however, can strip an alpine area of valuable nutrients. Generally, protected areas such as parks have regulations in place to protect the environment. If hikers follow such regulations, their impact can be minimized. Such regulations include forbidding wood fires, restricting camping to established camp sites, disposing or packing out faecal matter, imposing a quota on the number of hikers per mile.

Many hikers espouse the philosophy of Leave No Trace: hiking in a way such that future hikers cannot detect the presence of previous hikers. Practitioners of this philosophy obey its strictures, even in the absence of area regulations. Followers of this practice follow strict practices on dealing with food waste, food packaging, and alterations to the surrounding environment.

Human waste is often a major source of environmental impact from hiking. These wastes can contaminate the watershed and make other hikers ill. Bacterial contamination can be avoided by digging 'catholes' 10 to 25 cm (4 to 10 inches) deep, depending on local soil composition and covering after use. If these catholes are dug at least 60 m (200 feet) away from water sources and trails, the risk of contamination is minimized. Many hikers warn other hikers about the location of their catholes by marking them with sticks stuck into the ground.

Protecting the trails and nature areas can be taken further with the idea of taking out more than you brought in. If every responsible hiker took out one small bag of garbage left by others our trails and nature areas would gradually become pristine.

Sometimes hikers enjoy viewing rare or endangered species. However, some species (such as martens or bighorn sheep) are very sensitive to the presence of humans, especially around mating season. To prevent adverse impact, hikers should learn the habits and habitats of endangered species.

There is one situation where an individual hiker can make a large impact on an ecosystem: inadvertently starting a wildfire. For example, in 2005, a Czech backpacker burned 7% of Torres del Paine National Park in Chile by knocking over an illegal gas portable stove. Obeying area regulations and setting up cooking devices on designated areas (or if necessary on bare ground) will reduce the risk of wildfire.

Hazards

Hiking may produce threats to personal safety. These threats can be dangerous circumstances while hiking and/or specific accidents or ailments. Diarrhea has been found to be one of the most common illness afflicting long-distance hikers in the United States.

Dangerous hiking circumstances include losing the way, inclement weather, hazardous terrain, or exacerbation of pre-existing medical conditions. Specific accidents include metabolic imbalances (such as dehydration or hypothermia), topical injuries (such as frostbite or sunburn), attacks by animals, or internal injuries.

Hikers often propose a set of behavioral prescriptions to minimize these threats. A well-known example of such a set of prescription is the Ten Essentials.

Attacks by humans are also a reality. There are organizations that promote prevention, self defense and escape. The cell phone and GPS devices are used in some organizations.

In various countries, borders may be poorly marked. It is good practice to know where international borders are. Many nations, such as Finland, have specific rules governing hiking across borders.

CHAPTER 3

SURVIVAL SKILLS FOR ADVENTURE TOURISM

Survival skills are techniques a person may use in a dangerous situation (e.g. natural disasters) to save themselves or to save others (also see bushcraft.) Generally speaking, these techniques are meant to provide the basic necessities for human life: water, food, shelter, habitat, and the need to think straight, to signal for help, to navigate safely, to avoid unpleasant interactions with animals and plants, and for first aid. In addition, survival skills are often basic ideas and abilities that ancient humans had to use for thousands of years, so these skills are partially a reenactment of history. Many of these skills are the ways to enjoy extended periods of time in remote places, or a way to thrive in nature. Some people use these skills to better appreciate nature and for recreation, not just survival.

Background

Secondary sources on survival skills, including those produced by the United States Army, and the Boy Scouts of America (priorities for an individual or group in a survival situation), formulate lists of needs to be met for survival.

The needs for survival are differently conceptualized between sources; they may give six, or seven, or ten "needs" or "priorities." Furthermore, those sources often differ as to the relative priority of survival needs in a given survival situation. Some sources expressly acknowledge what seems manifest: that the order of priority of survival needs shifts according to the immediate situation faced.

One widely circulated concept to help set priorities is called the "Rule of Three": Employing a mnemonic device, the Rule of Three states:

1. Humans cannot survive more than three hours exposed to extremely high or low temperatures, unless individual is using proper gear to cope with heat/cold.
2. Humans cannot survive more than 3 days without water.
3. Humans cannot survive more than three weeks without food.

The Rule of Three is often otherwise formulated and is viewed by commentators as a rough guide. An aircrew reportedly lasted 8 days without water in a liferaft. People have survived without food for over twenty-one days; the survival of voluntary hunger strikes by persons in captivity over longer periods has been reported.

In 1999, Alaskan fireman Robert Bogucki survived for 12 days without water and 36 days with nearly no food in the Great Sandy Desert, Western Australia,

The Boy Scouts, in addition to listing seven priorities, use a mnemonic device, "STOP", to address the mental aspects of survival. "STOP" stands for "Stop, Think, Observe, Plan."

Shelter

Shelter is any thing that protects a person from his/her environment, including dangerous cold and heat and allow restful sleep, another human need.

A shelter can range from a "natural shelter"; such as a cave or a fallen-down (cracked but not split) thickly-foliaged tree, to an intermediate form of man-made shelter such as a debris shelter, a ditch dug next to a tree log and covered with foliage, or a snow cave, to completely man-made structures such as a tarp, tent, or house.

Fire

Making fire is recognized in the sources as to significantly increase the ability to survive physically and mentally. The skills required to light a fire without a lighter or matches, such as by using natural flint and steel with tinder, is a frequent subject of both books on survival and in survival courses. There is an emphasis placed on practicing fire-making skills before venturing into the wilderness.

Fire is presented as a tool meeting many survival needs. The heat provided by a fire allows the body to be warmed, wet clothes to be dried, water to be disinfected, and food to be cooked. Not to be overlooked is the psychological boost and the sense of safety and protection it gives. Fire may deter wild animals from interfering with the survivor, or wild animals may be attracted to the light and heat of a fire. The light and smoke emitted by a fire can also be used to work at night and can signal rescue units.

Water

A human being can survive an average of three to five days without the intake of water, assuming sea-level altitude, room temperature and favorable relative humidity. In colder or warmer temperatures, the need for water is greater. Need for water also increases with exercise.

A typical person will lose 2-3 litres of water per day under ordinary conditions, and more in hot, dry, or cold weather. Four to six litres of water or other liquids are generally required each day in the wilderness to avoid dehydration and to keep the body functioning properly. The U.S. Army survival manual recommends that you drink water whenever thirsty. Other groups recommend rationing water through "water discipline".

A lack of water causes dehydration, which may result in lethargy, headaches, dizziness, confusion, and eventually death. Even mild dehydration reduces endurance and impairs concentration, which is dangerous in a survival situation where clear thinking is essential. Dark yellow or brown urine is a diagnostic indicator of dehydration. To avoid dehydration, a high priority is typically assigned to locating a supply of drinking water and making provision to render that water as safe as possible.

Many sources in survival literature, as well as forums and online references, list the ways in which water may be gathered and rendered safer for consumption in a survival situation, such as boiling, filtering, chemicals, solar radiation + heat/SODIS, and distillation. Such sources also often list the dangers, such as pollutants, microorganisms, or pathogens which affect the safety of back country water.

Recent thinking is that boiling or commercial filters are significantly safer than use of chemicals, with the exception of chlorine dioxide.

The issues presented by the need for water dictate that unnecessary water loss by perspiration be avoided in survival situations.

To thus avoid these problems, culinary root tubers, fruit, edible mushrooms, edible nuts, edible beans, edible cereals or edible leaves, edible moss, edible cacti and algae can be searched and if needed, prepared (mostly by boiling). With the exception of leaves, these foods are relatively high in calories, providing some energy to the body. Plants are some of the easiest food sources to find in the jungle, forest or desert because they're stationary and can thus be had without exerting much effort.

Also, many commentators discuss the knowledge, skills, and equipment (such as bows, snares and nets) necessary to gather animal food in the wild through animal trapping, hunting, fishing.

Some survival books promote the "Universal Edibility Test". Allegedly, one can distinguish edible foods from toxic ones by a series of progressive exposures to skin and mouth prior to ingestion, with waiting periods and checks for symptoms. However, many other experts including Ray Mears and John Kallas reject this method, stating that even a small amount of some "potential foods" can cause physical discomfort, illness, or death. An additional step called the scratch test is sometimes included to evaluate the edibility of a potential food.

Focusing on survival until rescued by presumed searchers, The Boy Scouts of America especially discourages foraging for wild foods on the grounds that the knowledge and skills needed are unlikely to be possessed by those finding themselves in a wilderness survival situation, making the risks (including use of energy) outweigh the benefits.

First Aid

First aid (wilderness first aid in particular) can help a person survive and function with injuries and illnesses that would otherwise kill or incapacitate him/her. Common and dangerous injuries include:

- Lacerations, which may become infected
- Bites or stings from venomous animals, such as: snakes, scorpions, spiders, bees, stingrays, jellyfish, catfish, stargazers, etc.
- Bites leading to disease/septicemia, such as: mosquitoes, fleas, ticks, animals infected with rabies, sand flies, komodo dragons, crocodilians, etc.
- Infection through food, animal contact, or drinking non-potable water
- Bone fractures
- Sprains, particularly of the ankle
- Burns
- Poisoning from consumption of, or contact with, poisonous plants or poisonous fungi.

- Hypothermia (too cold) and hyperthermia (too hot)
- Heart attack
- Hemorrage

The survivor may need to apply the contents of a first aid kit or, if possessing the required knowledge, naturally-occurring medicinal plants, immobilize injured limbs, or even transport incapacitated comrades.

Navigation

Survival situations are sometimes resolved by finding one's way to safety, or one may need to move to find a more suitable location to wait for rescue. The sources observe that to do either of these safely requires some navigation equipment and skills. Types of navigation include:

- Celestial navigation, using the sun and the night sky to locate the cardinal directions and to maintain course of travel
- Using a map and compass together, particularly a topographic map or trail map.
- "Navigation by observation" of terrain features on a map or otherwise known
- Using a GPS receiver, if one is available
- dead reckoning -

In the Northern Hemisphere at mid-day, the sun is directly South of any observer. In the Southern Hemisphere at mid-day, the sun is directly North of any observer. Mid-day can be calculated by planting a stick or other upright structure in the ground as close to 90 degrees as possible and marking with sticks or rocks or any other feature, as often as possible, the length of the shadow it casts during a single daylight period. Wherever the shadow is the shortest during a daylight period, that direction is South if you are in the Northern Hemisphere and that direction is North if you are in the Southern Hemisphere. In lieu of a compass or natural terrain features to aid in navigation, this method will give a survivor a generally correct impression of direction. This method of orienteering is not useful when the survivor does not have a pre-existing general impression of the local environment (knowing which way is south will not help you if you don't know what should be south of you).

Training

Survival training has many components, mental competence and physical fitness being two. Mental competence includes the skills listed in this article, as well as the ability to admit the existence of a crisis, overcome panic, and think clearly. Physical fitness includes, among other abilities, carrying loads over long distances on rough terrain. Theoretical knowledge of survival skills is useful only if it can be applied effectively in the wilderness. Almost all Survival Skills are environment specific and require training in a particular environment.

Survival training may be broken down into three types, or schools; Modern Wilderness Survival, Bushcraft, and Primitive Survival Techniques.

Modern Wilderness Survival teaches the skills needed to survive Short-Term (1 to 4 Days) and Medium-Term (4 to 40 Days) survival situations.

"Bushcraft" is the combination of Modern Wilderness Survival and useful Primitive Survival Techniques. It normally splits its skill acquisition between Medium-Term Survival Techniques (4 to 40 Days) and Long-Term Survival Techniques (40 Days Plus).

Primitive Survival Techniques or "Primitive Living" teaches the skills needed to survive over the Long-Term (40 days plus). Many primitive technology skills require much more practice and may be more environment specific.

Several organizations offer wilderness survival training. Course ranges from one day to field courses lasting as long as a month. In addition to teaching survival techniques for conditions of limited food, water, and shelter, many organizations that teach bushcraft and Primitive Survival seek to engender appreciation and understanding of the lifestyles of pre-industrialized cultures.

There are several books that teach one how to survive in dangerous situations, and schools train children what to do in the event of an earthquake or fire. Some cities also have contingency plans in case of a major disaster, such as hurricanes or tornadoes.

Mental Preparedness

Commentators note that the mind and its processes are critical to survival. It is said that the will to live in a life and death situation often separates those that live and those that do not. Stories of heroic feats of survival by regular people with little or no training but a strong will to live are not uncommon. Laurence Gonzales in his book Deep Survival: Who Lives, Who Dies and Why describes the story of a young teenage girl named Juliane Köpcke who is the victim of a plane crash in the Amazon jungle. With no formal training and wearing only her confirmation clothes, she walked through the jungle for several days with parasitic insects boring under her skin. After eleven days, with very little food, she reached a hut and collapsed inside. Three hunters found her the next day and took her to a local doctor. Of those who survived the crash, she was the only one to make it out alive. Gonzales believes that her simple and indestructible will to live made the difference.

So stressful is a true survival situation, that those who appear to have a clear understanding of the stressors, even trained experts, are said to be mentally affected by facing deadly peril.

It seems that, to the extent that stress results from testing human limits, the benefits of learning to function under stress and determining those limits may outweigh the downside of stress. After all, stress is a natural reaction to adverse circumstances, developed by evolution to assist in survival - at least, in terms of brief, perilous encounters (such as being caught in the middle of a natural disaster, or being attacked by a wild animal.) If stress lingers for a prolonged period of time, it tends to produce the opposite effect, impeding one's ability to survive. In particular, the commentators note the following adverse effects of stress: forgetfulness, inability to sleep, increased propensity to make mistakes, lessened energy, outbursts of rage, and carelessness. None of these symptoms would seem to make survival easier or more likely.

Survival Manuals

A survival manual is a book used as reference in situations where a human's survival is threatened - expected or unexpected. Typically it will cover both preparation and guidance for dealing with eventualities.

There are many different types of survival manuals, but most have a section of standard advice. These are sometimes republished for public distribution: for example the SAS Survival Handbook, United States Army Survival Manual (FM 3-05.70) and United States Air Force Survival Manual (AF 64-4).

Other manuals have been written for more specific uses, such as wilderness or maritime survival.

Much of today's teaching principles on survival are derived from the work of SAS Survival Instructor Lofty Wiseman.

Lofty Wiseman's book has also been converted into the SAS Survival Guide - iPhone App for handy reference.

CHAPTER 4

BICYCLE TOURING

Bicycle touring is a form of cycling where riders travel long distances, prioritizing pleasure and endurance over utility or speed. Touring can vary from single day 'supported' rides — e.g., rides to benefit charities — where provisions are available to riders at stops along the route, to multi-day trips with solo or group riders carrying all necessary equipment, tool, food, clothing.

Origins

Bicycle touring is an activity as old as the bicycle. The historian James McGurn speaks of bets being taken in London in the 19th century for riders of hobby-horses – machines pushed by the feet rather than pedalled – outspeeding stage coaches. "One practitioner beat a four-horse coach to Brighton by half an hour," he says. "There are various accounts of 15 to 17-year-olds draisienne-touring around France in the 1820s. On 17 February 1869 John Mayall, Charles Spencer and Rowley Turner rode from Trafalgar Square, London, to Brighton in 15 hours for 53 miles. The Times, which had sent a reporter to follow them in a coach and pair, reported an "Extraordinary Velocipede Feat." Three riders set off from Liverpool to London, a journey of three days and so more akin to modern cycle-touring, in March that same year. A newspaper report said:

Their bicycles caused no little astonishment on the way, and the remarks passed by the natives were almost amusing. At some of the villages the boys clustered round the machines, and, where they could, caught hold of them and ran behind until they were tired out. Many enquiries were made as to the name of 'them queer horses', some called them 'whirligigs', 'menageries' and 'valparaisons'. Between Wolverhampton and Birmingham, attempts were made to upset the riders by throwing stones.

Enthusiasm extended to other countries. The New York Times spoke of "quantities of velocipedes flying like shuttles hither and thither". But while British interest had less frenzy than in the USA, it lasted longer.

The expansion from a machine that had to be pushed, or propelled through pedals on a small front wheel, made longer distances feasible. A rider calling himself "A Light Dragoon" told in 1870 or 1871 of a ride from Lewes to Salisbury, across southern England. The title of his book, Wheels and Woes, suggests a less than event-free ride but McGann says "it seems to have been a delightful adventure, despite bad road surfaces, dust and lack of signposts.

Journeys grew more adventurous. John Foster Fraser and two friends set off round the world on safety bicycles in July 1896. He, Edward Lunn and F. H. Lowe rode 19,237 miles, through 17 countries, in two years and two months. By 1878, recreational cycling was well enough established in Britain to lead to the formation of the Bicycle Touring Club, later renamed Cyclists' Touring Club. It is the oldest national tourism organisation in the world. Members, like those of other clubs, often rode in uniform. The CTC appointed an official tailor. The uniform was a dark green Devonshire serge jacket, knickerbockers and a "Stanley helmet with a small peak". The colour changed to grey when green proved impractical because it showed the dirt. Groups often rode with a bugler at their head to sound changes of direction or to bring the group to a halt. Confusion could be caused when groups met and mistook each other's signals.

Membership of the CTC inspired the Frenchman Paul de Vivie (b. April 29, 1853) to found what became the Fédération Française de Cyclotourisme, the world's largest cycling association, and to coin the French word cyclo-tourisme. The League of American Wheelmen in the USA was founded in Newport, Rhode Island on May 30, 1880. It shared an interest in leisure cycling with the administration of cycle racing. Membership peaked at 103,000 in 1898. The national cycle-touring organization in the USA is now the Adventure Cycling Association (ACA). The ACA, then called Bikecentennial, organized a mass ride in 1976 from one side of the USA to the other to mark the nation's 200th anniversary. The Bikecentennial route is still in use as the TransAmerica Trail.

Social Significance

The first cyclists, often aristocratic or otherwise rich, flirted with the bicycle and then abandoned it for the new motor car. It was the lower middle class which most profited from cycling and the liberation that it brought. The Cyclist of 13 August 1892 said: "The two sections of the community which form the majority of 'wheelmen' are the great clerk class and the great shop assistant class." H. G. Wells described this aspirant class liberated through cycling. Three of his heroes – in History of Mr Polly, Kipps and The Wheels of Chance – buy bicycles. The first two work in drapery shops. The third, Hoopdriver, goes on a cycling holiday. The authors Roderick Watson and Martin Gray say:

Hoopdriver is certainly liberated by his machine. It affords him not only a country holiday, in itself a remarkable event which he enjoys immensely, however ignorant of the countryside he may be, but also a brush with a society girl, riding on pneumatics and wearing some kind of Rational Dress. The book suggests the new social mobility created by the bike, which breaks the boundaries of Hoopdriver's world both literally and figuratively.

Hoopdriver sets off in a spirit of freedom, finally away from his job:

Only those who toil six long days out of the seven, and all the year round, save for one brief glorious fortnight or ten days in the summer time, know the exquisite sensations of the First Holiday Morning. All the dreary, uninteresting routine drops from you suddenly, your chains fall about your feet...There were thrushes in the Richmond Road, and a lark on Putney Heath. The freshness of dew was in the air; dew or the relics of an overnight shower glittered on the leaves and grass...He wheeled his machine up Putney Hill, and his heart sang within him.

Wells puts Hoopdriver in a new brown cycling suit to show the importance of the venture and the freedom on which he is embarking. Hoopdriver finds the bicycle raises his social standing, at least in his imagination, and he calls to himself as he rides that he's "a bloomin' dook" The New Woman that he pursues wears Rational Dress of a sort that scandalised society but made cycling much easier. The Rational Dress Society was founded in 1881 in London. It said:

The Rational Dress Society protests... against crinolines or crinolettes of any kind as ugly and deforming... [It] requires all to be dressed healthily, comfortably, and beautifully, to seek what conduces to birth, comfort and beauty in our dress as a duty to ourselves and each other.

Both Hoopdriver and the Young Lady in Grey, as he refers to her, are escaping social restraints through bicycle touring. Hoopdriver falls in love and rescues her from a lover who says marrying him is the only way that she, having left alone for a cycling holiday, can save her reputation. She lowers her social status; he raises his. McGurn says: "The shift in social perspectives, as exemplified by Wells' cyclists, led Galsworthy to claim, at a later date, that the bicycle had "been responsible for more movement in manners and morals than anything since Charles the Second."

Development

The bicycle gained from the outdoor movement of the 1930s. The Cyclists' Touring Club advertised a week's all-in tour, staying at hotels recommended to it by other cyclists, for £3 10s. The youth hostel movement started in Germany and spread abroad and a cycling holiday staying at hostels in the 1930s could be had for £2. Roderick Watson and Martin Gray estimate that there were ten million bicycles in Britain to one million cars.

A decline set in across Europe, but particularly in Britain, when millions of servicemen returned from World War II having learned to drive. Trips away were now to be taken, for the increasing number who had one, by car. The decline in the United States came even sooner. McGurn says:

The story of inter-war cycling was characterised by lack of interest and a steady decline... Cycling had lost out to the automobile, and to some extent to the new electric transport systems. In the 1930s cumbersome, fat-tyred 'balloon bombers', bulbously streamlined in imitation of motorcycles or aeroplanes, appealed to American children: the only mass market still open to cycle manufacturers. Wartime austerity gave cycling a short reprieve in the industrial world. The post-war peace was to lay the bicycle low.

Then came the US bicycle boom, that caught a back-to-nature trend of which the hippie movement had been a precursor. The author Charles Reich identified what he called a "consciousness" working against corporate consumer-culture in the USA. He said in The Greening of America in 1970: "When man allows machines and the machine-state to master his consciousness, he imperils not only his inner being but also the world he inhabits and upon which he depends." Such was the change that happened that 4,000 cyclists joined a ride from the Pacific to the Atlantic in 1976 to celebrate the nation's bicentennial. Its founder, Greg Siple, said:

My original thought was to send out ads and flyers saying, 'Show up at Golden Gate Park in San Francisco at 9 o'clock on June 1 with your bicycle.' And then we were going to bicycle across the country. I pictured thousands of people, a sea of people with their bikes and packs all ready to go, and there would be old men and people with balloon-tire bikes and Frenchmen who flew over just for this. Nobody would shoot a gun off or anything. At 9 o'clock everybody would just start moving. It would be like this crowd of locusts crossing America

The ride, called Bikecentennial, ran from Oregon to Williamsburg, Virginia, site of the first British settlements. It defined a new start for cycle-touring in the United States and led to the creation of the Adventure Cycling Association. The ACA has gone on to create mapped routes across America and into Canada, many of them rides taking three months to complete on a loaded bicycle.

Voyages

Bicycle touring can be of any distance and time. The French tourist Jacques Sirat speaks in lectures of how he felt proud riding round the world for five years – until he met an Australian who had been on the road for 27 years. The German rider, Walter Stolle, lost his home and living in the Sudetenland in the aftermath of World War II, settled in Britain and set off from Essex on 25 January 1959, to cycle round the world. He rode through 159 countries in 18 years, denied only those with sealed borders. He paid his way by giving slide shows in seven languages. He gave 2,500 at US$100 each. In 1974, he rode through Nigeria, Dahomey, Upper Volta, Ghana, Leone, Ivory Coast, Liberia and Guinea. He was robbed 231 times, wore out six bicycles and had five more stolen.

Another German set off three years after Stolle and is still riding. Heinz Stücke left his job as a die-maker in North Rhine-Westphalia in 1962 when he was 22. He has never been home since. By 2006 he had cycled more than 539,000 km (335,000 miles) and visited 192 countries. He pays his way by selling photographs to magazines. Outside the West, Gua Dahao left China in May 1999 to ride across Siberia, the Middle East, Turkey, western Europe, Scandinavia, then another 100,000 km across Africa, Latin America and Australia.

Journeys can equally be shorter and more anonymous. Cyclo-Camping International makes a point of including shorter tours with children in its annual presentation in Paris. But children have been the stimulus for longer journeys. Among tours featured by Cyclo-Camping International has been one by Brigitte and Nicolas Mercat and their three children, five, seven and nine when they left France in July 2002. They rode through Peru, Bolivia, Argentina, Chile, New Zealand, New Caledonia and Indonesia. They taught their children from school books as they rode and returned to Chambéry to find that not only were they ahead of their classmates but they had learned several languages on the way.

Types

Distances vary considerably. Depending on fitness, speed and the number of stops, the rider usually covers between 50–150 kilometres (30–90 mi) per day. A short tour over a few days may cover as little as 200 kilometres (120 mi) and a long tour may go right across a country or around the world.

There are many different types of bicycle touring:

Lightweight Touring

Informally called credit-card touring, a rider carries a minimum of equipment and a lot of money. Overnight accommodation is in youth hostels, hotels, pensions or B&Bs. Food is bought at cafes, restaurants or markets.

Fully-loaded Touring

Also known as self-supported touring, cyclists carry everything they need, including food, cooking equipment, and a tent for camping. Some cyclists minimize their load, carrying only basic supplies, food, and a Bivouac sack or lightweight tent.

Expedition Touring

Cyclists travel extensively, often through developing nations or remote areas. The bicycle is loaded with food, spares, tools, and camping equipment so that the traveller is largely self-supporting.

Mixed Terrain Cycle-Touring

Also called rough riding, cyclists travel over a variety of surfaces and topography on a single route, with a single bicycle. Focusing on freedom of travel and efficiency over varied surfaces, cyclists often adopt an ultralight camping approach and carry their own minimal gear.

Supported Touring

Cyclists are supported by a motor vehicle, which carries most equipment. This can be organized independently by groups of cyclists or commercial holiday companies. These companies sell places on guided tours, including booked lodging, luggage transfers, route planning and often meals and rental bikes.

Day Touring

These rides vary highly in their size of the group (from solo cyclists, group rides, to large organized rides with hundreds to thousands of riders), in their length (from a few miles to Century rides of 100 miles — or longer), in their purpose (from riding for pleasure to raising money for a charitable organization) and in their methods of support (from self-supported day rides, to organized rides where cyclists pay for support or accommodations provided by event organizers — including rest and refreshment stops, marshalling to aid safety, and SAG service.

Touring Bicycle

A touring bicycle is a bicycle designed or modified to handle bicycle touring. To make the bikes sufficiently robust, comfortable and capable of carrying heavy loads, special features may include a long wheelbase (for ride comfort and to avoid pedal-to-luggage conflicts), frame materials that favor flexibility over rigidity (for ride comfort), heavy duty wheels (for load capacity), and multiple mounting points (for luggage racks, fenders, and bottle cages).

Types

Touring bicycle configurations are highly variable and may include road, sport/touring, trail, recumbent, or tandem configurations.

Road Touring

Road touring bicycles have a frame geometry designed to provide a comfortable ride and stable, predictable handling when laden with baggage, provisions for the attachment of fenders and mounting points for carrier racks and panniers.

Modern road tourers may employ 700C (622mm) wheels — the same diameter as a road (racing) bicycle. Other road touring bikes may feature wider rims and more clearance in the frame for wider bicycle tires. Before the 1980s, many touring bikes for the North American market were built with 27-inch (630mm) wheels which have a slightly larger diameter.

Other touring bikes use 26-inch wheels for touring bikes, for both off-road and on-road use. Advantages of the slightly smaller wheel include additional strength, worldwide tire availability, and lighter weight. Some touring bicycles, such as the Surly Long Haul Trucker, offer frames designed for 26" (ISO 559) wheels or for 700C wheels, with the frame geometry optimal for the selected wheel size. Specially-made touring tires for 26" wheels are now widely available, especially in developing countries, where 700C may be difficult to obtain. Hence, on the mass ride from Paris to the Beijing Olympics in 2008, the Fédération Française de Cyclotourisme asked all riders to use 26-inch wheels.

Factors that affect rolling resistance include tire air pressure, tread and tire width as well as wheel size.

Sport Touring

The sport/touring bicycle is a very lightweight touring bike fitted with lighter wheels and narrower 25–28 mm (1 - 1.125-inch) tires. It may also be described as a road racing bike fitted with heavier tires and slightly more relaxed frame geometry (though still quicker than the average road touring bike). It is designed as a fast-handling, responsive and quick day touring machine. As such, it is intended to carry only the rider and very light loads, such as encountered in credit card touring, where riders typically carry little more than a pocketbook and credit cards to book overnight lodging at any handy motel, pension, or bed-and-breakfast while on a journey. Gearing is often a mix of closely-spaced ratios for speed, combined with a few low gears for long climbs. Sport/touring bikes may sometimes have provisions for mounting slim fenders and a rear carrier or pannier rack, though in the interests of weight savings and quicker handling, most do not.

Expedition Touring

There are numerous variants on the traditional road tourer depending on the weight carried and the type of terrain expected. Expedition tourers are strongly built bicycles designed for carrying heavy loads over the roughest roads in remote and far-flung places. These range from simply stronger built mountain bikes, equipped with racks, panniers, mudguards and heavy-duty tires, to purpose-built bicycles built to cope with long-haul touring on tracks and unsealed roads in developing countries throughout Asia, Africa, and the other continents. Their frames are often made of steel as any breakages can be more easily repaired in towns all around the world.

A typical expedition touring bike would be made of relatively heavy duty steel tubing, with 26 inch wheels, and componentry chosen for robustness and ease of maintenance. The main design criteria for such a bike would be to allow all day comfort on the bike, have good handling characteristics under heavy load, and be capable of running smoothly on good roads, but also on the roughest of tracks. Some bike tourers have made their own expedition bikes, by building up on mountain bike frames. The key difference between a mountain bike and an expedition touring bike would be the addition of racks for panniers, and tougher, all purpose tires. They will have a longer wheelbase to allow for more comfortable cruising, at the expense of the manoeverability of an mtb. Most tourers also prefer heavier, stronger wheels than would be normal on a production mountain bike and although some are now equipped with disc brakes to cope with the extra loads and weight. Most expedition bikes will have the same range of gears as a mountain bike and for reliability some use the Rohloff Speedhub at the expense of its high cost.

It is a small, specialist market, so only a small number of bikes are sold under this description, few if any by the biggest manufacturers. Examples are the EXP and Raven from Thorn Cycles, and the Roberts Roughstuff, all made in the UK. Koga-Miyata produce the Signature range of bikes that allows users to specify many aspects of the bikes components to ultimately achieve an expedition bike.

Mixed Terrain Touring

Mixed Terrain Cycle-Touring bikes are a cross between mountain and road bikes. Also called all-rounders, 29er touring or monster cross, these bikes strive for a balance of efficiency and speed on and off road. Typically they are built with light steel frames and drop handlebars. Unlike expedition touring bikes they typically sport 700c or 650b sized wheels. Yet like other touring bikes, they stress a relaxed geometry for all day comfort. Low mountain bike gearing is often used and these bikes can usually carry a medium weight load without trouble. Mixed terrain touring bikes fall into this category and are used for mixed terrain touring in the mountains. A few manufacturers like Rawland Cycles, Surly Bikes, and Singular Cycles are now producing these bikes. Salsa has also come up with a related model called the Fargo. But many riders convert older, non-suspension mountain bikes and cyclo-cross bikes for the purpose.

Folding/Collapseable Touring

There is an increasing number of specially-designed and built or adapted folding bicycles used in bicycle touring. Most are built with 20" wheels (406mm rims), although some are built with 16" wheels, and the Moulton is built around a specially-made 17" wheel. Many have ride characteristics just as good as touring bicycles with 26" or 700C wheels, but they have the advantage that they can be folded or collapsed for much easier transportation in trains and in Airline Luggage. The Raleigh Twenty is also a popular frame format used to construct collapseable touring bicycles. Other bicycles such as the Surly Travelers Check and the Santana Travel Tandem are full-sized bicycles which do not fold, but instead use Bicycle Torque Couplings to enable separating the frame into two parts for easier transport.

Recumbent Touring

Recumbents are different in that the rider sits with his legs in front. Recumbents have their handlebars not in front, as with conventional bicycles, but above or below the seat. Depending on design, the ability to carry gear on the front wheel may be limited or absent. This limitation may be offset by pulling a trailer.

Tandem Touring

Tandems are bikes built for two riders and many couples tour on them. They can make it easier for two riders of different abilities to ride together, but the tandem frame does not allow for any more luggage than a single bike does. As with recumbents, this limitation can be overcome by pulling a trailer.

Specifications

Touring bicycles are usually equipped with luggage racks front and rear, designed to hold panniers or other forms of luggage. To carry heavy loads, to be field-repairable and for reliability, touring bicycles typically have steel (CroMo) frames and forks. They may also have durable hubs, double-wall rims and 36-spoke wheels with 3 or 4-cross spoke lacing. To accommodate long rides, touring bikes have comfortable handlebars and saddles. In fact there are many different bicycle handlebar arrangements available to touring cyclists, the choice of which is highly individual. One of the few remaining hand-built bicycle saddle manufacturers based in the UK is Brooks England. They produce leather saddles often used by touring cyclists due to their comfort when long hours are required in the saddle.

Touring bicycles may appear similar to road bicycles if they have drop handlebars. However, they greatly differ by typically having a much longer wheelbase and more stable steering geometry, with numerous attachments for luggage racks, fenders (mudguards), lights, high capacity water bottles, tools and spare parts. Chainstays must be long enough to accommodate panniers without them brushing the rider's heels, and the entire structure must be stiff enough to safely handle long, fast descents with the machine fully loaded.

Touring bicycles may also be fitted with 26" (ISO 559) wheels in preference over 700C (ISO 622). This is because ISO 559 wheels are used on mountain bicycles and are more durable and often easier to source in remote locations than 700C wheels. World bicycle tourers Tim and Cindie Travis are notable advocates of ISO 559 wheels for touring bicycles.

Instead of panniers, some riders prefer a bicycle trailer. Trailers are easy to use and allow touring with bikes on which it is impossible to attach racks. However, double wheeled trailers decrease maneuverability and are not particularly suited for touring in mountainous regions or on rugged terrain. On the other hand, single wheel trailers are extremely maneuverable, with the trailer wheel tracking very closely with the rear wheel. These can easily be ridden on single track trails (about 40 cm width), over some very technical terrain. Trailers have an advantage over panniers on single track trails because the bike itself carries no extra weight, except some on the rear axle attachment (the trailer itself can be loaded with up to 70 kg). This allows the rider to shift weight as if without load and clear logs or rocks (trailers will typically follow over anything the bottom bracket clears).

Touring bicycles traditionally use wide-ratio derailleur gears, often with a very low gear, in some countries called a "granny gear", for steep hills under load. Typically the gearing has a triple chainring similar to mountain bicycles, whereas most road bicycles have only two chainrings. Raleigh's 1985 catalogue lists touring bicycles that usually fitted with a 14-32 tooth 6-speed freewheel and 28/45/50-tooth chainrings, typically giving a gear range of 23 to 96 gear inches. A modern popular combination is to use an 11-34 tooth cassette with 22/32/44-tooth chainrings, typically giving a gear range from 18 to 104 gear inches. Internal-geared hubs with 5, 7, 8 or even 14 gear ratios have become an option in recent years because of their robustness and low maintenance. In particular, the Rohloff 14-speed hub with a gear range of over 500% has been used on at least two around-the world bicycle tours. Internal-geared hubs have a couple of advantages over traditional derailleur gears, in that they can use stronger chainsas generally a single sprocket and chainring combination will be used. Secondly the spread of gears can be made more evenly, that is to say there are many duplicated and unusable gears in a derailler geared setup.

Touring bicycles usually have linear-pull brakes or cantilever brakes, instead of the caliper brakes used on racing bicycles. Caliper brakes are less suitable because, to fit around mudguards (fenders) and wide tires, they become large and may flex when trying to stop a heavy bike. Some newer touring bikes use disc brakes, because of their greater stopping power in wet and muddy conditions and also to avoid outer rim wear. However, they are more complicated, so repairing them in remote locations can be difficult; they also weigh more than a cantilever brakes, increase the stresses on spokes, and require the front wheel to be dished, which reduces the durability of the wheels.

Thus, touring bikes trade speed for utility and ruggedness. This combination is popular with commuters and couriers as well.

Challenge Riding

Challenge riding is a form of cycling where the riders challenge themselves rather than each other. Some challenge rides are charity events or pledge rides. Some are organised as pre- or early-season training events (sometimes in the UK called reliability trials). Others, often referred to as Randonnées, brevets or Audax events occur simply for the sake of the challenge; cyclosportive events allow cyclists to test themselves over challenging race routes used, for example L'Étape du Tour in the Tour de France. Most challenge rides are open to all comers, but a few require qualification to attend.

Challenge rides may be day rides of fixed distance (e.g. 50 km, 100 km, 100 miles) or multi-day trips that span a state, country or province, such as RAGBRAI in Iowa and the End to End in the United Kingdom.

Audax (cycling)

Audax is a style of long distance cycling event mostly popular in France, but also in Holland, Belgium and Germany. The term is now also commonly used to describe a different style of long distance cycling event found in many countries including France, Great Britain, Singapore, Australia, Canada and the USA.

The original form of the audax style involves riding in strict group formation at a steady pace set by a road captain. The group attempts to maintain a pace of 22.5 km/h between stops. The route is pre-planned with designated stopping points. For longer audax events the group may ride between 16 and 20 hours in a day before stopping at a designated sleeping location. The goal of the audax is to finish inside the prescribed time limit with all members of the group present. A support vehicle is allowed to follow each group of riders.

In some countries such as Australia and Great Britain, the term Audax is also used for randonnées. These are also long distance bicycle events, but riders are free to cycle at their own pace (French: allure libre), stop or sleep wherever they want and form groups randomly, provided they stay within the time limit.

The national organising bodies for allure libre riding in these counties (Audax Australia and Audax UK) both include the word 'audax' in their names. In addition, Audax Club Parisien now holds events such as the Paris–Brest–Paris (PBP) for the allure libre style, not the original audax style.

This has contributed to some confusion over the use of the term 'audax'.

The allure libre style is also favoured in the USA, where the governing body is the Randonneurs USA.

History

On June 12, 1897, twelve Italian cyclists attempted the challenge of cycling from Rome to Naples, a distance of 230 km, during daylight hours. Nine succeeded. This is credited as an early example of randonneuring. Their attempt was described as 'daring' where the word audax is a form of the Italian/Latinate word "audace" meaning "audacious"

In 1904, Henri Desgrange in France was attracted to this style of cycling and created the French Audax club. On April 3, 1904 the first 200 km audax ride was held, followed by the first 100 km ride on June 26 of the same year. This style of riding led to the creation of the Paris–Brest–Paris cycle race, which was open for professional and for non-professional riders as well. The event evolved later into two separate non-professional events:

1. the allure libre event, held on a four year cycle,
2. the audax event, held on a five year cycle.

On July 14, 1921 the Union of Parisian Audax Cyclistes (UACP) was formed, which became the Union of French Audax in January 1956.

Organisations

The official organisation for the original audax style is the Union des Audax in France.

Bicycle Safety

Bicycle safety is the use of practices designed to reduce risk associated with cycling. Some of this subject matter is hotly debated: for example, the discussions as to whether bicycle helmets or cyclepaths really deliver improved safety. The merits of obeying the rules of the road including the use of bicycle lighting at night are less controversial.

Bicycle Crashes

According to a Department for transport report cyclists have in the UK a killed and serious injury (KSI) rate per million vehicle kilometres that is a half of the rate for Motorcyclists and eight times the rate for Motorists.

The first recorded bicycle accident is probably a collision in 1842, reportedly between Kirkpatrick McMillan, an early rider of the velocipede, and a young girl in Glasgow. The report, however, is vague and the identification disputed.

Causes of crashes vary according to local conditions. A study conducted in 2000 by SWOV (Institute for Road Safety Research) in the Netherlands found that single bicycle accidents accounted for 47% of all bicycle accidents, collisions with obstacles and animals accounted for 12%, and collisions with other road users accounted for 40% (with the remaining 1% having unknown or unclassified cause). In most countries the dominant cause of serious cyclist injury is collisions with motor traffic.

Motorists' Perceptions of Cyclists

The authors of the Drivers' perceptions of cyclists research report concluded that:

it is clear that motorists hold negative views about cyclists and tend to view cycle users as an 'out group' with significantly different characteristics from most road users ... the 'out group' status of cyclists brings with it a tendency among drivers to impute the poor or incompetent behaviour of some cyclists to all cyclists.

the effect of infrastructure that clearly defines ownership of space, in the case of these experiments the provision of cycle lanes in the virtual reality worlds, appears to increase driver confidence and, hence, potentially risky behaviour, such as higher vehicle speeds and less speed reduction when encountering cyclists.

Defining Safety

Although many accidents involve a cyclist alone, collisions that also involve a motor vehicle account for a much greater number of serious injuries. A cyclist who is hit by a car is more likely to be killed than one who just falls off.

This is what one would expect; a cyclist only accident only provides a small amount of kinetic energy due to relatively small mass and low speeds, whereas a motor vehicle can provide more. Falling off and hitting obstructions tend to be relatively minor, seldom requiring medical attention, hence sparsely represented in statistics.

As long ago as the early 1930s there were efforts to clear cyclists off the roads to make way for private cars, then largely a preserve of the elite. These were successful in Germany, then an authoritarian regime, and spread during the war to German-occupied countries such as the Netherlands where civilian motor transport was also crippled by fuel rationing, but was resisted in other countries.

During the mid-part of the twentieth century, the traffic engineering response to the increased use of motor vehicles in the United Kingdom, as in the rest of the industrialised world, was to look for solutions which not only eased the passage of traffic through the streets, but which also protected vulnerable road users from the dangers of the motor car. In the 1940s, an influential proponent of this ideology was Herbert Alker Tripp, an assistant commissioner of London's Metropolitan Police. Tripp argued in his book Town Planning and Road Traffic that: "If we could segregate pedestrians completely from the wheeled traffic, we could of course abolish pedestrian casualties". This philosophy was also pursued by Colin Buchanan, his 1963 report for the UK Government Traffic in Towns, defined future government policy until the end of the century. Buchanan himself knew that segregation had not been proven to work in the case of cyclists, he famously wrote in his 1958 book Mixed Blessing "The meagre efforts made to separate cyclists from motor traffic have failed, tracks are inadequate, the problem of treating them at junctions and intersections is completely unsolved, and the attitude of the cyclists themselves to these admittedly unsatisfactory tracks has not been as helpful as it might have been".

Primary Safety

The state of knowledge regarding primary safety has advanced significantly through programmes such as Effective Cycling and the development of Britain's new National

Standards for cycle training. In addition to technical improvements in brakes, tyres and bicycle construction generally (for example, it is now rare for a chain to snap and throw the rider when accelerating away from a stop), there are well-understood behavioural models which actively manage the risk posed by others. Most important among these is the understanding of road position.

SEGREGATED CYCLE FACILITIES

Segregated cycle facilities are roads, tracks, paths or marked lanes designated for use by cyclists from which motorised traffic is generally excluded. The names and definitions of the various cycle facility types vary from country to country, but besides local naming conventions, one of the main subdivisions is whether the facility is physically separated from other (especially motor vehicle) traffic, or whether the segregation is only due to markings.

Terminology and Usage

The term cycleway (UK) refers to a road (UK) or path (USA), for cyclists only, on its own separate right of way. The USA equivalents include bike trails or mountain-bike trails, which are unsurfaced trails, and bike paths, which are surfaced trails which meet more rigorous standards for width, grade and accessibility. Sometimes, pedestrians and cyclists are expected to share the same road or path. Such a shared facility is often called a shared-use path, multi-use path, or recreational path.

The term cycle track / cycle path (UK) or sidepath (USA) refers to a footway- or sidewalk-type structure, for cyclists only, alongside (not on) a carriageway (UK) or roadway (USA).

The category off-road facility includes all of the above: cycleways, bike trails, mountain-bike trails and bike paths.

The term cycle lane (UK) or bike lane (USA) refers to a lane, for cyclists only, marked on an existing portion of a carriageway (UK), roadway or shoulder (USA).

The category on-road facility includes cycle lanes and bike lanes.

History

Pre-motorisation

By the end of the 19th century, cycling was growing from a hobby to an established form of transport. Cyclists campaigned to improve the existing, often poorly surfaced, roads and tracks. A US group was the Good Roads Movement. In the UK, the Cyclists' Touring Club (CTC) distributed a treatise entitled Roads:Their construction and maintenance. In Germany, concerns arose regarding conflicts between cyclists, horse traffic and pedestrians, leading to sections of routes being upgraded to provide smoother surfaces and separate portions for the different groups.

An example of an early segregated cycle facility was the nine-mile dedicated Cycle-Way built in 1897 to connect Pasadena, California to Los Angeles. Its right of way followed the stream bed of the Arroyo Seco and required 1,250,000 board feet (2,950 m3) of pine to construct. The roundtrip toll was 15 US and it was lit with electric lights along its entire length. The route did not succeed, and the right of way later became the route for the Arroyo Seco Parkway, an automobile freeway opened in 1940.

Pre World War II

With the advent of the motor car, conflict arose between the increasingly powerful car lobby and bicycle users. By the 1920s and 1930s the German car lobbies initiated efforts to have cyclists removed from the roads so as to improve the convenience of motoring. In the UK, the cycling lobby was attempting to remove motor vehicles from the roads by calling for the building of special "motor roads" to accommodate them. This idea was opposed by the Motorists' Union, who feared that it would lead to motorists' losing the freedom to use public roads.

United Kingdom

In 1926 the CTC discussed an unsuccessful motion calling for cycle tracks to be built on each side of roads for "the exclusive use of cyclists", and that cyclists could be taxed, providing the revenue was used for the provision of such tracks. The first (and one of the very few) dedicated roadside optional cycle tracks was built, as an experiment for the Ministry of Transport, beside Western Avenue between Hanger Lane and Greenford Road in 1934. It was thought that "the prospect of cycling in comfort as well as safety would be appreciated by most cyclists themselves". However, the idea ran into trenchant opposition from cycling groups, with the CTC distributing pamphlets warning against the threat of cycle paths. Local CTC branches organised mass meetings to reject the use of cycle tracks and any suggestion that cyclists should be forced to use such devices. In 1935, a packed general meeting of the CTC adopted a motion rejecting ministerial plans for cycle path construction. The CTC were listened to, and the use of cycle tracks largely fell out of favour in the UK.

Post World War II

In the UK, little use of separate cycleway/cycle track systems took place except in the so-called "new towns" such as Stevenage and Harlow. From the end of the 1960s in Nordic countries, the Swedish SCAFT guidelines on urban planning were highly influential and argued that non-motorised traffic must be segregated from motorised traffic wherever possible. Under the influence of these guidelines cyclists and pedestrians were treated as a homogeneous group to be catered for using similar facilities. The guidelines strongly influenced cities such as Helsinki and Västerås to build large cycle path networks. By the late 1960s and 1970s, with the cyclists mainly gone, many German towns began removing cycle tracks so as to accommodate more car parking. Increasing traffic congestion and the 1970s oil shocks contributed to a resurgence in cycling in some countries. Outside of SCAFT-inspired developments in Nordic countries, the use of segregated cycle facilities was mainly confined to university towns with established populations of bicycle users.

1970s

In 1970 in the United Kingdom, the Milton Keynes Development Corporation produced the "Master Plan for Milton Keynes". One of the important elements of this plan, and of its subsequent implementation, was the Milton Keynes redway system of segregated cycle/pedestrian paths. These are fully separated from the road system, only occasionally running along side it. One of the aims of the redways was to make travel for pedestrians and cyclists convenient, safe, pleasant and accident free, but a study suggests that the system has only partially met these expectations. More recent statistical data shows that the accident rate for pedestrians in Milton Keynes is just 46% of the average for England and the rate for cyclists is 87%. However, the secluded semi-rural nature of many redways that make them pleasant by day can make some people feel unsafe to use them after dark.

In 1971 in the United States, the California state government contracted with University of California, Los Angeles (UCLA) for the design of bikeways (bicycle paths, bicycle side-paths, bicycle lanes). UCLA largely copied Dutch bicycle facilities practice (primarily sidepaths) to create their bikeway designs, but the derived designs were not made public. The California Statewide Bicycle Committee (CSBC) was created. Initially composed of representatives of governmental and motoring organisations. When John Forester, a cyclist representative, became a member he concluded that its real motivation for moving cyclists aside was the convenience of motorists, although the stated reason was the safety of cyclists. Serious safety issues were identified with the proposed designs. The resulting cyclist opposition discredited the designs and prevented enactment of a mandatory side-path law. This forced the state to start over with new bikeway design standards in 1976. Those designs were subsequently adapted by the Association of American State Highway and Transportation Officials (AASHTO) to form the first edition of the AASHTO Guide for Bicycle Facilities, which is widely followed in the USA.

1980s to Present

The 1980s saw the start of experimental cycle route projects in Danish towns such as Århus, Odense and Herning, and the beginning of a large programme of cycle facilities construction as part of a "bicycle masterplan" in the Netherlands. Following the "bicycle boom" of the early 1980s, German towns began revisiting the concept. The use of segregated cycle facilities is promoted by a large segment of the cycling community, for example lane and path cyclists, and also by many organisations associated with the environmental movement. The rise of the "Green" movement in the 1990s has been accompanied by requests for the construction of cycle networks in many countries. This has led to various high-profile cycle network projects, in Bogotá, Montreal, Dublin, Portland, New York and many other cities.

Safety Issues

The issue of the safety of segregated cycling facilities is one of controversy. Proponents tout segregation of cyclists as necessary to the provision of a safe cycling environment. In contrast, some research imply increases, some significant, in the rate and severity of car/bicycle collisions due to such segregation. Traffic reform advocates including David Engwicht and John Adams suggest that the added perception of risk in shared facilities increases safety.

Since the 1930s, the established cycling lobby in the UK and Ireland has taken a critical and measured view of the utility and value of segregating cyclists. In 1947, in response to official suggestions that cyclists should use cycle-tracks, the CTC adopted a motion expressing determined opposition to cycle paths alongside public roads. In 2007, official claims of safety for cycle tracks provoked a position paper from the umbrella body for UK cyclists' groups, stating "Cycle Campaign Network knows of no evidence that cycle facilities and in particular cycle lanes, generally lead to safer conditions for cycling".

In the 1970s the California Statewide Bicycle Committee arranged with Kenneth D. Cross for a study of car-bike collisions, expecting that this study would support their arguments on collision prevention. When presented to the Committee in Sacramento on 19 June 1974, Cross's study showed the opposite: only 0.5% of car-bike collisions had occurred between straight-ahead cyclists and overtaking straight-ahead motorists. Cross later had a contract with the National Highway Traffic Safety Administration (NHTSA) to produce an improved study (on a pseudo-random national sample), and the results were much the same. A 2006 report concludes that "bicycle safety data are difficult to analyse, mostly because bicycle trip data (and thus accident probability per trip) are hard to uncover" (see NCHRP Report 552, 2006, "Guidelines for Analysis of Investment in Bicycle Facilities", National Cooperative Highway Research Program, Transportation research Board of the National Academies, page F-1). The Netherlands and Denmark, which have the highest rates of cycle usage combined with the best records for safety, used to give their segregated cycle path networks primary importance in achieving these goals. However, the largest study undertaken into the safety of Danish cycle facilities has found that safety has decreased as a result. More recently, shared space redesigns of urban streets in those and other countries have achieved significant improvements in safety (as well as congestion and quality of life) by replacing segregated facilities with integrated space.

Urban Roads

Nature of Accidents

The source of the direct safety problem lies in the nature of the predominant car/bicycle collision types. The majority of collisions on urban roads occur at junctions and involve turning vehicles. Rear-end type collisions are only a major factor on arterial or interurban roads. More width for cyclists to use on rural/arterial roads with few junctions might lower the net number of collisions, but the data does not help answer the question of whether separating cyclist from other users would make a significant difference one way or the other.

Segregated Facilities and Location of Accidents

Cycle paths can be particularly dangerous at intersections with roads. When the path entrance is set back from the road, motorists often have difficulty seeing cyclists approaching from the path. Research presented at a conference at Lund University in 1990 found that "crash risk" for cycle users crossing the intersection on a set-back path are up to 11.9 times higher than when cycling on the roadway in a bike lane (see diagrams).

Segregated Facilities and Roundabouts

Particular concern attaches to the use of cycle lanes in urban situations such as large roundabouts. For adults, the standard vehicular cycling advice for handling roundabouts is to try to maintain a prominent position while circulating. The use of cycle lanes runs counter to this advice and places cyclists outside the main "zone of observation" of entering motorists, who represent the overwhelming source of risk (50% of collisions). In 2002, cycle lanes were removed from a roundabout in the English town of Weymouth after 20 months because the casualty rate had increased significantly. German research has indicated that cyclists are safer negotiating roundabouts in traffic rather than on separate cycle lanes or cycle paths. A recent paper on German roundabout design practice states "Cycle lanes at the peripheral margin of the circle are not allowed since they are very dangerous to cyclists". See also cycle facilities at roundabouts.

Segregated Facilities and Accident Numbers

For urban roads with many junctions, accident analysis suggests that segregated cycling facilities are likely to produce a net increase in the number of collisions. These conclusions are supported by the experience of countries that have implemented segregated cycling facilities. In the United States, UK,[not in citation given] Germany, Sweden, Denmarkand Finland, it has been found that cycling on roadside urban cycle tracks/sidepaths results in up to 12-fold increases in the rate of car/bicycle collisions. At a 1990 European conference on cycling, the term Russian roulette was used to describe the use of roadside cycle paths.

In Helsinki, research has shown that cyclists are safer cycling on roads with traffic than when using the city's 800 kilometres (500 mi) of cycle paths. The Berlin police and Senate conducted studies which led to a similar conclusion in the 1980s. In Berlin 10% of the roads have cycle paths, but these produce 75% of fatalities and serious injuries among cyclists. In the English town of Milton Keynes it has been shown that cyclists using the off-road Milton Keynes redway system have on a per-journey basis a significantly higher rate of fatal car-bicycle collisions than cyclists on ordinary roads. Cycle lanes and bike lanes are less dangerous than cycle paths in urban situations but even well-implemented examples have been associated with 10% increases in casualty rates,though incidentally, cycle lanes have been credited with reducing pedestrian crossing crash numbers by up to 30%.

Rural and Arterial Roads

Direct rear impacts with cyclists are a more prominent collision type in arterial/rural road type situations. When they occur in such circumstances they are also associated with significantly increased risk of fatality. Data collated by the OECD indicates that rural locations account for 35% or more of cycling fatalities in Denmark, Finland, France, Great Britain, Japan, the Netherlands and Spain.

In the UK, cycling collision data recorded by police indicates that at non-junction locations, where a cyclist was struck directly from behind there was an overall fatality rate of 17%. The rate of fatality increases with speed limit of the road:

- 5% on 30 mph (48 km/h),
- 13% on 40 mph (64 km/h),
- 21% on 60 mph (97 km/h) and
- 31% on 70 mph (110 km/h) roads.

The use of appropriately designed segregated space on arterial or interurban routes appears to be associated with reductions in overall risk. In Ireland, the provision of hard shoulders on interurban routes in the 1970s reportedly resulted in a 50% decrease in accidents. It is reported that the Danes have also found that separate cycle tracks lead to a reduction in rural collisions.

Cycleways

The safety of cycleways or roads and trails open exclusively to non-motorised modes, is difficult to assess. In terms of car/ bicycle collisions this is clearly mediated by how the cycleway network rejoins the main road network. The consequences of other risks — falls, cyclist–cyclist collisions and cyclist–pedestrian collisions — are frequently not recorded in official accident figures and may be available only via local hospital surveys. As a general rule those cycleways with the highest perceived safety tend to be those engineered on the assumption of vehicular rather than pedestrian traffic. Thus the most popular examples tend to be converted road or railway alignments or constructed to the same standards used by road and railway engineers.

Indirect Safety

There is evidence that one of the main factors influencing the individual safety of cyclists is the base number of cyclists using the roads - see safety in numbers effect. Therefore it is arguable that if a segregated cycle facility attracts more people to cycle, this should contribute to an increase in safety. For instance, a study of the accident impacts of re-engineering bicycle crossings in the Swedish city of Gothenburg attributes collision rate reductions in part to significant increases in cyclist volumes at the treated sites. In addition it has been shown that in Western countries the health benefits of regular cycling significantly outweigh the risks due to traffic danger. Therefore, notwithstanding a net increase in collisions, measures that promote cycling should produce an overall societal health benefit. Dutch analysts have argued as a statistical exercise that given that three times as many cyclists as car occupants are injured in collisions, and that cars harm about three times the number of other road users that bicycles do, in situations where casualties due to car traffic predominate increasing the number of cycling journeys and reducing the number of car journeys will reduce the total number of casualties] However, given their historical purpose, a positive relationship between the use of segregated cycle facilities and increased cyclist numbers cannot be assumed.

The "safety in numbers" argument has also been used to explain the apparent success of cycle facilities in some cities. In most cases, the most prominent examples of "successful" cycle networks were implemented in towns that already had significant numbers of cyclists. It is argued that in such cases this existing large cycling population already exerts a strong "safety in numbers" effect, and it is this, rather than their diversion onto off-road tracks, that accounts for the better safety record. More people might start cycling if the perceived safety of doing so improved sufficiently. Segregated cycle facilities are one way to improve the perception of safety. There are other approaches, such as shared space, which improve actual safety in part by decreasing the difference between real and perceived safety. See the Utility cycling article for other examples of measures to improve both actual and perceived safety.

Remedial Measures

Various remedial measures have been developed in an attempt to solve the identified safety problems of segregated cycle facilities. In some environments these represent established engineering practice while in others they may have to be retroactively applied in response to complaints and safety concerns. Examples include the addition of a separate system of traffic signals for bicycle traffic. This can result in greater cost and complexity in implementation particularly if there are already separate traffic signal phases for pedestrians, motorised traffic and public transport.

Some treatments involve raising the cycle track onto a speed ramp type structure where it crosses side roads. In addition, various road markings have been developed in an attempt to remedy the issue of increased junction collisions. Examples of these include the use of special road markings, e.g. "sharks teeth" or "elephants footprints", and treatments using red, green or blue coloured tarmac. Cycle-facility sceptics counter these improvements often simply "restore" the level of safety that existed before the marking or construction of the segregated cycle facility. Other approaches include efforts to "traffic calm" the bicycle traffic by introducing tight curves or bends to slow the cyclists down as they near a junction. Alternatively, traffic engineers may remove priority from the cyclists and require them to yield to turning traffic at every side road. In 2002, engineers proposing a sidepath scheme in the Irish university city of Galway stated that cyclists would be required to dismount and "become pedestrians" at every junction on the finished route.

Road traffic legislation and its implications

One of the potential pitfalls for observers trying to interpret the operation of segregated cycle facilities is that the same legal assumptions do not apply in all environments. For instance, in contrast to most English speaking countries, some European countries, including Germany, France, Denmark, Belgium and the Netherlands have defined liability legislation. Thus there is a legal assumption that motorists are automatically considered liable in law for any injuries that occur if they collide with a cyclist. This may hold regardless of any fault on the part of the cyclist and may significantly affect the behaviour of motorists when they encounter cyclists. In some countries it is legal for cyclists to overtake motor-vehicles on the inside, and cyclists doing so may enjoy the protection of the law. In this case, the use of segregated cycle facilities conforms to existing traffic law. In other jurisdictions similar "undertaking" manoeuvres by cyclists are illegal. Such distinctions form the basis of the argument that segregated cycle facilities encourage behaviours that flout existing traffic law and in which cyclists enjoy no legal protection.

This variation also applies to the operation of traffic signals and cyclist-specific traffic lights. For instance, in Germany and elsewhere at junctions with segregated facilities all the traffic in a given direction (motorists, pedestrians and cyclists) may get a green signal at the same time. Turning motor traffic is obliged to wait for cyclists and pedestrians to clear the junction before proceeding. In this situation all the transport modes get equal green time. In contrast, UK and Irish practice restricts pedestrians to a dedicated signal phase, separate from and usually much shorter than the green phase for motorists (e.g. 6–12 seconds, vs. signal cycle times of up to 120 seconds). If cyclists were to be segregated and treated in a similar manner this would imply a significant reduction in green time for cycle traffic at every junction. In the English city of Cambridge the use of cyclist-specific traffic signals is reported to have resulted in increased delays for cyclists, leading some to ignore the cycle-facilities and stay on the road. A similar example occurred in a Parisian bikepath scheme in 1999. Cyclists faced twice the number of traffic signals as motorised traffic and were expected to wait over one minute to get seven seconds of green time. Conversely, in Copenhagen cyclist-specific traffic signals on a major arterial bike lane have been linked to provide "green waves" for rush hour cycle-traffic.

Design Issues

Other potential pitfalls in interpreting the operation of segregated cycle facilities are the issues of design vehicles and design users. The Netherlands is a flat country and Dutch town planning keeps cycling distances short. The typical Dutch town bike or "granny bike" has no gears or a three-speed hub gear and back pedal brakes. In countries with different geographies and cycling cultures bicycles tend to have 7-15 gears (not counting duplicates), and a reasonably fit adult commuter can expect to reach speeds of 30 km/h (20 mph) Sports cyclists can travel even faster: with tailwinds or downhill gradients, some cyclists may exceed 50 km/h (30 mph). While a Dutch sidepath system may work for Dutch cyclists, serious questions have been raised since at least the 1970s that other cyclists using faster bicycle types cannot use such a system safely at their higher normal cycling speeds. The Danish Roads Directorate acknowledges that the advent of faster bicycle types has not increased safety, since their cycle track system "functions best when cyclists travel at relatively low speeds"

In some cases designers may focus on a particular design user. The UK's Sustrans guidelines for the National Cycle Network are based on recreational use with a design user who is an unaccompanied twelve-year-old. The Dublin Transportation Office has advertised their cycle facilities as being based on an unaccompanied ten-year-old design user. This raises the issue of what happens if different cyclist types find themselves forced onto such devices either by legal coercion or as a result of motorist aggression. This issue is captured in a 1996 review of the Sustrans approach from the Proceedings of the Institution of Civil Engineers.

The fast cycle commuter must not be driven off the highway onto a route that is designed for a 12-year-old or a novice on a leisure trip, because if that happens, the whole attempt to enlarge the use of the bicycle will have failed

Maintenance Issues

Moving motor vehicles generate a "sweeping" effect that pushes road debris such as grit and broken glass to the edge of the roadway. By excluding motor traffic, cycle lanes and cycle tracks become parts of the road that are no longer routinely "swept", thus collecting more broken glass and gravel. In addition, some off-road designs are not accessible to standard road sweeping equipment. One UK study estimated that cycle path users are seven times more likely to get punctures than are road cyclists.

Many cyclists will simply refuse to use poorly maintained facilities that offer obvious dangers. Some question the prudence of funding new cycle facilities unless there is a simultaneous commitment to maintenance and sweeping.

In areas subject to high leaf-fall in autumn, or high snowfall in winter, any cycle facilities must be subject to regular clearing if they are to remain usable. Danish guidance specifies three different categories of cycle track. Category "A" tracks must be kept clear of snow 24 hours a day, category "B" tracks are swept or cleared daily, and category "C" receive less regular winter maintenance. In 2007 the city of Copenhagen spent DKK 9.9 million (US$1.72 million, •1.33 million) annually on maintaining its cycle track network. German federal law requires local authorities to declassify cycle tracks that do not conform to strict design and maintenance criteria. In the UK, facilities for non-motorized traffic are not normally salted or gritted in icy conditions, making them dangerous or completely unrideable; those who are willing to continue cycling in such conditions are safer on the main road if that has been appropriately treated.

Segregated cycle facilities and transportation cycling

n some cases, cycle paths have been constructed so bicycles could be prohibited from the main roadway. It is controversial in the cycle path debate whether this is for the benefit of motorists or bicyclists.

In 1996 the UK Cyclists' Touring Club and the Institute of Highways and Transportation jointly produced a set of Cycle-Friendly Infrastructure guidelines that placed segregated cycling facilities at the bottom of the hierarchy of measures designed to promote cycling. Planners at the Directorate Infrastructure Traffic and Transport in Amsterdam place cyclists and motorists together on roads with speed limits at or below 30 km/h (19 mph), and segregate them through bicycle lanes at higher limits. This is in a context where most of the measures prioritised by Cycle-Friendly Infrastructure (HGV restrictions, area-wide traffic calming, speed limit enforcement etc.) are already in place - see Utility cycling for more detail.

The typical cost of constructing a striped bike lane is US$10,000 - $50,000 per round-trip mile.

Evidence

Between the late 1980s and early 1990s the Netherlands spent 1.5 billion guilders (US$945 million) on cycling infrastructure, yet cycling levels stayed practically the same. When the flagship Delft Bicycle Route project was evaluated, the results were "not very positive: bicycle use had not increased, neither had the road safety. A route network of bicycle facilities has, apparently, no added value for bicycle use or road safety".

In the UK, a ten-year study of the effect of cycle facilities in eight towns and cities found no evidence that they had resulted in any diversion from other transport modes. A similar finding had been reported for Denmark in 1989, where it was found that there was no correlation between cycle facilities and increased cycling unless active traffic restraint measures were also present. In Denmark as a whole, the establishment of a huge cycling infrastructure has been accompanied by cycling levels that have stayed roughly stable (with minor fluctuations) since 1975. The construction of 320 kilometres (200 mi) of "Strategic cycle network" in Dublin has been accompanied by a 15% fall in commuter cycling and 40% falls in cycling by second and third level students. In contrast, in the late 1970s and early 1980s cycling underwent robust growth in Germany, the UK and Ireland while there was little or no investment in cycling infrastructure.

Issue of Demonstrated Need

A key concern raised by critics of such schemes is that the focus is often on constructing "cycle facilities" rather than "facilitating cyclists". This was in part the motivation behind the "Hierarchy of Provision" approach set out in Cycle Friendly Infrastructure. This document states; There is little point providing a limited number of cycle facilities if conditions are made more difficult on the remainder of the road network. It is readily apparent that there are many cities that have extensive cycle networks and also high levels of cycling. However, there is a debate over whether many people took up cycling because the facilities were available or whether those cities constructed cycle facilities because of a large cycling population. For instance, bike planning in Davis, California was driven by the prior existence of a "dramatic volume" of cyclists in the 1960s. Research on the German bicycle boom of the 1980s paints a picture of German local authorities struggling to keep up with the growth of cycling rather than this growth being driven by their interventions In relation to the UK, it has been argued that locally high levels of cycling are more likely to result from factors other than cycle facilities. These include an existing cycling culture and historically high levels of cycle use, compact urban forms, lack of hills and lack of barriers such as high speed intersections.

However, U.S.-based observers have stated that "the provision of separate cycling facilities" appears to be one of the keys to the achieving of high levels of cycling in the Netherlands, Denmark and Germany.

The safety of cycling and the number of cyclists results from a complex interaction of spatial planning, population density, legislative environment, and wider traffic/transportation management policies (see utility cycling for more detailed discussion). The essence of the debate is whether segregated cycle facilities play a primary role of themselves, or are secondary to these other factors.

Cycle Facilities in Promoting Recreational Cycling

Separate cycleways and bike trails are less controversial when used to promoting recreational cycling. In Northern European countries, cycling tourism represents a significant proportion of overall tourist activity. Extensive interurban cycleway networks can be found in countries such as Denmark, which has had a national system of cycle routes since 1993. These may use roads dedicated to exclusively cycle traffic or minor rural roads whose use is otherwise restricted to local motor traffic and agricultural machinery. The UK has recently implemented the National Cycle Network.

Where available these routes often make use of abandoned railway corridors - see picture right of Mosel Maar cycle route. A prominent example in the UK is the Bristol & Bath Railway Path, a 13 miles (21 km) off-road cycleway that is part of National Cycle Route 4. Other UK examples include The Ebury Way Cycle Path, The Alban Way, the Hillend Loch Railway Path and the Nicky Line. In 2003 the longest continuous cycleway in Europe was opened, along the Albacete-Valdeganga highway in Spain, a distance of 22 kilometres (14 mi). Bogota's Bike Paths Network or "Ciclo-Ruta" in Spanish, designed and built during the administration of Mayor Enrique Peñalosa attracts significant recreational use.

Sharing as opposed to segregation

- Shared space

- Sharrows
- Bicycle boulevard
- Hans Monderman

In terms of multi-use trails, a "shared trail" may refer to a shared trail corridor with or without segregation within the corridor. In this context, segregated cycle facilities are a subset of shared facilities. Segregation may be supported by physical separation.

Cyclists' Touring Club

CTC and the UK's national cyclists' organisation are the trading names of the Cyclists' Touring Club.

CTC is the United Kingdom's largest cycling membership organisation. It also has members and district associations in the Republic of Ireland. It was established in 1878, originally as the 'Bicycle Touring Club', making it the oldest national tourism organisation of any description in the World, and was renamed the Cyclists' Touring Club in 1883. Since January 2007, CTC's president has been the newsreader and journalist, Jon Snow.

History

CTC was founded at Harrogate, Yorkshire, on 5 August 1878 by an Edinburgh medical student, Stanley Cotterell. It was originally called the Bicycle Touring Club and its headquarters were wherever Cotterell happened to be living. It had 80 members, all men. The first woman, a Mrs W. D. Welford, joined in 1880. In 1883, the Bicycle Touring Club was renamed the Cyclists' Touring Club to open membership to tricyclists. Membership rose to 10,627 and CTC opened a headquarters at 139-140 Fleet Street, London EC4.

Uniform

Members, like those of other clubs, often rode in uniform. CTC appointed an official tailor. The uniform was a dark green

Devonshire serge jacket, knickerbockers and a "Stanley helmet with a small peak". The colour changed to grey when green proved impractical because it showed the dirt. Groups often rode with a bugler at their head to sound changes of direction or to bring the group to a halt. Confusion could be caused when groups met and mistook each other's signals.

Cycling Accommodation

In earlier times, the Cyclists' Touring Club gave seals of approval, in the form of a cast metal plaque showing the winged-wheel symbol of CTC, for mounting on an outside wall of hotels and restaurants which offered good accommodation and service to cyclists. A few of the metal plaques still exist, as do a handful of road signs put up by CTC to warn cyclists of steep hills: usually steep going down, which was as much a problem for riders of large-wheel ordinaries, or "penny-farthings", as going up. Nowadays, CTC no longer puts up general road signs—although the right to do so is retained—and approved establishments are offered a plastic window-sticker carrying the blue and yellow logo shown above.

In 1898 CTC became embroiled in a court case to defend a member denied what she thought adequate service at a hotel carrying the club's badge.

Florence Wallace Pomeroy, Lady Harberton (1843-1911) of Cromwell Road, Kensington — wife of James Pomeroy, 6th Viscount Harberton and president of the Western Rational Dress Society — cycled on the morning of 27 October 1898 to have lunch at the Hautboy Hotel in Ockham, Surrey. Her campaigning for society to accept that women could wear "rational" dress on a bicycle and not ankle-length dresses led her to wear a jacket and a pair of long and baggy trousers which came together just above the ankle. She walked into the coffee room and asked to be served. The landlady, a Mrs Martha Sprague, showed her instead into the bar parlour.

CTC went into action, mounting a prosecution for "refusing food to a traveller". The landlady was acquitted and CTC lost the unusually large amount of money it had allotted to the case, which had been considered at the root of cyclists' rights and the values of CTC.

CTC and Motorists

In 1906 CTC asked the High Court to amend its constitution so that it could admit all tourists, including car-drivers. A majority of members - 10,495 to 2,231 - had voted the previous year for the change to take place. The court ruled that CTC could not protect the interests of cyclists and drivers at the same time and denied permission.

In 1926 the CTC discussed an unsuccessful motion calling for cycle tracks to be built on each side of roads for "the exclusive use of cyclists", and that cyclists could be taxed, providing the revenue was used for the provision of such tracks.

Modern CTC

Today CTC is concerned with the promotion of cycling for recreation, travel and transport, and has about 70,000 members. Among its successes have been a benchmarking project to spread best practice in cycle-friendly infrastructure design, and a grant of nearly £1 million to promote national standards for cycle training, standards CTC helped to develop.

CTC is organised at a district level, with CTC Local Groups organising cycle rides on most Sundays and often during the week. The more leisurely rides are planned around café stops, the quality of the ride often being judged on the standard of the cakes; CTC has been referred to as[by whom?] "Café To Café" or "Coffee, Tea and Cakes".

CTC is a founder of the Slower Speeds Initiative, an unincorporated association dedicated to reducing traffic speeds on all roads. CTC works with organisations such as Transport

2000 and Sustrans, and has charitable offshoots, the CTC Charitable Trust and the Cyclists' Defence Fund.

In 2008, the CTC Charitable Trust launched their Cycle Champions' programme. Utilising funding from the National Lottery's Wellbeing Fund, CTC employ 13 Community Cycling development Officers around England to promote cycling in all sectors of the community, particularly those not traditionally associated with cycling. They recruit 'Cycle Champions' within the community to work towards these goals as volunteers.

In 2009, CTC, in partnership with ContinYou and UK Youth, launched Bike Club, a programme funded by Cycling England with the intention of promoting cycling, and its associated learning experiences, among children and young people aged 10-20. Locally-based officers advise on the establishment of clubs and the application for funding.

The members' magazine, Cycle, covers subjects including ride reports, product reviews and legal and technical advice. Members benefit from public liability insurance, which is extended to cover rides organised under the auspices of CTC Local Groups.

CTC is a member of the European Cyclists' Federation.

Mixed Terrain Cycle-Touring

Mixed Terrain Cycle-Touring nicknamed "rough riding" involves cycling over a variety of surfaces and topography on a single route, with a single bicycle. The recent popularity of mixed terrain touring is in part a reaction against the increasing specialization of the bike industry. Focusing on freedom of travel and efficiency over varied surfaces, mixed terrain bicycle travel has a storied past, one closely linked with warfare. By comparison, today's mixed terrain riders are generally adventure oriented, although many police departments rely on the bicycle's versatility. In many remote (and not so remote) parts of the world with unreliable pavement, the utility bicycle has become a dominant form of mixed terrain transportation. A new style of travel called adventure cycle-touring or expedition touring involves exploring these remote regions of the world on sturdy bicycles designed for the purpose.

Specialized Versus All-round Transportation

Mountain biking has become increasingly more specialized for travel over technical dirt (hiking width) trails called single track, while road cycling focuses increasingly on maximizing travel over pavement. Traditional bicycle touring is typically considered road biking with travel primarily on paved roads, often carrying heavy loads of camping gear. Rough riding, in contrast, incorporates travel on both dirt and pavement; it stresses efficient travel on any surface or topography, a greater freedom of travel, and self reliance.

Types of Mixed Terrain Bicycle Travel

Adventure Cycle-Touring or expedition touring involves bicyclists attempting extended travel in remote regions of the world. Some "use bikes to go even further off the beaten track: they want to go where buses don't go at all and perhaps where other vehicles cannot get to either." Adventure tourists expect poor road conditions, unpaved roads and other mixed terrain.

Alpine Cycle-Touring is rough riding in the mountains. Different than pure mountain biking, in alpine touring paved mountain roads are combined with dirt roads and single track for an efficient route through tough mountain terrain. Mountain features are not always avoided and are sometimes incorporated into the route, which may require alternative bicycle hauling techniques. This type of bicycle travel has a mountaineering flair, but it is generally done as adventure cycle-touring in developed countries where services are more prevalent and bike technology is slightly different allowing for more efficiency and speedier travel.

Mixed Terrain Bicycle Racing includes Cyclo-cross, a popular racing style in America. Begun in Europe in the early

1900s, racers compete on mixed terrain courses on relatively flat courses. Mountain-cross, another form of mixed terrain racing staged on mountain courses is a recent invention.

Mixed Terrain Commuting may have contributed to the reaction against bicycle specialization. As bikes become more specialized, they become less suited for general commuting. Often commuters must travel on mixed surfaces or rough pavement even in urban environments. Often safer routes can be found away from heavy traffic, encouraging alternative and varied route selection.

Snow Biking, also called icebiking is another example of mixed terrain bicycle travel and a great example of the bicycle's flexible technology. Nearly any bike which allows medium or wide tires can be outfitted with special snow studded tires. Surly Bikes and other manufactures make bikes with extra wide tires specifically designed for deep snow. Events for racing and adventure riding across the snow have been created. The Iditarod Trail Invitational is a 1100 mile race billed as the "worlds longest winter ultra race across frozen Alaska". Another form of bicycle snow travel is called Skibobbing or ski biking which replaces wheels for skis. Ski bikes can be seen at many ski areas in North America.

Preferred Bicycles

The preferred bike for mixed terrain travel in the West is called an "all-in-one" or "all-rounder". Sometimes called cross bikes, they are a synthesis between road bikes and mountain bikes. There are cyclocross bikes that are used for on and off road racing, and monster cross bikes that accommodate mountain bike sized tires and allow for single track riding. Furthermore, there are also Brevet or Randonneur bikes which originated in mixed long terrain rides. This breed of bike retains much of the speed and efficiency of a road bike on pavement, while maintaining the necessary features for dirt and gravel. These unusual bikes have light frames with 700c or 650B tires and drop handlebars. Expedition touring bikes for allow for travel in third world countries in contrast compromise some speed for increased durability, heavy load carrying capacity and easy maintenance anywhere in the world. This has come to mean an expensive sturdy steel framed bike with 26" mountain bike sized wheels, no suspension, and either road style drop or mountain bike style flat handlebars. There are many producers of touring and cross bicycles, ranging from major manufacturers to your local custom frame builder.

Organizations and Clubs

A few organizations and clubs promote mixed terrain touring. The biggest is probably the Adventure Cycling Association located in Missoula Montana. They are responsible for mapping the Great Divide Trail, the world's longest mapped mixed terrain route. The oldest, still functioning, club dedicated to rough riding may be The Rough Stuff Fellowship of Great Britain founded in 1955. The Rough Riders of Southern California and the Colorado Rough Riders in Golden, Colorado are two American clubs dedicated to mixed terrain bicycle travel.

History

The history of mixed terrain bicycle travel begins with the bicycle itself. Early roads were rarely paved. In fact, the popularity of bicycle riding may have encouraged the paving of roads. Bicycle travel became very popular around 1885 with the development of the modern bicycle configuration which we still see in wide use today. By 1886 the United States Army started experimenting with bicycle infantry as a replacement for horses in mixed terrain environments. The Army's 25th Infantry Regiment unit (African American Buffalo Soldiers) stationed at Fort Missoula, Montana was chosen for the test. These hearty riders traveled from Missoula to Yellowstone National Park during one trip and from Missoula to St. Louis, Missouri for their final trial. Much of the mixed terrain route was on unimproved roads or through roadless areas. Although they succeeded in beating the best horse travel times, the Army abandoned bicycle travel in anticipation of yet a faster new technology just being developed, the automobile . Although the U.S. military has not relied on bicycles, other militaries throughout the world, out of necessity, have used bicycles extensively for travel in mixed terrain. During the Second Boer War (1899–1901) both sides used bicycles in combat. Bike were primarily used for messenger service.

By World War I, the Italian Army developed a folding bicycle that could be carried on a soldier's back for easy transport over difficult mixed terrain and alpine obstacles. The Germans, French and British also used bicycles for mixed terrain travel in WWI. Mechanized transport was still fairly limited so bicycle travel was relied upon heavily. Mechanized transport during WWII was much more prevalent, but the bicycle was still used by Japanese, German and Italian troops to some extent. The Allies supplied a limited number of paratroopers with folding bikes. British paratroopers on folding bicycles raided a German radar unit at Ste. Bruneval, France.

Up until recently (2003), the Swiss Army still had a bicycle infantry unit. The Swiss were great believers in the virtues of mixed terrain bicycle travel. " A fully equipped man can fly down the mountainside at speeds up to 50mph, and up to a distance of about 30 miles the entire troop can reach a potential battle zone faster than mechanized troops. 'We can go through the woods, we can take short-cuts,' said Jean-Pierre Leuenberger, commander of the training school near Romont. But the important point, he added, was that his men were able to fight when they got there."

Some armies around the world still use bicycles even today. In the West, many police departments now rely on mixed terrain travel by police bicycle. These cops on bikes can quickly chase down a runner, maneuver through tight areas not available to cars and yet cruise down any paved road or path. Paramedic and emergency medical technician groups also use the bicycle for ease of access where ambulance travel is difficult.

Mixed terrain bicycle travel for pleasure & commerce has seen varying degrees of interest over the years. Cyclo-cross racing likely got its start when European road racers in the early 1900s began cutting through farm fields and over fences as a way to train and keep warm during the winter off season. Club riding in early 1900's Europe often included mixed terrain (called rough stuff or storm passing) as an integral part of typical routes. Early recreational cyclists would extend their biking range to include off road cycling. "Evidence of how much rough stuff was viewed as an integral part of the experience for the touring cyclist can be found in the format of the BCTC (British Cycle Tourist Competition). Run by the CTC and inaugurated in 1952 until the late 80's its aim was to find Britain's best tourist. Rough stuff riding was a key element and the organizers often went to great lengths to find awkward tracks, fords etc that would test a rider's skill."

By the 1950s in Europe, bike clubs were formed specifically around mixed terrain and off road touring. In Great Britain, a club called Rough Stuff Fellowship was formed around mixed terrain and off road touring. "The history of the RSF goes way back to its foundation in 1955, long before anyone had ever heard of Marin County. It was formed by cyclists who wanted to get away from roads and cycle on tracks, and byways." The Rough Stuff Fellowship is still an active club today. France also had a mixed terrain club called Velo Cross Club Parisien formed between 1951 and 1956. Not content with cyclo-cross racing of the day, around twenty French cyclists modified their 650-b bikes for mixed and off road travel.

The beach cruiser bicycle entered the market in the early 1930s. These heavy single speed bikes sporting "balloon" tires could handle a variety of mixed terrain including moderately loose flat sandy beaches. Paper boys and couriers favored these bikes since they could handle the occasional gravel road with ease. However, as heavy single speed bikes they were not good for hilly terrain and climbing. These bikes have made a comeback in recent years for their retro look. They are still good flat lander all-rounder bikes, great for cruising the beach or urban landscape. In the late 1970s cruiser bicycles, by then called "clunkers" became the inspiration for mountain bikes. Offering cheap material for experimentation, these clunkers were slowly turned into the modern mountain bike. Wider tires on lighter frames, with multiple gears proved to be a wildly successful combination for mixed terrain and truly rugged single track. Early mountain bike designs still make good mixed terrain vehicles, with slight modification. Unfortunately with current mountain bike advancements in suspension systems and other technical mountain bike features, the mountain bike of today is overkill and inefficient for mixed terrain touring. Recently a new synthesis between road bikes and mountain bikes has begun to take shape as riders look away from specialization and back towards bicycles that can handle mixed terrain travel.

Chapter 5

Grand Tour

The Grand Tour was the traditional travel of Europe undertaken by mainly upper-class European young men of means. The custom flourished from about 1660 until the advent of large-scale rail transit in the 1840s, and was associated with a standard itinerary. It served as an educational rite of passage. Though primarily associated with the British nobility and wealthy landed gentry, similar trips were made by wealthy young men of Protestant Northern European nations on the Continent, and from the second half of the 18th century some American and other overseas youth joined in. The tradition was extended to include more of the middle class after rail and steamship travel made the journey less of a burden, and Thomas Cook made the "Cook's Tour" a byword.

Recently The New York Times described the Grand Tour in this way:

Three hundred years ago, wealthy young Englishmen began taking a post-Oxbridge trek through France and Italy in search of art, culture and the roots of Western civilization. With nearly unlimited funds, aristocratic connections and months (or years) to roam, they commissioned paintings, perfected their language skills and mingled with the upper crust of the Continent.

The primary value of the Grand Tour, it was believed, lay in the exposure both to the cultural legacy of classical antiquity and the Renaissance, and to the aristocratic and fashionably polite society of the European continent. In addition, it provided the only opportunity to view specific works of art, and possibly the only chance to hear certain music. A grand tour could last from several months to several years. It was commonly undertaken in the company of a knowledgeable guide or tutor. The Grand Tour had more than superficial cultural importance; as E.P. Thompson stated, "ruling-class control in the 18th century was located primarily in a cultural hegemony, and only secondarily in an expression of economic or physical (military) power."

In essence the Grand Tour was neither a scholar's pilgrimage nor a religious one, though a pleasurable stay in Venice and a cautious residence in Rome were essential. Catholic Grand Tourists followed the same routes as Protestant Whigs. Since the 17th century a tour to such places was also considered essential for budding young artists to understand proper painting and sculpture techniques, though the trappings of the Grand Tour— valets and coachmen, perhaps a cook, certainly a "bear-leader" or scholarly guide— were beyond their reach. The advent of popular guides, such as the Richardsons', did much to popularize such trips, and following the artists themselves, the elite considered travel to such centres as necessary rites of passage. For gentlemen, some works of art were essential to demonstrate the breadth and polish they had received from their tour: in Rome antiquaries like Thomas Jenkins provided access to private collections of antiquities, among which enough proved to be for sale that the English market raised the price of such things, as well as for coins and medals, which formed more portable souvenirs and a respected gentleman's guide to ancient history.Pompeo Batoni made a career of painting English milordi posed with graceful ease among Roman antiquities. Many continued on to Naples, where they viewed Herculaneum and Pompeii, but few ventured far into southern Italy and fewer still to Greece, still under Turkish rule.

History

In Britain, Thomas Coryat's travel book Coryat's Crudities (1611), published during the Twelve Years' Truce, was an early influence on the Grand Tour but it was the far more extensive tour through Italy as far as Naples undertaken by the 'Collector' Earl of Arundel, together with his wife and children in 1613-14 that established the most significant precedent. This is partly because he asked Inigo Jones, not yet established as an architect but already known as a 'great traveller' and masque designer, to act as his cicerone (guide).. Larger numbers of tourists began their tours after the Peace of Münster in 1648. According to the Oxford English Dictionary, the first recorded use of the term (perhaps its introduction to English) was by Richard Lassels (c. 1603–1668), an expatriate Roman Catholic priest, in his book The Voyage of Italy, which was published posthumously in Paris in 1670 and then in London. Lassels's introduction listed four areas in which travel furnished "an accomplished, consummate Traveller": the intellectual, the social, the ethical (by the opportunity of drawing moral instruction from all the traveller saw), and the political.

The idea of traveling for the sake of curiosity and learning was a developing idea in the 17th century. With John Locke's Essay Concerning Human Understanding (1690) it was argued, and widely accepted, that knowledge comes entirely from the external senses, that what one knows comes from the physical stimuli to which one has been exposed, thus, one could "use up" the environment, taking from it all it offers, requiring a change of place. Travel, therefore, was necessary for one to develop the mind and expand knowledge of the world. As a young man at the outset of his account of a repeat Grand Tour the historian Edward Gibbon remarked that "According to the law of custom, and perhaps of reason, foreign travel completes the education of an English gentleman." Consciously adapted for intellectual self-improvement, Gibbon was "revisiting the Continent on a larger and more liberal plan"; most Grand Tourists did not pause more than briefly in libraries. On the eve of the Romantic era he played a significant part in introducing, William Beckford wrote a vivid account of his Grand Tour that made Gibbon's unadventurous Italian tour look distinctly conventional.

The typical 18th century sentiment was that of the studious observer traveling through foreign lands reporting his findings on human nature for those unfortunate enough to have stayed home. Recounting one's observations to society at large to increase its welfare was considered an obligation; the Grand Tour flourished in this mindset.

The Grand Tour not only provided a liberal education but allowed those who could afford it the opportunity to buy things otherwise unavailable at home, and it thus increased participants' prestige and standing. Grand Tourists would return with crates of art, books, pictures, sculpture, and items of culture, which would be displayed in libraries, cabinets, gardens, and drawing rooms, as well as the galleries built purposely for their display; The Grand Tour became a symbol of wealth and freedom. Artists who especially thrived on Grand Tourists included Carlo Maratti, who was first patronized by John Evelyn as early as 1645, Pompeo Batoni the portraitist, and the vedutisti such as Canaletto, Pannini and Guardi. The less well-off could return with an album of Piranesi etchings.

The "perhaps" in Gibbon's opening remark cast an ironic shadow over his resounding statement. Critics of the Grand Tour derided its lack of adventure. "The tour of Europe is a paltry thing", said one 18th century critic, "a tame, uniform, unvaried prospect". The Grand Tour was said to reinforce the old preconceptions and prejudices about national characteristics, as Jean Gailhard's Compleat Gentleman (1678) observes: "French courteous. Spanish lordly. Italian amorous. German clownish." The deep suspicion with which Tour was viewed at home in England, where it was feared that the very experiences that completed the British gentleman might well undo him, were epitomised in the sarcastic nativist view of the ostentatiously "well-travelled" maccaroni of the 1760s and 70s.

After the arrival of steam-powered transportation, around 1825, the Grand Tour custom continued, but it was of a qualitative difference—cheaper to undertake, safer, easier, open to anyone. During much of the 19th century, most educated young men of privilege undertook the Grand Tour. Germany and Switzerland came to be included in a more broadly defined circuit. Later, it became fashionable for young women as well; a trip to Italy, with a spinster aunt chaperon, was part of the upper-class woman's education, as in E.M. Forster's novel A Room with a View.

Travel Itinerary

The most common itinerary of the Grand Tour shifted across generation in the cities it embraced, but the tourist usually began in Dover, England and crossed the English Channel to Ostend, in Belgium, or Calais, or Le Havre in France. From there the tourist, usually accompanied by a tutor (known colloquially as a "bear-leader") and if wealthy enough a league of servants, could rent or acquire a coach (which could be resold in any city or disassembled and packed across the Alps, as in Giacomo Casanova's travels, who resold it on completion), or opt to make the trip by boat as far as the alps, either traveling over the Seine to Paris, or the Rhine to Basel.

Upon hiring a French-speaking guide, the tourist and his entourage would travel to Paris. There the traveler might undertake lessons in French, dancing, fencing, and riding. The appeal of Paris lay in the sophisticated language and manners of French high society, including courtly behavior and fashion. Ostensibly this served the purpose of preparing the young man for a leadership position at home, often in government or diplomacy.

From Paris he would typically go to urban Switzerland for a while, often to Geneva (the cradle of the Protestant Reformation) or Lausanne. ("Alpinism," or mountaineering, was a development of the 19th century.) From there the traveler would endure a difficult crossing over the Alps into northern

Italy (such as at St. Bernard Pass), which included dismantling the carriage and luggage. If wealthy enough, he might be carried over the hard terrain by servants.

Once in Italy the tourist would visit Turin (and, less often, Milan), then might spend a few months in Florence, where there was a considerable Anglo-Italian society accessible to traveling Englishmen "of quality" and where the Tribuna of the Uffizi gallery brought together in one space the monuments of High Renaissance paintings and Roman sculptures that would inspire picture galleries dressed with antiquities at home, with side trips to Pisa, then move on to Padua, Bologna, and Venice. The British idea of Venice as the "locus of decadent Italianate allure" made it an epitome and cultural setpiece of the Grand Tour.

From Venice the traveler went to Rome to study the ruins of ancient Rome. Some travelers also visited Naples to study music, and (after the mid-18th century) to appreciate the recently-discovered archaeological sites of Herculaneum and Pompeii and perhaps for the adventurous thrilling ascent of Mount Vesuvius. Later in the period the more adventurous, especially if provided with a yacht, might attempt Sicily (the site of Greek ruins) or even Greece itself. But Naples or later Paestum further south was the usual terminus.

From here the traveler traversed the Alps heading north through to the German-speaking parts of Europe. The traveler might stop first in Innsbruck before visiting Berlin, Dresden, Vienna and Potsdam, with perhaps some study time at the universities in Munich or Heidelberg. From there travelers visited Holland and Flanders (with more gallery-going and art appreciation) before returning across the Channel to England.

Published Aaccounts

Published (and often polished) accounts of personal experiences on the Grand Tour provide illuminating detail and a first-hand perspective of the experience. Of some accounts offered in their own lifetimes, Jeremy Black detects the element of literary artifice in these and cautions that they should be approached as travel literature rather than unvarnished accounts. He lists as examples Joseph Addison, John Andrews, William Thomas Beckford, whose Dreams, Waking Thoughts, and Incidents was a published account of his letters back home in 1780, embellished with stream-of-consciousness associations, William Coxe, Elizabeth Craven, John Moore, tutor to successive dukes of Hamilton, Samuel Jackson Pratt, Tobias Smollett, Philip Thicknesse, and Arthur Young.

The Grand Tour on Television

In 2009, the Grand Tour featured prominently in a PBS miniseries based on the novel Little Dorrit by Charles Dickens. Produced with masterful attention to detail, and in sumptuous settings, mainly Venice, it faithfully portrayed the Grand Tour as an essential ritual for entry to English high society.

Kevin McCloud presented Kevin McCloud's Grand Tour on Channel 4 during the late summer and early autumn of 2009. The four part series saw Kevin retrace the popular tour by British architects through the last four centuries.

In 2005, British art historian Brian Sewell followed in the footsteps of the Grand Tourist for a 10 part television series Brian Sewell's Grand Tour. Produced by UK's Channel Five, Sewell travelled across Italy by car stopping off in Rome, Florence, Vesuvius, Naples, Pompeii, Turin, Milan, Cremona, Siena, Bologna, Vicenza, Paestum, Urbino, Tivoli. His journey concluded in Venice at a masked ball.

In 1998, the BBC produced an art history series Sister Wendy's Grand Tour presented by Carmelite nun Sister Wendy. Ostensibly an art history series, the journey takes her from Madrid to St. Petersburg with stop offs to see the great masterpieces.

CHAPTER 6

CAMPING

Camping is an outdoor recreational activity. The participants (known as campers) leave urban areas, their home region, or civilization and enjoy nature while spending one or several nights outdoors, usually at a campsite. Camping may involve the use of a tent, caravan, cabin, a primitive structure, or no shelter at all.

Camping as a recreational activity became popular in the early 20th century. Campers frequent national parks, other publicly owned natural areas, and privately owned campgrounds. Camping is a key part of the program of many youth organizations around the world, such as Scouting. It is used to teach self-reliance and team work.

Camping is also used as a cheap form of accommodation for people attending large open air events such as sporting meetings and music festivals. Organizers often provide a field and other basic amenities.

Definition

Camping describes a range of activities. Survivalist campers set off with little more than their boots, whereas recreational vehicle travelers arrive equipped with their own electricity, heat, and patio furniture. Camping is often enjoyed in conjunction with activities, such as: hiking, whitewater kayaking, hill walking, climbing, canoeing, mountain biking, motorcycling, swimming, and fishing. Camping may be combined with hiking either as backpacking or as a series of day hikes from a central location.

Some people vacation in permanent camps with cabins and other facilities (such as hunting camps or children's summer camps), but a stay at such a camp is usually not considered 'camping'. The term camping (or camping out) may also be applied to those who live outdoors, out of necessity (as in the case of the homeless), or for people waiting overnight in queues. It does not, however, apply to cultures whose technology does not include sophisticated dwellings. Camping may be referred to colloquially as roughing it.

Range of Amenities

Campers span a broad range of age, ability, and ruggedness, and campsites are designed in many ways as well. Many campgrounds have sites with facilities such as fire rings, barbecue grills, utilities, shared bathrooms and laundry, as well as access to nearby recreational facilities, but not all campsites have similar levels of development. Campsites can range from a patch of dirt, to a level, paved pad with sewer and electricity. (For more information on facilities, see the campsite and RV park articles.)

Today's campers have a range of comforts available to them, whether their shelter is a tent or a recreational vehicle. Today, backcountry campers can pack-in comfortable mattresses, compact chairs, and solar powered satellite phones. Those choosing to camp closer to their car ("car camping") with a tent have access to potable hot water, tent interior lighting and fans, and other technological changes to camping gear. For those camping in recreational vehicles (RVs), options include air conditioning, bathrooms, kitchens, showers, and home theatre systems. In the United States, Canada and Europe, some campgrounds offer hookups where recreational vehicles are supplied with electricity, water, and sewer services.

Other vehicles used for camping include motorcycles, touring bicycles, boats, canoes, pack animals, and even bush planes; although backpacking on foot is a popular alternative.

Tent camping sites often cost less than campsites with full amenities, and most allow direct access by car. Some "walk-in" sites lie a short walk away from the nearest road, but do not require full backpacking equipment. Those who seek a rugged experience in the outdoors prefer to camp with only tents, or with no shelter at all ("under the stars").

Although many people see in camping a chance to get out of the daily routine and improve their survival skills, others would rather benefit from the many amenities that campsites are nowadays equipped with. If a few decades ago camping meant a great deal of responsibility and knowledge about wild nature, today any individual who wants to spend a weekend away in the woods may also expect a high level of comfort.

The amenities that can be found in a campsite vary greatly depending on the position of the campsite and on the price campers must pay to use them. Usually, the most visited places tend to be more comfortable and more sought after as well. The costs of the different campsites may also reflect the security level of the place. The prices vary depending on the facilities and they may range from less than $10 to over $30. The cheapest option when it comes to camping still remains backpacking or tent camping, though much lesser comfortable.

As camping constantly increases in popularity, many companies manufacturing camping accessories produce different types of equipment or gear that is intended to make camping a more comfortable activity. The gear used in camping is crucial and it can be a life saver. The right tent or food storage unit can easily save campers from insects or even bear attacks.

Mobile Camping

Backpacking is a mobile variety of tent camping. Backpackers use lightweight equipment that can be carried long distances on foot. They hike across land, cross rivers, and camp at remote locations, and select campsites at will if resource protection rules allow. Backpacking equipment typically costs more than that for car camping, but still far less than a trailer or motor home, and backpacking campsites are generally cheap.

Mobile camping may be done using riding animals such as horses and mules. Pack animal increase the limited carrying capacity of riders or may assist hikers by carrying much of the load. Some pack animals such as dogs and llama cannot be ridden but can carry much of the weight of camp supplies. Horse trails and horse camps may be kept separate from hiking areas due to the extra wear they put on areas.

Canoe camping is similar to backpacking, but uses canoes for transportation; much more weight and bulk can be carried in a canoe or kayak than in a backpack. Canoe camping is common in North America.

Sail Camping is a form of camping while sailing or boating. Sailers will visit islands and campgrounds along the shorelines, dock their boats, and set up camp. This form of sail camping gives a variety activities to the boater they may want a break from being on the water.

One form of bicycle touring combines camping with cycling. The bicycle is used to carry the gear and as the primary means of transportation, allowing greater distances to be covered than backpacking. A small number of "bike-in" campsites exist along trails only accessible by mountain biking.

Motorcycle camping is more comparable to bicycle camping than car camping due to the limited storage capacity of the motorbike. Motorcycle camping riders, as well as bicycle touring riders, often use some of the same equipment as backpackers because of the lighter weights and compact dimensions associated with backpacking equipment.

Backpacking is constantly increasing in popularity, especially amongst youth who are willing to go through a challenging experience. Although it can be among the cheapest ways to camp, backpacking is also the most uncomfortable and it is usually performed by individuals who are in a general good condition. Given the fact that the equipment one needs for camping must be carried on the camper's back makes it an athletic activity not suited to everyone. However, the technological development and the increased interest in camping this way lead to an improvement in the equipment carried by backpackers. Many camping companies nowadays produce a wide range of equipment that is lightweight or otherwise specialized for backpacking. Special types of backpacks are manufactured for this particular type of activity. The quality of backpacking gear is revealed by its price and if they generally cost around $100 some modern models with different features may easily exceed $300. For many campers, backpacking allows them to experience the true wilderness but there is little chance to avoid severe weather and injury in the backcountry can lead to serious issues.

Canoe camping is quite popular as a camping opportunity although the equipment needed is more expensive than the one needed when camping with a car. The advantage of this type of camping is that the canoe provides an easier way to transport everything is needed when camping; however, paddling can be a challenging experience. Rivers and lakes that are not suitable for canoeing may be dangerous, especially for novices. Electric motors or small gas ones may be attached on some canoes where allowed for a faster journey on the river, although they are not generally used as they are thought to diminish the essence of the experience. Waterproof bags and fishing gear are often used because of the always present water.

People who enjoy riding their bikes consider bicycle camping a great alternative to enjoy the beauty and quiet of the nature. Due to the lack of protection against bad weather, individuals who are bicycle camping usually carry a different type of equipment, which is helpful especially when raining. Poor road conditions and low temperatures are safety issues when camping during the winter. This type of camping keeps increasing in popularityin people of all ages because it is more "pure" than car camping and yet easier than backpacking.

Specialized Camping

Survivalist campers learn the skills needed to survive in any out-door situation. This activity may require skills in obtaining food from the wild, emergency medical treatments, orienteering, and pioneering.

"Winter camping" refers to the experience of camping outside during the winter - often when there is snow on the ground. Campers and outdoorspeople have adapted their forms of camping and survival to suit extremely cold nights and limited mobility or evacuation. Methods of survival when winter camping includes: building snow shelters such as quinzhees, igloos, or snow caves, dressing in "layers," staying dry, using low-temperature sleeping bags, and fueling the body with appropriate food.

Workcamping allows campers to trade their labor for a free campsite, and sometimes even for utilities and additional pay. Workcamping is usually seasonal, from May to October, although in warm weather countries or states such as Florida and Arizona they can be year round. Work campers are mainly individuals or couples who come into a recreational facility with their own RV and offer their labor in maintain that particular facility. In exchange they can camp for free and sometimes they might receive wages. Camp host programs allow people to camp for free for extended periods in exchange for acting as a volunteer to introduce visitors to campground facilities and organizing some activities.

Adventure camping is a form of camping by people who race (possibly adventure racing or mountain biking) during the day, and camp in a minimalist way at night. They might use the basic items of camping equipment such as a micro-camping stove, sleeping bag, and Bivouac bag.

Boutique Camping is found at music festivals in the UK. Also called glamping, posh camping or comfy camping. It allows people to escape the hassles of finding camp space, carrying their tents, and erecting and taking down their own tents. Companies deliver accommodation units to the festival, as well as build and breakdown the units for their guests. Various companies with various products exist. These products include: tents, bell tents, podpads, yurts, and tipis.

Historical camping is camping using the methods and tools of a specific time in the past. Historical reenactors often camp with gear correct or similar to that available in the period they represent (Wild West, Medieval, Civil War, etc.). Such camping is done for personal enjoyment and for instructional purposes. Their equipment is often made by specialized blacksmiths, leatherworkers and tentmakers or may be self-made.

Camping Equipment

The equipment used in camping varies with the particular type of camping. For instance, in survival camping the equipment consists in small items which have the purpose of helping out the camper in providing food, heat and safety. The equipment used in this type of camping must be lightweight and it is restricted at only the mandatory items. Another types of camping such as winter camping involve having specially designed equipment in terms of tents or clothing which is strong enough to protect the camper's body from the wind and cold.

Survival camping involves certain items that campers are recommended to have with them in case something goes wrong and they need to be rescued. A survival kit includes mandatory items but which are small and must fit in one's pocket or could be carried on one's person. This kit is useless in these circumstances if it is kept in the backpack. Such a kit should include a small metal container which can be used to heat water over a campfire, a small length of duct tape which is small and which can prove useful in many situations and an emergency space blanket. These blankets are specially designed to occupy least space and are perfect for making emergency shelters, keeping the camper warm. Also because of the aluminum-like color this blanket is also reflective which means it can be easily seen from an aircraft. Candle stubs are good in starting a fire as well as in warming an enclosed space. One or two band-aids are mandatory in this type of camping. Any camper, and not only the survival ones need waterproof matches and a large safety pin or fish hook which can be used in fishing. Baking soda is good in rehydrating a dehydrated camper and at the same time, if it is mixed into a paste it helps hastening the cure of mosquito bites. Rubber gloves, antiseptic wipes, tinfoil, jackknife, or halazone tablets (which purify the water) are also to be included into a survival kit. Although these seem too many items to be carried on one person, they are in fact small, lightweight and definitely useful.

Winter camping can be dangerous without respecting the basic rules when it comes to this particular activity. Firstly, the cold is fought against with clothing of three types of layers as following: a liner layer against the camper's skin (longjohns), an insulation layer (fleece), and a water- and wind-proof outer shell. Although cotton is one of the best quality fabrics there is, it is not recommended to be worn on winter camping because if it gets wet it dries out very slowly and the wearer could freeze. Rather than cotton, winter campers should wear wool or synthetic materials. The boots must be waterproof and the head must be protected against the cold given that more than half of the body's heat can be lost through this part of the body. Although it seems a good choice, campers are advised not to wear too many pairs of socks as they might restrict the blood flow to the feet resulting in cold feet. Gaiters should also be worn to avoid snow and rain wetting the boots. Secondly, one should include carbohydrates into their diet to keep their body warm as well as to provide energy. Hydration is very important so winter campers should drink plenty of water to keep themselves well hydrated. Thirdly, the tent must be carefully chosen to shelter from the wind.

Camping equipment includes:

- First aid kit
- Tent, lean-to to act as a shelter.
- Hammer to drive tent stakes into soil.
- Sleeping bag and/or blankets for warmth.
- Sleeping pad or air mattress is placed underneath the sleeping bag for cushioning from stones and twigs as well as for insulation from the ground.
- Lantern or flashlight
- Hatchet, axe or saw for cutting firewood for a campfire.
- Fire starter or other ignition device for starting a campfire.
- Folding chairs for placement around campfire.
- Ropes for stringing clothes line and for securing the shelter.
- Tarp for adding additional layer of storm protection to a tent, and to shelter dining areas.
- Raincoat or poncho
- Hiking boots
- Fishing pole
- Chuck box to hold camp kitchen items for food preparation, consumption and cleanup.
- Trash bags particularly one with handles can be tied to a tree limb, or clothesline off the ground. For handling of waste in backcountry see Leave no trace.
- Insect repellent particularly one that has DEET.
- Sunscreen for protecting the skin.
- Personal care products and towel
- Cooler to store perishables and beverages. If electricity is available, a thermoelectric or stirling engine cooler can be used without the need for ice.
- Beverages or portable water filter for areas that have access to rivers or lakes.

- Campers at modern campgrounds will normally bring perishable foods in coolers while backcountry campers will bring non-perishable foods such as dried fruits, nuts, jerky, and MREs.
- A tripod chained grill, Dutch oven, or La Cotta clay pot can be used for cooking on a campfire. A portable stove can be used where campfires are forbidden or impractical. If using a campground with electricity an electric frying pan or slow cooker can be used.

Firewood for Camp Fires

Much of the remaining needed camping equipment is commonly available in the home, including: dishes, pots and pans; however, many people opt not to use their home items, but instead utilize equipment better tailored for camping. These amenities include heavy plastic tableware and salt and pepper shakers with tops that close in order to shelter the shakers from rain. Backpackers use lightweight and portable equipment.

Social Camping

Many campers enjoy socializing with small groups of fellow campers. Such groups will arrange events throughout the year to allow members with similar interests or from similar geographical areas in order to collaborate. This allows families to form small close knit societies, and children to form lasting friendships. There are two large organizations in the UK who facilitate this sort of camping: the Caravan Club and the Camping and Caravanning Club.

Some who participate in this sort of camping feels that it brings a closer form of bonding, as members become more mutually dependant, than they would otherwise be in modern society. Social camping can also bring more closure between members of the same family and between different families. It is common for many campers to organize this type of activities with their friends or neighbors. Social camping goes beyond uniting families and it may also give the opportunity of lonely campers to enjoy this type of activity with individuals who share their enthusiasm in this matter.

Because of the bonding this type of camping promotes, it can also be used as a personnel training facility. In fact, many companies offer their employees this type of training because it helps connect people who do not necessarily know each other but who need to work in the same environment and need to get along successfully. Including this type of activity in a personnel training package is becoming more and more popular and it is also recommended because of their benefits.

In more recent years, those who camp alone have been able to share their experiences with other campers, through blogs and online social networking. There are many online websites especially designed for people who are looking for camping companions or for those who only want to share their experiences with other people. In this case, campers may provide the others with useful tips resulted from their own experience. Individuals who are willing to camp are likely to access this type of websites and connect with other campers, especially if they are novices because it gives them the opportunity to learn more about this activity.

Camping Coach

Camping coaches were offered by many railway companies in the United Kingdom as accommodation for holiday makers in rural or coastal areas.

The coaches were old passenger vehicles no longer suitable for use in trains, which were converted to provide basic sleeping and living space at static locations. Many of the coaches would be removed from their stations in the winter and overhauled at the railway's workshops ready to be returned in the spring, being placed on sidings. The local railway staff looked after the coaches as part of their duties.

The charges for the use of these coaches were designed to require groups of people to travel by train to the stations where they were situated; they were also encouraged to make use of the railway to travel around the area during their holiday.

History

They were first introduced by the London and North Eastern Railway in July 1933, when there was a great deal of popular enthusiasm in the urban population for hiking and camping as holiday activities. Initially ten vehicles were provided, chiefly at inland beauty spots.

The following year, two other railway companies followed suit: the London, Midland and Scottish Railway, with what it originally called "caravans", and the Great Western Railway which called them "camp coaches". In 1935 they were introduced on the Southern Railway and on the L.M.S. Northern Counties Committee in Northern Ireland. In the same year the L.N.E.R. introduced a touring camping coach.

As a result of World War II, the facility was not made available after the 1940 season and many of the vehicles were used as temporary accommodation for railway staff or others in connection with the war effort. The Southern Railway reintroduced coaches at some sites in 1947, but their large-scale return came under British Railways ownership in 1952. In 1960 some sites started to receive conversions from Pullman lounge cars. The sites at which larger numbers of coaches were located tended to be on the west coast including Abergele in North Wales, and, in Lancashire, Heysham (pre-war), Squires Gate in Blackpool, and Hest Bank.

The number of camping coaches offered for hire declined from the mid-1960s as other forms of holidays became more popular, the condition of the vehicles deteriorated, and the number of staffed stations at which they could be sited decreased. The last were offered to the public by the London Midland Region of British Railways in 1971, although some were retained for many years after this for railway staff to hire for their holidays at Dawlish Warren in Devon and Marazion in Cornwall.

A few heritage railways and private companies have now taken to offering camping coaches at select locations. While ideal for railway enthusiasts, they are also marketed to the general public. Privately-owned cars serving a similar purpose may also be found, for example at North Conway on the Conway Scenic Railroad in the United States.

Campsite

A campsite (also known as a camping pitch in British English) is a place used for overnight stay in the outdoors. The term campsite generally means an area where an individual, family, group, or military unit might camp. There are two types of campsites:

- an impromptu area (as one might decide to stop while backpacking or hiking)
- a dedicated area with improvements and various facilities (see below).

A campground is a group of dedicated campsites with common amenities.

Description

The term camp comes from the Latin word campus, meaning "field". Therefore, a campsite consists typically of open pieces of ground where a camper can pitch a tent or park a camper. More specifically a campsite is a dedicated area set aside for camping and for which often a user fee is charged. Campsites typically feature a few (but sometimes no) improvements.

Dedicated campsites usually have some amenities. Common amenities include, listed roughly in order from most to least common:

- Fireplaces or fire pits in which to build campfires (this can be a circle of rocks, a metal enclosure, a metal grate, a concrete spot, or even just a hole).
- Road access for vehicles
- A gravel or concrete pad on which to park a vehicle
- Picnic tables
- Marked spaces indicating a boundary for one camper or a group of campers
- Reservations to ensure there will be available space to camp
- Utility hookups, such as gas, propane, water, electricity and sewer, primarily for the use of Travel trailers, Recreational vehicles, or similar
- Raised platforms on which to set up tents
- Piped potable water

Campgrounds may include further amenities:

- Pit toilets (outhouses)
- Flush toilets and showers
- Sinks and mirrors in the bathrooms
- A small convenience store
- Shower facilities (with or without hot water)
- Wood for free or for sale for use in cooking or for a campfire
- Garbage cans or large rubbish bins in which to place refuse.

Camping outside a designated campsite may be forbidden by law. It is thought to be a nuisance, harmful to the environment, and is often associated with vagrancy. However some countries have specific laws and/or regulations allowing camping on public lands (see Freedom to roam). In the United States, many national and state parks have dedicated campsites and sometimes also allow impromptu backcountry camping by visitors. U.S. National Forests often have established campsites, but generally allow camping anywhere, except within a certain distance of water sources.

RV Parks/caravan Parks

In North America many campgrounds have facilities for Recreational Vehicles and are also known as RV parks . Similar facilities in the UK are known as Caravan Parks. The Kampgrounds of America (KOA) is a large chain of commercial campgrounds located throughout the United States and Canada. Many travellers prefer to use KOA, or similar campsites, as an alternative to hotels or motels.

Both commercial and governmental campgrounds typically charge a nominal fee for the privilege of camping there, to cover expenses, and in the case of an independent campground, to make a profit. Some RV parks provide year-round spaces.

Trailer Parks

Frequently confused with campsites, campgrounds and RV parks, trailer parks are made up of long term or semi-permanent residents occupying mobile homes, park trailers or RVs.

Holiday Park

The holiday park is a United Kingdom version of the North American trailer park. Created to allow coastal resorts to enable temporary and high-income accommodation to be easily created, under UK planning laws, no residents are permanent, and the park must be wholly shut to all for at least two months each year. All of the mobile homes are either available for rent from the land owner, or pitches are leased on a long-term basis from the land owner and the lease's own mobile home placed on the pitch. Permanent sites owners lease includes the provision by the land owner of water, sewerage and general site and grounds maintenance. Some holiday parks includes a small campsite for those touring the area, where they can pay to pitch tents or site touring caravans and motorhomes. Touring campsites have full access to the Holiday parks facilities, including clothes washing and showering. Most holiday parks include a central entertainments block, which can include a shop, restaurants, and a multi-purpose theatre used for both stage and activity-based entertainment.

Backcountry Camping

In the U.S., backcountry camping is common in large undeveloped protected areas. These areas can only be reached on foot, canoe or on horseback. The camping areas are usually established campsites or "zones", which have a predetermined maximum number of persons that are allowed to stay in the section per night. Strict regulations are imposed regarding food storage and resource protection. In most cases, open fires are not permitted and all cooking must be done with small portable stoves. Usually in organized parks or wilderness areas, backcountry campsites require a free permit obtainable at visitor centers and ranger stations. Dispersed camping in other areas may not require a permit.

Military Camp

A military camp or bivouac is a semi-permanent facility for the lodging of an army. Camps are erected when a military force travels away from a major installation or fort during training or operations, and often have the form of large campsites. In the Roman era the military camp had highly stylized parameters and served an entire legion. Archaeological investigations have revealed many details of these Roman camps at sites such as Vindolanda (England) and Raedykes (Scotland).

RV Park

A recreational vehicle park (RV park) or caravan park is a place where people with recreational vehicles can stay overnight, or longer, in alloted spaces known as "pitches" ("sites" in the United States, Europe, and Australia). They are also referred to as campgrounds, though a true campground also provides facilities for tent camping; many facilities calling themselves

"RV parks" also offer tent camping or cabins with limited facilities.

Services

Allocated space (pitch/site) facilities may include:

- AC power connection. (Usually rated by capacity such as 16, 20, 30 or 50 amperes.)
- Drinking water connection
- Sewer connection
- Television connection (relevant to local area standards)
- Telephone connection (rare outside North America)
- Hotspot (Wi-Fi)

Park facilities may include:

- Barbecue area
- Bathhouses
- Convenience store
- Dump station
- Exercise equipment
- Gift shop
- Golf Courses
- Hot tubs
- Laundry
- Picnic tables
- Restrooms
- Recreation Hall
- Showers
- Swimming pool
- Bar/restaurant

RV parks by region

Australia

In Australia there is generally no differentiation between an RV park and a trailer park. The term "caravan park" is used to refer to both, and "RV park" and "trailer park" are never used, even to the point of not being understood by some Australians. The term "holiday park" is becoming increasingly common, with many parks increasing their stock of on-site cabins, often accompanied by a reduction in the number of caravan sites.

Europe

Caravan sites in Europe range in facilities depending on their age. Most new sites will be built to high environmentally friendly standards and have facilities compatible with the newest vehicles.

The Caravan Club has 1 million members in Europe with around 200 self-owned campsites and over 2,500 certified third party locations. . The Camping and Caravanning Club is a non-profit organisation which has been running for over a century and has over 400,000 members and 100 campsites in the United Kingdom.

In France, Germany and Italy, to a lesser degree also in Norway and Netherlands, a large network of dedicated stopover sites for motorhomes has grown since about 1980. These sites are called Reisemobil-Stellplatz in German or Aire de Camping-car in French. While these sites can usually not be compared to North American RV sites regarding size and facilities, they still fulfill the same purpose.

New Zealand

In New Zealand motor camp, caravan park or holiday park are the usual terms for overnight or long term vehicle based camping. As well powered caravan or campervan sites the parks usually offer tent sites and cabins, a rudimentary building with cooking and other facilities shared with other users.

North America

RV parks range from rustic facilities with no or limited utility hookups, as often found in state/provincial parks and national parks, to luxury resorts with amenities that rival fine hotels. Some high-end resorts restrict the type of RV that can stay to motorhomes of a certain length or longer, and/or newer than a certain year.

Most RV parks are open to allcomers and rent spaces on a nightly or weekly basis, much like a motel or hotel. A few parks operate on a time-share basis. Membership campground networks like Thousand Trails operate like clubs, with members paying an initial membership fee and annual dues. There are over 13,000 privately owned RV parks and over 1,600 state parks that cater to RVers in the USA.. Many of these RV parks offer WiFi hotspot access on a daily, weekly, or monthly basis; occasionally, WiFi is included in the campsite fee.

Most RV parks are independent or operated by a government entity. In the USA Kampgrounds of America, KOA, is the largest and best-known chain of RV parks, with Yogi Bear's Jellystone Park Campgrounds a distant second. Good Sam Parks are mostly independently owned RV campgrounds endorsed by the Good Sam Club, a large association of US RVers that is operated for profit by the Affinity Group, Inc. Listings of RV parks can be found in printed directories; the best known are the annual ones by Woodall's and Trailer Life Magazine. Online RV directories are provided by eCampGuide, CampRate, Reserve RV, RVThereYet, RVParkReviews, AmericaOnWheels.com and others. Overnight rates for most USA RV parks are US$15 to US$50, although some in city and country parks may be US$10 or less, even free.

There is a subculture of "fulltiming" RV owners who live in their recreational vehicles on a permanent basis. They typically move from one RV park to another. The length of time that someone is allowed to stay in an RV park varies from park to park.

Chapter 7

Traveler's Diarrhea

Traveler's diarrhea or traveller's diarrhoea, abbreviated to TD, is the most common illness affecting travelers. Traveler's diarrhea is defined as three or more unformed stools in 24 hours passed by a traveler, commonly accompanied by abdominal cramps, nausea, and bloating. It does not imply a specific organism, but enterotoxigenic Escherichia coli is the most common. Most cases are self-limited and the pathogen is most often not identified.

Incidence

Each year 20%–50% of international travelers, an estimated 10 million people, develop diarrhea. TD is also known to mountaineers, as it can occur in camps due to poor sanitary conditions.

Risk Factors

The primary source of infection is ingestion of fecally contaminated food or water.

The most important determinant of risk is the traveler's destination. High-risk destinations are the developing countries of Latin America, Africa, the Middle East, and Asia. Among backpackers, additional risk factors for this class of infections include drinking untreated surface water and failure by the individual and his or her companions to maintain personal hygiene practices and clean cookware. Campsites often have very primitive sanitation facilities, if any, making them as potentially dangerous as any third-world country.

People at particular high-risk include young adults, immunosuppressed persons, persons with inflammatory-bowel disease or diabetes, and those taking H-2 blockers or antacids. Attack rates are similar for men and women.

Although traveler's diarrhea usually resolves within three to five days (mean duration: 3.6 days), in about 20 percent of persons the illness is severe enough to cause bed confinement and in 10 percent of cases the illness lasts more than one week.

For those who get serious infections, TD can occasionally be life-threatening. The serious infections include bacillary dysentery, amoebic dysentery, and cholera.

Symptoms

The onset of TD usually occurs within the first week of travel, but may occur at any time while traveling, and even after returning home. When it appears depends in part on the specific infectious agent. The incubation period for giardiasis averages about 14 days and that of cryptosporidiosis about seven days. Certain other bacterial and viral agents have shorter incubation periods, although hepatitis may take weeks to manifest itself. Most TD cases begin abruptly.

The illness usually results in increased frequency, volume, and weight of stool. Altered stool consistency also is common. Typically, a traveler experiences four to five loose or watery bowel movements each day. Other commonly associated symptoms are nausea, vomiting, diarrhea, abdominal cramping, bloating, low fever, urgency, and malaise, and appetite is usually low or non-existent.

It is much more serious if there is blood or mucus in the diarrhea, abdominal pain, or high fever. With serious cases of cholera, there is a rapid onset of symptoms, which include weakness, malaise (feeling rotten), and torrents of watery diarrhea with flecks of mucus (called "rice water" stools). Dehydration is a serious consequence, with death occurring in as quickly as 24 hours with cholera.

Causes

Infectious agents are the primary cause of travelers' diarrhea. Bacterial enteropathogens cause approximately 80% of cases.

The most common causative agent isolated in countries surveyed has been enterotoxigenic Escherichia coli (ETEC). Enteroaggregative E. coli is increasingly recognized and many studies do not look for this important bacterium. Shigella spp. are the other most common bacteria involved. Incidents in which other bacteria, such as Salmonella, Campylobacter, Yersinia, Aeromonas, and Plesiomonas spp., have caused diarrhea are isolated and occur less often. Protozoan parasites such as Giardia lamblia and Cryptosporidium may also cause diarrhea.

Some bacteria release toxins which bind to the intestines and cause diarrhea; others damage the intestines themselves by their direct presence. In infants and children, it is estimated that nearly 70% of diarrhea is due to viruses; for adult travelers, this drops to around 30%. Diarrhea caused by viral agents is usually self-limited.

Pathogens implicated in travelers' diarrhea are:

E. coli, enterotoxigenic	20-75%
E. coli, enteroaggregative	0-20%
E. coli, enteroinvasive	0-6%
Shigella spp	2-30%
Salmonella spp	0-33%
Campylobacter jejuni	3-17%
Vibrio parahemolyticus	0-31%
Aeromonas hydrophila	0-30%

Giardia lamblia	0 to less than 20%
Entameba histolytica	0-5%
Cryptosporidium sp	0 to less than 20%
Rotavirus	0-36%
Norwalk virus	0-10%

A sub-type of travelers' diarrhea afflicting hikers and campers, sometimes known as wilderness diarrhea, may have a somewhat different frequency distribution of pathogens.

Treatment

TD usually is a self-limited disorder and often resolves without specific treatment; however, oral rehydration therapy is often beneficial to replace lost fluids and electrolytes. Clear, disinfected water or other liquids are routinely recommended for adults. Water that is purified is best, along with oral rehydration salts to replenish lost electrolytes. Carbonated water (soda), which has been left out so that the carbonation fizz is gone, is useful if nothing else is available.

Travelers who develop three or more loose stools in a 24-hour period — especially if associated with nausea, vomiting, abdominal cramps, fever, or blood in stools — should be treated by a doctor and may benefit from antimicrobial therapy. Antibiotics usually are given for 3–5 days, but single dose azithromycin or levofloxacin have been used. If diarrhea persists despite therapy, travelers should be evaluated and treated for possible parasitic infection. There are different medications needed for bacterial dysentery, for amoebic dysentery, for giardia and for worms. There can be 100% recovery from cholera when properly treated, which usually only means rehydration, usually through an intravenous line.

Antimotility Agents

Antimotility agents (loperamide, diphenoxylate, and paregoric) primarily reduce diarrhea by slowing transit time in the gut, and, thus, allow more time for absorption. Some persons believe diarrhea is the body's defense mechanism to minimize contact time between gut pathogens and intestinal mucosa. In several studies[who?], antimotility agents have been useful in treating travelers' diarrhea by decreasing the duration of diarrhea. However, these agents should never be used by persons with fever or bloody diarrhea, because they can increase the severity of disease by delaying clearance of causative organisms (specifically those diarrheal diseases caused by either Shigella or Salmonella). Because antimotility agents are now available over the counter, their injudicious use is of concern. Adverse complications (toxic megacolon, sepsis, and disseminated intravascular coagulation) have been reported[who?] as a result of using these medications to treat diarrhea.

Prevention

Among the primary measures to prevent gastrointestinal illness are keeping good hygiene, getting specific vaccines and prophylactic medications. Studies show a decrease in the incidence of TD with use of bismuth subsalicylate and with use of antimicrobial chemoprophylaxis. Options for prophylaxis of traveler's diarrhea include norfloxacin, ciprofloxacin, ofloxacin, or trimethoprim/sulfamethoxazole. Prolonged intake of penicilline derivatives may decrease effectiveness of such drugs, however, should a serious infection occur.

Dukoral has been shown to prevent TD and cholera - one dose a few weeks before travel, and another about a week before travel. Additionally, vaccine candidates are in various stages of development for enterotoxigenic E. coli, the leading cause of traveler's diarrhea, and Shigella.

Travelan, a proprietary mix of antibodies against the common strains of E.Coli involved in travellers diarrhoea, taken in pill before every meal while on holiday, has been shown to work in preventing TD in up to 93% of cases. The antibodies work to inhibit the ETEC's attachment to the intestinal wall.

This avoids killing beneficial flora because these antibodies are specific to strains of ETEC.

Traveler's diarrhea is fundamentally a sanitation failure, leading to bacterial contamination of drinking water and food. It is best prevented through proper water quality management systems as found in responsible hotels and resorts. In the absence of that, the next best option for travelers is to take precautions to prevent the disease:

- Maintain good hygiene and only use safe water for drinking and teeth brushing.
- Use only safe bottled water and avoid ice. Reports of locals filling bottles with tap water, then sealing them and then selling the bottled water as purified water have come out of several countries.
- Drink safe beverages — these include bottled carbonated beverages, hot tea or coffee and water boiled or appropriately treated by the traveler. Caution with this because water used for hot beverages may have been only heated, not boiled.
- Active intervention involves boiling water for three to five minutes (depending on elevation), filtering water with appropriate filters or using chlorine bleach (2 drops per litre) or tincture of iodine (5 drops per litre) in the water. The wide availability of safe bottled water makes these interventions usually unnecessary for all but the most remote destinations.
- Avoid eating raw fruits and vegetables unless the traveler peels them.
- Recently an ultraviolet (UV) water purification device entered the market that allows people to quickly and conveniently treat small amounts of water, even in restaurant settings. The method of action is UV light bonding thymine rungs of the DNA molecule, destroying the organisms' ability to live or replicate. The major

advantage (besides convenience) is that UV light also kills viruses when filtration does not. Many travelers are opting for this method because it adds no taste to the water, allows the drinking of cold water, and is extremely economical compared with the cost of buying bottled water.

If handled properly, well-cooked and packaged foods are usually safe. Eating raw or undercooked meat and seafood should be avoided. Unpasteurized milk, dairy products, mayonnaise and pastry icing are associated with increased risk for TD, as are foods or drinking beverages purchased from street vendors or other establishments where unhygienic conditions are present.

Several probiotics (Saccharomyces boulardii and a mixture of Lactobacillus acidophilus and Bifidobacterium) have significant efficacy. In a meta-analysis by McFarland (2005), no serious adverse reactions were reported in the 12 trials. Probiotics may offer a safe and effective method to prevent TD.

According to a study published in June, 2008, in the Lancet, researchers found that patients given a travelers' diarrhea vaccine (made by the Iomai Corporation) were significantly less likely to suffer from clinically significant diarrhea than those who received a placebo. The study, which followed 170 healthy travelers ages 18–64 to Mexico and Guatemala, found that of the 59 individuals who received the new vaccine, only three suffered from moderate or severe diarrhea, while roughly two dozen of the 111 who received a placebo suffered from moderate or severe diarrhea. Only one of the 59 volunteers in the vaccine group reported severe diarrhea, compared with 12 in the placebo group.

Immunity

Travelers often get diarrhea from eating and drinking products that do not cause any problems to local people. This is due to immunity that is developed after repeated exposure to pathogens. It is not fully clear how much exposure is needed and up to what extent the immune system can deal with pathogens, but a study among expatriates in Nepal suggests that it can take seven years to develop immunity, presumably in the case of adults who mostly avoided exposure to pathogens. On the other hand, immunity that US-originated students acquired while living in Mexico appeared to disappear within as little as 8 weeks of non-exposure.

Colloquial Names

There are a number of colloquialisms for travelers' diarrhea contracted in various localities, such as "Montezuma's revenge", "turistas", or "Aztec two step" for travelers' diarrhea contracted in Mexico, "Pharaoh's Revenge," "mummy's tummy," or "Cairo two-step" in Egypt, "Kurtz Hurtz" in Uzbekistan, "Bombay belly" or "Delhi belly" in India, "kabulitis" in Afghanistan, "holiday tummy" in United Kingdom, although this is not directed at tourists in the UK but at British tourists abroad, "Bali belly" in Bali, or "Katmandu quickstep" in Nepal. In Canada it is termed "beaver fever". A recent local term in Pattaya, Thailand, is "Thai-dal wave".Peacekeepers to Arabic-speaking countries have called it "yalla yalla" (Arabic for "fast, fast") referring to the extreme urgency it causes.

Montezuma's Revenge

"Montezuma's revenge" redirects here. For other uses, see Montezuma's revenge (disambiguation).

Montezuma's revenge (var. Moctezuma's revenge) is the colloquial term for any cases of traveler's diarrhea contracted by tourists visiting Mexico. The name refers to Moctezuma II (1466-1520), the Tlatoani (ruler) of the Aztec civilization who was defeated by Hernán Cortés, the Spanish conquistador.

It is estimated that 40% of foreign traveler vacations in Mexico are disrupted by infection. Most cases are mild and resolve in a few days with no treatment. Severe or extended cases, however, may result in extensive fluid loss and/or dangerous electrolytic imbalance which pose a severe medical risk and may prove fatal if mismanaged. The oversight of a medical professional is advised.

WILDERNESS DIARRHEA

Wilderness diarrhea (WD), also called wilderness-acquired diarrhea (WAD) or backcountry diarrhea, is the name preferred by some backpackers, hikers, campers and other outdoor recreationalists for traveler's diarrhea that appears in wilderness or "backcountry" situations while still in their home country. It is due to the same agents as all other traveler's diarrhea, which are usually bacterial and viral in short expeditions and may be giardiasis in longer expeditions. and is largely due to the absence of treated water and poor hygiene. Some people reserve the name backpacker's diarrhea as a synonym for giardiasis.

Causes

Infectious diarrhea acquired in the wilderness is caused by various bacteria, viruses, and parasites (protozoa). The most commonly reported are the protozoa Giardia and Cryptosporidium. Other infectious agents may play a larger role than generally believed and include Campylobacter, hepatitis A virus, hepatitis E virus, enterotoxogenic E. coli, c. coli 0157:H7, Shigella, and various other viruses. More rarely, Yersinia enterocolitica, Aeromonas hydrophila, and Cyanobacterium may also cause disease.

Giardia lamblia does not tolerate freezing but can remain viable for nearly three months in river water when the temperature is 10°C and about one month at 15–20°C in lake water. Cryptosporidium may survive in cold waters (4°C) for up to 18 months, and can even withstand freezing, although its viability is thereby greatly reduced. Many other varieties of diarrhea-causing organisms, including Shigella and Salmonella typhi, and hepatitis A virus, can survive freezing for weeks to months. Virologists believe all surface water in the United States and Canada has the potential to contain human viruses, which cause a wide range of illnesses including diarrhea, polio and meningitis.

Modes of acquiring infection from these causes are limited to fecal-oral transmission, and contaminated water and food. The major factor governing pathogen content of surface water is human and animal activity in the watershed. The risk of WAD from untreated water may have been over-stated relative to the risk from insufficient hygiene.

Symptoms

The average incubation periods for giardiasis and cryptosporidiosis are each 7 days. Certain other bacterial and viral agents have shorter incubation periods, although hepatitis may take weeks to manifest itself. The onset usually occurs within the first week of return from the field, but may also occur at any time while hiking.

Most cases begin abruptly and usually result in increased frequency, volume, and weight of stool. Typically, a hiker experiences at least four to five loose or watery bowel movements each day. Other commonly associated symptoms are nausea, vomiting, abdominal cramping, bloating, low fever, urgency, and malaise, and usually the appetite is affected. The condition is much more serious if there is blood or mucus in stools, abdominal pain, or high fever. Dehydration is a possibility. Life-threatening illness resulting from WAD is extremely rare but can occur in people with weakened immune systems.

Some people may be carriers and not exhibit symptoms.

Diagnosis

It may be difficult to associate a particular case of diarrhea with a recent wilderness trip of a few days because incubation of the disease may outlast the trip. Studies of trips that are much longer than the average incubation period, e.g. a week for Cryptosporidium and Giardia, are less susceptible to these errors since there is enough time for the diarrhea to occur during the trip. Other bacterial and viral agents have shorter incubation periods, although hepatitis may require weeks.

A suspected case of wilderness acquired diarrhea may be assessed within the general context of intestinal complaints. During any given four-week period, as many as 7.2% of Americans may experience some form of infectious or non-infectious diarrhea. There are an estimated 99 million annual cases of intestinal infectious disease in the United States, most commonly from viruses, followed by bacteria and parasites, including Giardia and Cryptosporidium. Giardia alone may infect up to 10% of Americans at any one time. However, because most carriers are asymptomatic, there are only an estimated 2 million U.S. cases of symptomatic giardiasis annually spread mostly by fecal-oral or food-borne transmission.

Treatment

WAD is typically self-limited, generally resolving without specific treatment. Oral rehydration therapy with rehydration salts is often beneficial to replace lost fluids and electrolytes. Clear, disinfected water or other liquids are routinely recommended.

Hikers who develop three or more loose stools in a 24-hour period — especially if associated with nausea, vomiting, abdominal cramps, fever, or blood in stools — should be treated by a doctor and may benefit from antibiotics, usually given for 3–5 days. Alternatively, a single dose azithromycin or levofloxacin may be prescribed. If diarrhea persists despite therapy, travelers should be evaluated and treated for possible parasitic infection.

Cryptosporidium can be quite dangerous to patients with compromised immune systems. Alinia (nitazoxanide) is approved by the FDA for treatment of Cryptosporidium.

Prevention

Since wilderness acquired diarrhea can be caused by insufficient hygiene, contaminated water, and (possibly) increased susceptibility from vitamin deficiency, prevention methods should address these causes.

Hygiene

The risk of fecal-oral transmission of pathogens that cause diarrhea can be significantly reduced by good hygiene, including washing hands with soap and water after urination and defecation, and washing eating utensils with warm soapy water. Additionally a three-bowl system can be used for washing eating utensils.

Treating Water

Water can be treated in the wilderness through filtering, chemical disinfectants, a portable ultraviolet light device, pasteurizing or boiling. Factors in choice may include the number of people involved, space and weight considerations, the quality of available water, personal taste and preferences, and fuel availability.

In a study of long-distance backpacking, it was found that water filters were used more consistently than chemical disinfectants. Inconsistent use of iodine or chlorine may be due to disagreeable taste, extended treatment time or treatment complexity due to water temperature and turbidity.

Because methods based on halogens, such as iodine and chlorine, do not kill Cryptosporidium, and because filtration misses some viruses, the best protection may require a two-step process of either filtration or coagulation-flocculation, followed by halogenation. Boiling is effective in all situations.

Iodine resins, if combined with microfiltration to remove resistant cysts, are also a viable single-step process, but may not be effective under all conditions. New one-step techniques using chlorine dioxide, ozone, and UV radiation may prove effective, but still require validation.

Ultraviolet (UV) light for water disinfection is well established and widely used for large applications, like municipal water systems. A small portable UV device, called a SteriPEN, is now available for hikers. According to the manufacturer, it meets standards set forth in the U.S. EPA Guide Standard and Protocol for Testing Microbiological Water Purifiers. Another approach to portable UV water purification is solar disinfection which is called SODIS. Clear water is sterilized by putting it in a clear polyethylene (PET) bottle and leaving it in direct sunlight for 6 hours.

Water Risk Avoidance

Different types of water sources may have different levels of contamination:

More contamination may be in water that

1. likely could have passed through an area subject to heavy human or animal use.
2. is cloudy, has surface foam, or has some other suspicious appearance.

Less contamination may be in water from.

1. springs (provided the true source is not surface water a short distance above).
2. large streams (those entering from the side may have less contamination than those paralleling the trail).
3. fast-flowing streams.
4. higher elevations.
5. l akes with undisturbed sediments (10 days undisturbed water storage can result in 75-99% removal of coliform bacteria by settling to the bottom).
6. freshly melted snow.
7. deep wells (provided they aren't subject to contamination from surface runoff).
8. regions where there was a heavy snow year when streams run full and long compared to dry years..

Rain storms can either improve or worsen water quality. They can wash contaminants into water and stir up contaminated sediments with increasing flow, but can also dilute contaminants by adding large amounts of water.

Unfortunately, there have not been any epidemiological studies to validate the above, except possibly for the case of spring water.

Vitamins

One study suggests that on very long trips in the wilderness, taking multivitamins may reduce the incidence of diarrhea.

Epidemiology

The risk of acquiring infectious diarrhea in the wilderness arises from inadvertent ingestion of pathogens. Various studies have sought to estimate diarrhea attack rates among wilderness travelers, and results have ranged widely. The variation of diarrhea rate between studies may depend on the time of year, the location of the study, the length of time the hikers were in the wilderness, the prevention methods used, and the study methodology.

The National Outdoor Leadership School (NOLS), which emphasizes strict hand-washing techniques, water disinfection and washing of common cooking utensils in their programs, reports that gastrointestinal illnesses occurred at a rate of only 0.26 per 1000 program days. By contrast, studies of hiking trips on the Appalachian Trail that averaged almost 5 months, reported that more than half of the hikers experienced at least one episode of diarrhea that lasted an average of 2 days. The occurrence of diarrhea was positively associated with the duration of exposure in the wilderness. A number of behaviors each individually reduced the incidence of diarrhea: treating water; routinely washing hands with soap and water after urination (as did after defecation); cleaning cooking utensils with soap and warm water; and taking multi-vitamins.

A variety of pathogens can cause diarrhea, and most cases among backpackers appear to be caused by bacteria from feces. A study at Grand Teton National Park found 69% of diarrhea affected visitors had no identifiable cause, that 23% had diarrhea due to Campylobacter and 8% of patients with diarrhea had giardiasis. Campylobacter enteritis occurred most frequently in young adults who had hiked in wilderness areas and drunk untreated surface water in the week prior. In another study, there were no identifiable cases of giardiasis.

Fecal-oral transmission may be the most common vector for wilderness acquired diarrhea. There are differing opinions regarding the importance of routine disinfection of water during relatively brief backcountry visits.

Backcountry Water Quality Surveys

Infection by fecal coliform bacteria, which indicate fecal pollution, represent a much higher risk than giardiasis. Risks are highest in surface water near trails used by pack animals and cattle pastures.

Most surveys of backcountry water in the United States have found very low or no Giardia cysts. However, very few studies have addressed the issue of transient contamination. According to one researcher, the likely model for the risk of Giardia from wilderness water is pulse contamination, that is, a brief period of high cyst concentration from fecal contamination.

Travel Medicine

Travel medicine or emporiatrics is the branch of medicine that deals with the prevention and management of health problems of international travelers.

Globalization and Travel

Globalization facilitates the spread of disease and increases the number of travelers who will be exposed to a different health environment. Major content areas of travel medicine include the global epidemiology of health risks to the traveler, vaccinology, malaria prevention, and pre-travel counseling designed to maintain the health of the approximately 600 million international travelers. It has been estimated that about 80 million travelers go annually from developed to developing countries.

Mortality and Morbidity

Mortality studies indicate that the cardiovascular disease accounts for most deaths during travel (50-70%), while injury and accident follow (~25%). Infectious disease accounts for about 2.8-4% of deaths during/from travel. Morbidity studies suggest that about half of the people from a developed country that stay one month in a developing country will get sick. Traveler's diarrhea is the most common problem encountered.

Disciplines

The field of travel medicine encompasses a wide variety of disciplines including epidemiology, infectious disease, public health, tropical medicine, high altitude physiology, travel related obstetrics, psychiatry, occupational medicine, military and migration medicine, and environmental health.

Special itineraries and activities include cruise ship travel, diving, mass gatherings (e.g. the Hajj), and wilderness/remote regions travel.

Basically, travel medicine can divide into 4 main topics: prevention (vaccination and travel advice), assistance (dealing with repatriation and medical treatment of travelers), wilderness medicine (e.g. high-altitude medicine, cruise ship medicine, expedition medicine, etc.) and access to health care, provided by travel insurance.

Focus

Travel medicine includes pre-travel consultation and evaluation, contingency planning during travel, and post-travel follow-up and care. Information is provided by the WHO that addresses health issues for travelers for each country as well as the specific health risks of air travel itself. Also, the CDC publishes valuable and up-to-date information. Key areas to consider are vaccination and the six I's:

1. Insects: repellents, mosquito nets, antimalarial medication.
2. Ingestions: safety of drinking water, food.
3. Indiscretion: HIV, sexually transmitted disease.
4. Injuries: accident avoidance, personal safety.
5. Immersion: schistosomiasis.
6. Insurance: coverage and services during travel, access to health care.

Specific Disease Problems

Yellow fever is endemic to certain areas in Africa and South America. The CDC site delineates the risk areas and provides information about vaccination and preventive steps.

Meningococcal meningitis is endemic in the tropical meningococcal belt of Africa. Vaccination is required for pilgrims going to Mecca. Detailed information is available on the CDC site.

Malaria prevention consists of preventing or reducing exposure to mosquitos by using screened rooms, air-conditioning, and nets, and use of repellents (usually DEET). In addition, chemoprophylaxis is started before the travel, during the time of potential exposure, and for 4 weeks (chloroquine, doxycycline, or mefloquine) or 7 days (atovaquone/proguanil or primaquine) after leaving the risk area. See detailed CDC site.

Medication Kit

The traveler should have a medication kit to provide for necessary and useful medication. Based on circumstances, it should include also malaria prophylaxis, condoms, and medication to combat traveler's diarrhea. In addition, a basic first aid kit can be of use.

Studies have shown there are four main medical problems that travellers develop - diarrhoea or gut problems, respiratory problems, wounds and pain. The medical kit should at least address these common things.

Research has also shown that the best treatment for travellers diarrhoea is to take an antibiotic (e.g. ciprofloxacin) plus a stopper (e.g. loperamide). Due to bacterial resistance, different parts of the world require different antibiotics. It is best to consult a travel doctor to sort out the best medical kit for the exact destination and medical history of the person travelling.

Wilderness Medicine

Wilderness medicine (also known as expedition medicine) is the practice of medicine where definitive care is more than one hour away, and often days to weeks away. The practice of wilderness medicine is defined by difficult patient access, limited equipment, and environmental extremes. The development of wilderness medicine has paralleled the evolution of pre-hospital care in the urban setting, beginning with the Napoleonic Wars.

History

Today, wilderness or expedition medicine is practiced by Wilderness First Responders, Wilderness EMTs, Remote/Offshore Paramedics and Physicians on expeditions, in outdoor education, search and rescue, mountain rescue, remote area operations including research, exploration, and offshore oil platforms, as well as tactical environments. In mainland Europe, where mountain rescue is done by paid professionals, there are courses for physicians that help qualify them to be mountain rescue or expedition doctors. Many of these courses lead to an International Diploma in Mountain Medicine, which is recognized by the Union Internationale des Associations Alpinistes.

In the United States, where mountain and other wilderness rescue on land is usually done by volunteers, there is no equivalent diploma. However, there are many wilderness medicine conferences at which medical professionals can earn continuing education credits, and some medical schools (for example, at the University of New Mexico) have begun offering electives in wilderness medicine.

The Internationally active Wilderness Medical Society is an organization dedicated to wilderness medicine education and research, and they conduct multiple conferences annually in this area. Anyone who is interested in wilderness medicine can join the organization as an associate member, and receive their magazine, Wilderness Medicine. Their peer-reviewed journal, Wilderness and Environmental Medicine, is archived on their web site (www.wms.org), and back issues are accessible to the public at no cost.

Training in wilderness medicine is specialized, involving advanced practices and protocols due to the distance from hospitals and physicians. Common US certifications include Wilderness First Aid, Wilderness First Responder, and Wilderness EMT. While there is no legislation on standards of care for wilderness emergency care, there is a consensus of wilderness medical experts published by the Wilderness Medical Society

Wilderness Medicine is popular in medical school communities, and many student groups hold their own Wilderness Medicine Conferences. Examples include the Mid-Atlantic Student Wilderness Conference and the Southeast Student Wilderness Medicine Conference . These events commonly feature prominent members of the Wilderness Medical Society as guest speakers and workshop leaders. Additionally, many top tier emergency physicians and surgeons are active in the field.

Many organizations offer training in wilderness emergency care to lay people, which may include techniques that go beyond urban first aid or EMT training, such as reducing dislocations. The National Ski Patrol (www.nsp.org), a volunteer organization with a congressional charter, has an 80-hour course to train patrollers, Outdoor Emergency Care, which meets the standards for an EMT (Emergency Medical Technician) course. The Wilderness Medicine Institute of NOLS, Wilderness Medical Associates, Aerie Backcountry Medicine, SOLO, and Remote Medical International offer courses up to the Wilderness EMT level. The American Safety & Health Institute (www.ashinstitute.org) has a Wilderness Emergency Care program that offers a full range of courses including Wilderness First Aid, Wilderness First Responder, and Wilderness EMT Upgrade. Most outdoor organizations that take people into wilderness settings now require their trip leaders, guides or camp councilors to be certified in such a course.

Wilderness Medical Society

The Wilderness Medical Society was created on the 15th of February 1983 by three doctors from California. The doctors in question were Dr Paul Auerbach, Dr Ed Geehr, and Dr Ken Kizer. It provides advice and guidance to medical personnel working in wilderness or backcountry environments. It also publishes Wilderness & Environmental Medicine Journal and Practice Guidelines for Wilderness Emergency Care.

Mission Statement

"To advance healthcare, research, and education related to wilderness medicine."

Academy of Wilderness Medicine

The academy seeks to provide a system of adult education and certificaton in a modern and standardised way to provide a set level of knowledge and education for practitioners working in the wilderness arena.

The goals of the academy are to:

- Professional designation for achievement in Wilderness Medicine.
- Validation for the public, patients, and clients of practitioner education in Wilderness Medicine.
- Recognition for completing high quality standards in Wilderness Medicine.
- Continuing medical education (CME) credit for acquisition of knowledge and hands-on experiences in Wilderness Medicine.
- The advancement of an internationally recognized curriculum of Wilderness Medicine categories, topics, and skills.

FAWM Curriculum

The curriculum for participants wishing to gain fellowship is modular and is divided into Electives, Required Topics and Experience:

Required/Core Topics are divided into twelve sub-headings:

- Diving and Hyperbaric Medicine.
- Tropical and Travel Medicine.
- High Altitude & Mountaineering Medicine.
- Expedition Medicine.
- Field Craft and Equipment.
- Rescue and Evacuation.
- Sports Medicine and Physiology.
- Preventive Medicine, Field Sanitation & Hygiene.
- General Environmental Medicine.
- Improvised and Alternative Medicine.

- Disaster & Humanitarian Assistance.
- Wilderness Emergencies and Trauma Management.

FAWM credits can be gained in a number of ways such as;

- Attending WMS conferences.
- Completing online tests after reading journal articles.
- Watching online lectures.
- Publishing articles.
- Teaching in the area of Wilderness Medicine.

Activities

The Wilderness Medical Society organize annual conferences and meetings for members and interesting parties.

Notable Fellows

- Dr Paul Auerbach - Founder and past president of the WMS.
- Dr Sean Hudson - One of the first holders of the FAWM in England.

Affiliated Groups

- Expedition and Wilderness Medicine.
- Advanced Wilderness Life Support (AWLS).
- Aerie Backcountry Medicine.
- Wilderness Medicine Institute of NOLS.
- American College of Emergency Physicians - Wilderness Section.
- International Hypoxia Symposia.
- Everest ER.
- Institute for Altitude Medicine.
- Wilderness Medical Associates.
- Wilderness Medicine Programs - Roane State Community College.

CHAPTER 8

SCOUTING

Scouting, also known as the Scout Movement, is a worldwide youth movement with the stated aim of supporting young people in their physical, mental and spiritual development, so that they may play constructive roles in society.

Scouting began in 1907 when Robert Baden-Powell, Lieutenant General in the British Army, held the first Scouting encampment at Brownsea Island in England. Baden-Powell wrote the principles of Scouting in Scouting for Boys (London, 1908), based on his earlier military books, with influence and support of Frederick Russell Burnham (Chief of Scouts in British Africa), Ernest Thompson Seton of the Woodcraft Indians, William Alexander Smith of the Boys' Brigade, and his publisher Pearson. During the first half of the 20th century, the movement grew to encompass three major age groups each for boys (Cub Scout, Boy Scout, Rover Scout) and, in 1910, a new organization, Girl Guides, was created for girls (Brownie Guide, Girl Guide and Girl Scout, Ranger Guide).

The movement employs the Scout method, a program of informal education with an emphasis on practical outdoor activities, including camping, woodcraft, aquatics, hiking, backpacking, and sports. Another widely recognized movement characteristic is the Scout uniform, by intent hiding all differences of social standing in a country and making for equality, with neckerchief and campaign hat or comparable head wear. Distinctive uniform insignia include the fleur-de-lis and the trefoil, as well as merit badges and other patches.

In 2007, Scouting and Guiding together had over 38 million members in 216 countries. The two largest umbrella organizations are the World Organization of the Scout Movement (WOSM), for boys-only and co-educational organizations, and the World Association of Girl Guides and Girl Scouts (WAGGGS), primarily for girls-only organizations but also accepting co-educational organizations. That year marked the centenary of Scouting world wide, and member organizations planned events to celebrate the occasion.

History

Origins

As a military officer, Baden-Powell was stationed in British India and Africa in the 1880s and 1890s. Since his youth, he had been fond of woodcraft and military scouting, and—as part of their training—showed his men how to survive in the wilderness. He noticed that it helped the soldiers to develop independence rather than just blindly follow officers' orders.

In 1896, Baden-Powell was assigned to the Matabeleland region in Southern Rhodesia (now Zimbabwe) as Chief of Staff to Gen. Frederick Carrington during the Second Matabele War, and it was here that he first met and began a life-long friendship with Frederick Russell Burnham, the American born Chief of Scouts for the British. This would become a formative experience for Baden-Powell not only because he had the time of his life commanding reconnaissance missions into enemy territory, but because many of his later Boy Scout ideas took hold here. During their joint scouting patrols into the Matobo Hills, Burnham began teaching Baden-Powell woodcraft, inspiring him and giving him the plan for both the program and the code of honor of Scouting for Boys. Practiced by frontiersmen of the American Old West and Indigenous peoples of the Americas, woodcraft was generally unknown to the British, but well known to the American scout Burnham. These skills eventually formed the basis of what is now called scoutcraft, the fundamentals of Scouting. Both men recognised that wars in Africa were changing markedly and the British Army needed to adapt; so during their joint scouting missions, Baden-Powell and Burnham discussed the concept of a broad training programme in woodcraft for young men, rich in exploration, tracking, fieldcraft, and self-reliance. It was also during this time in the Matobo Hills that Baden-Powell first started to wear his signature campaign hat like the one worn by Burnham, and it was here that Baden-Powell acquired his Kudu horn, the Ndebele war instrument he later used every morning at Brownsea Island to wake the first Boy Scouts and to call them together in training courses.

Three years later, in South Africa during the Second Boer War, Baden-Powell was besieged in the small town of Mafeking by a much larger Boer army (the Siege of Mafeking). The Mafeking Cadet Corps was a group of youths that supported the troops by carrying messages, which freed the men for military duties and kept the boys occupied during the long siege. The Cadet Corps performed well, helping in the defense of the town (1899–1900), and were one of the many factors that inspired Baden-Powell to form the Scouting movement. Each member received a badge that illustrated a combined compass point and spearhead. The badge's logo was similar to the fleur-de-lis that Scouting later adopted as its international symbol.

In the United Kingdom, the public followed Baden-Powell's struggle to hold Mafeking through newspapers, and when the siege was broken, he had become a national hero. This rise to fame fueled the sales of a small instruction book he had written about military scouting, Aids to Scouting.

On his return to England, he noticed that boys showed considerable interest in the book, which was used by teachers and youth organizations. He was suggested by several to rewrite this book for boys, especially during an inspection of the Boys' Brigade, a large youth movement drilled with military precision.

Baden-Powell thought this would not be attractive and suggested that it could grow much larger when scouting would be used. He studied other schemes, parts of which he used for Scouting.

In July 1906, Ernest Thompson Seton sent Baden-Powell a copy of his book The Birchbark Roll of the Woodcraft Indians. Seton, a British-born Canadian living in the United States, met Baden-Powell in October 1906, and they shared ideas about youth training programs. In 1907 Baden-Powell wrote a draft called Boy Patrols. In the same year, to test his ideas, he gathered 21 boys of mixed social backgrounds (from boy's schools in the London area and a section of boys from the Poole, Parkstone, Hamworthy, Bournemouth,, and Winton Boys' Brigade units) and held a week-long camp in August on Brownsea Island in Poole Harbour, Dorset, England. His organizational method, now known as the Patrol System and a key part of Scouting training, allowed the boys to organize themselves into small groups with an elected patrol leader.

In the autumn of 1907, Baden-Powell went on an extensive speaking tour arranged by his publisher, Arthur Pearson, to promote his forthcoming book, Scouting for Boys. He had not simply rewritten his Aids to Scouting, but left out the military aspects and transferred the techniques (mainly survival) to non-military heroes: backwoodsmen, explorers (and later on, sailors and airmen). He also added innovative educational principles (the Scout method) by which he extended the attractive game to a personal mental education.

Scouting for Boys first appeared in England in January 1908 as six fortnightly installments, and was published in England later in 1908 in book form. The book is now the fourth-bestselling title of all time, and is now commonly considered the first version of the Boy Scout Handbook.

At the time, Baden-Powell intended that the scheme would be used by established organizations, in particular the Boys' Brigade, from the founder William A. Smith. However, because of the popularity of his person and the adventurous outdoor game he wrote about, boys spontaneously formed Scout patrols and flooded Baden-Powell with requests for assistance. He encouraged them, and the Scouting movement developed momentum. As the movement grew, Sea Scout, Air Scout, and other specialized units were added to the program.

Growth

The Boy Scout movement swiftly established itself throughout the British Empire soon after the publication of Scouting for Boys. The first recognized overseas unit was chartered in Gibraltar in 1908, followed quickly by a unit in Malta. Canada became the first overseas dominion with a sanctioned Boy Scout program, followed by Australia, New Zealand and South Africa. Chile was the first country outside the British dominions to have a recognized Scouting program. The first Scout rally, held in 1909 at The Crystal Palace in London, attracted 10,000 boys and a number of girls. By 1910, Argentina, Denmark, Finland, France, Germany, Greece, India, Malaya, Mexico, the Netherlands, Norway, Russia, Sweden, and the United States had Boy Scouts.

The program initially focused on boys aged 11 to 18, but as the movement grew, the need became apparent for leader training and programs for younger boys, older boys, and girls. The first Cub Scout and Rover Scout programs were in place by the late 1910s. They operated independently until they obtained official recognition from their home country's Scouting organization. In the United States, attempts at Cub programs began as early as 1911, but official recognition was not obtained until 1930.

Girls wanted to become part of the movement almost as soon as it began. Baden-Powell and his sister Agnes Baden-Powell introduced the Girl Guides in 1910, a parallel movement for girls, sometimes named Girl Scouts. Agnes Baden-Powell became the first president of the Girl Guides when it was formed in 1910, at the request of the girls who attended the Crystal Palace Rally. In 1914, she started Rosebuds—later renamed

Brownies—for younger girls. She stepped down as president of the Girl Guides in 1920 in favor of Robert's wife Olave Baden-Powell, who was named Chief Guide (for England) in 1918 and World Chief Guide in 1930. At that time, girls were expected to remain separate from boys because of societal standards, though co-educational youth groups did exist. By the 1990s, two thirds of the Scout organizations belonging to WOSM had become co-educational.

Baden-Powell could not single-handedly advise all groups who requested his assistance. Early Scoutmaster training camps were held in London in 1910 and in Yorkshire in 1911. Baden-Powell wanted the training to be as practical as possible to encourage other adults to take leadership roles, so the Wood Badge course was developed to recognize adult leadership training. The development of the training was delayed by World War I, so the first Wood Badge course was not held until 1919. Wood Badge is used by Boy Scout associations and combined Boy Scout and Girl Guide associations in many countries. Gilwell Park near London was purchased in 1919 on behalf of The Scout Association as an adult training site and Scouting campsite. Baden-Powell wrote a book, Aids to Scoutmastership, to help Scouting Leaders, and wrote other handbooks for the use of the new Scouting sections, such as Cub Scouts and Girl Guides. One of these was Rovering to Success, written for Rover Scouts in 1922. A wide range of leader training exists in 2007, from basic to program-specific, including the Wood Badge training.

Influences

Important elements of traditional Scouting have their origins in Baden-Powell's experiences in education and military training. He was a 50-year-old retired army general when he founded Scouting, and his revolutionary ideas inspired thousands of young people, from all parts of society, to get involved in activities that most had never contemplated. Comparable organizations in the English-speaking world are the Boys' Brigade and the non-militaristic Woodcraft Folk;

however, they never matched the development and growth of Scouting.

Aspects of Scouting practice have been criticized as too militaristic. Military-style uniforms, badges of rank, flag ceremonies, and brass bands were commonly accepted in the early years because they were a part of normal society, but since then have diminished or been abandoned in both Scouting and society.

Local influences have also been a strong part of Scouting. By adopting and modifying local ideologies, Scouting has been able to find acceptance in a wide variety of cultures. In the United States, Scouting uses images drawn from the U.S. frontier experience. This includes not only its selection of animal badges for Cub Scouts, but the underlying assumption that American native peoples are more closely connected with nature and therefore have special wilderness survival skills which can be used as part of the training program. By contrast, British Scouting makes use of imagery drawn from the Indian subcontinent, because that region was a significant focus in the early years of Scouting. Baden-Powell's personal experiences in India led him to adopt Rudyard Kipling's The Jungle Book as a major influence for the Cub Scouts; for example, the name used for the Cub Scout leader, Akela (whose name was also appropriated for the Webelos), is that of the leader of the wolf pack in the book.

The name "Scouting" seems to have been inspired by the important and romantic role played by military scouts performing reconnaissance in the wars of the time. In fact, Baden-Powell wrote his original military training book, Aids To Scouting, because he saw the need for the improved training of British military-enlisted scouts, particularly in initiative, self-reliance, and observational skills. The book's popularity with young boys surprised him. As he adapted the book as Scouting for Boys, it seems natural that the movement adopted the names Scouting and Boy Scouts.

"Duty to God" is a principle of Scouting, though it is applied differently in various countries. The Boy Scouts of America

(BSA) take a strong position, excluding atheists. The Scout Association in the United Kingdom permits variations to its Promise, in order to accommodate different religious obligations, but does not allow for atheists. Scouts Canada defines Duty to God broadly in terms of "adherence to spiritual principles" and leaves it to the individual member or leader whether they can follow a Scout Promise that includes Duty to God.

Movement Characteristics

Scouting is taught using the Scout method, which incorporates an informal educational system that emphasizes practical activities in the outdoors. Programs exist for Scouts ranging in age from 6 to 25 (though age limits vary slightly by country), and program specifics target Scouts in a manner appropriate to their age.

Scout Method

The Scout method is the principal method by which the Scouting organizations, boy and girl, operate their units. WOSM describes Scouting as "...a voluntary nonpolitical educational movement for young people open to all without distinction of origin, race or creed, in accordance with the purpose, principles and method conceived by the Founder..." It is the goal of Scouting "to contribute to the development of young people in achieving their full physical, intellectual, social and spiritual potentials as individuals, as responsible citizens and as members of their local, national and international communities."

The principles of Scouting describe a code of behavior for all members, and characterize the movement. The Scout method is a progressive system designed to achieve these goals, comprising seven elements: law and promise, learning by doing, team system, symbolic framework, personal progression, nature, and adult support. While community service is a major element of both the WOSM and WAGGGS programs, WAGGGS includes it as an extra element of the Scout method: service in the community.

The Scout Law and Promise embody the joint values of the Scouting movement worldwide, and bind all Scouting associations together. The emphasis on "learning by doing" provides experiences and hands-on orientation as a practical method of learning and building self-confidence. Small groups build unity, camaraderie, and a close-knit fraternal atmosphere. These experiences, along with an emphasis on trustworthiness and personal honor, help to develop responsibility, character, self-reliance, self-confidence, reliability, and readiness; which eventually lead to collaboration and leadership. A program with a variety of progressive and attractive activities expands a Scout's horizon and bonds the Scout even more to the group. Activities and games provide an enjoyable way to develop skills such as dexterity. In an outdoor setting, they also provide contact with the natural environment.

Since the birth of Scouting in 1907, Scouts worldwide have taken a Scout Promise to live up to ideals of the movement, and subscribe to the Scout Law. The form of the promise and laws have varied slightly by country and over time, but must fulfil the requirements of the WOSM to qualify a National Scout Association for membership.

The Scout Motto, 'Be Prepared', has been used in various languages by millions of Scouts since 1907. Less well-known is the Scout Slogan, 'Do a good turn daily'.

Activities

Common ways to implement the Scout method include having Scouts spending time together in small groups with shared experiences, rituals, and activities, and emphasizing good citizenship and decision-making by young people in an age-appropriate manner. Weekly meetings often take place in local centres known as Scout dens. Cultivating a love and appreciation of the outdoors and outdoor activities is a key element. Primary activities include camping, woodcraft, aquatics, hiking, backpacking, and sports.

Camping is most often arranged at the unit level, such as one Scout troop, but there are periodic camps (known in Australia as "jamborettes" and in the US as "camporees") and "jamborees". Camps occur a few times a year and may involve several groups from a local area or region camping together for a weekend. The events usually have a theme, such as pioneering. World Scout Moots are gatherings, originally for Rover Scouts, but mainly focused on Scout Leaders. Jamborees are large national or international events held every four years, during which thousands of Scouts camp together for one or two weeks. Activities at these events will include games, scoutcraft competitions, badge, pin or patch trading, aquatics, woodcarving, archery and activities related to the theme of the event.

In some countries a highlight of the year for Scouts is spending at least a week in the summer engaging in an outdoor activity. This can be a camping, hiking, sailing, or other trip with the unit, or a summer camp with broader participation (at the council, state, or provincial level). Scouts attending a summer camp work on merit badges, advancement, and perfecting scoutcraft skills. Summer camps can operate specialty programs for older Scouts, such as sailing, backpacking, canoeing and whitewater, caving, and fishing.

At an international level Scouting perceives one of its roles as the promotion of international harmony and peace. Various initiatives are in train towards achieving this aim including the development of activities that benefit the wider community, challenge prejudice and encourage tolerance of diversity. Such programs include co-operation with non-scouting organisations including various NGOs, the United Nations and religious institutions as set out in The Marrakech Charter.

Uniforms and Distinctive Insignia

The Scout uniform is a widely recognized characteristic of Scouting. In the words of Baden-Powell at the 1937 World Jamboree, it "hides all differences of social standing in a country and makes for equality; but, more important still, it covers differences of country and race and creed, and makes all feel that they are members with one another of the one great brotherhood". The original uniform, still widely recognized, consisted of a khaki button-up shirt, shorts, and a broad-brimmed campaign hat. Baden-Powell also wore shorts, because he believed that being dressed like a Scout helped to reduce the age-imposed distance between adult and youth. Uniform shirts are now frequently blue, orange, red or green and shorts are frequently replaced by long trousers all year or only in winter.

While designed for smartness and equality, the Scout uniform is also practical. Shirts traditionally have thick seams to make them ideal for use in makeshift stretchers—Scouts were trained to use them in this way with their staves, a traditional but deprecated item. The leather straps and toggles of the campaign hats or Leaders' Wood Badges could be used as emergency tourniquets, or anywhere that string was needed in a hurry. Neckerchiefs were chosen as they could easily be used as a sling or triangular bandage by a Scout in need. Scouts were encouraged to use their garters for shock cord where necessary.

Distinctive insignia for all are Scout uniforms, recognized and worn the world over, include the Wood Badge and the World Membership Badge. Scouting has two internationally known symbols: the trefoil is used by members of the World Association of Girl Guides and Girl Scouts (WAGGGS) and the fleur-de-lis by member organizations of the WOSM and most other Scouting organizations.

The swastika was used as an early symbol by the British Boy Scouts and others. Its earliest use in Scouting was on the Thanks Badge introduced in 1911. Lord Baden-Powell's 1922 design for the Medal of Merit added a swastika to the Scout fleur-de-lis to symbolize good luck for the recipient. Like Rudyard Kipling, he would have come across this symbol in India. In 1934, Scouters requested a change to the design because of the later use of the swastika by the Nationalsozialistische Deutsche

Arbeiterpartei (Nazi Party). A new British Medal of Merit was issued in 1935.

Age Groups and Sections

Scouting and Guiding movements are generally divided into sections by age or school grade, allowing activities to be tailored to the maturity of the group's members. These age divisions have varied over time as they adapt to the local culture and environment.

Scouting was originally developed for adolescents—youths between the ages of 11 and 17. In most member organizations, this age group composes the Scout or Guide section. Programs were developed to meet the needs of young children (generally ages 6 to 10) and young adults (originally 18 and older, and later up to 25). Scouts and Guides were later split into "junior" and "senior" sections in many member organizations, and some organizations dropped the young adults' section. The exact age ranges for programs vary by country and association.

Original age groups as developed by Baden-Powell:

Age range	Scouting section	Guiding section
7 to 10	Cub Scout	Brownie Guide
11 to 17	Boy Scout	Girl Guide or Girl Scout
18 and up	Rover Scout	Ranger Guide

The national programs for younger children include Tiger Cubs, Cub Scouts, Brownies, Daisies, Rainbow Guides, Beaver Scouts, Joey Scouts, Keas, and Teddies. Programs for post-adolescents and young adults include the Senior Section, Rover Scouts, Senior Scouts, Venture Scouts, Explorer Scouts, and the Scout Network. Many organizations also have a program for members with special needs. This is usually known as Extension Scouting, but sometimes has other names, such as Scoutlink. The Scout Method has been adapted to specific programs such as Air Scouts, Sea Scouts, Rider Guides and Scoutingbands .

In many countries, Scouting is organized into neighborhood Scout Groups, or Districts, which contain one or more sections. Under the umbrella of the Scout Group, sections are divided according to age, each having their own terminology and leadership structure.

Adults and Leadership

Adults interested in Scouting or Guiding, including former Scouts and Guides, often join organizations such as the International Scout and Guide Fellowship. In the United States and the Philippines, university students might join the co-ed service fraternity Alpha Phi Omega. In the United Kingdom, university students might join the Student Scout and Guide Organisation, and after graduation, the Scout and Guide Graduate Association.

Scout units are usually operated by adult volunteers, such as parents and carers, former Scouts, students, and community leaders, including teachers and religious leaders. Scout Leadership positions are often divided into 'uniform' and 'lay' positions. Uniformed leaders have received formal training, such as the Wood Badge, and have received a warrant for a rank within the organization. Lay members commonly hold part-time roles such as meeting helpers, committee members and advisors, though there are a small number of full-time lay professionals.

A unit has uniformed positions—such as the Scoutmaster and assistants—whose titles vary among countries. In some countries, units are supported by lay members, who range from acting as meeting helpers to being members of the unit's committee. In some Scout associations, the committee members may also wear uniforms and be registered Scout leaders.

Above the unit are further uniformed positions, called Commissioners, at levels such as district, county, council or province, depending on the structure of the national organization. Commissioners work with lay teams and professionals. Training teams and related functions are often formed at these levels. In the UK and in other countries, the national Scout organization appoints the Chief Scout, the most senior uniformed member.

Around the World

Following its foundation in the United Kingdom (UK), Scouting spread around the globe. The first association outside the UK was opened in Malta, which is independent now but was a British colony at the time. In most countries of the world, there is now at least one Scouting (or Guiding) organization. Each is independent, but international cooperation continues to be seen as part of the Scout Movement. In 1922 the WOSM started as the governing body on policy for the national Scouting organizations (then male only). In addition to being the governing policy body, it organizes the World Scout Jamboree every four years.

In 1928 the WAGGGS started as the equivalent to WOSM for the then female-only national Scouting/Guiding organizations. It is also responsible for its four international centres: Our Cabaña in Mexico, Our Chalet in Switzerland, Pax Lodge in the United Kingdom, and Sangam in India.

Today at the international level, the two largest umbrella organizations are:

- World Organization of the Scout Movement (WOSM), for boys-only and co-educational organizations.
- World Association of Girl Guides and Girl Scouts (WAGGGS), primarily for girls-only organizations but also accepting co-educational organizations.

Co-educational

There have been different approaches to co-educational Scouting. Countries such as the United States have maintained separate Scouting organizations for boys and girls. In other countries, especially within Europe, Scouting and Guiding have merged, and there is a single organization for boys and girls, which is a member of both the WOSM and the WAGGGS. In others, such as Australia and the United Kingdom, the national Scout association has opted to admit both boys and girls, but is only a member of the WOSM, while the national Guide association has remained as a separate movement and member of the WAGGGS. In some countries like Greece, Slovenia and Spain there are separate associations of Scouts (members of WOSM) and guides (members of WAGGGS), both admitting boys and girls.

The Scout Association in the United Kingdom has been co-educational at all levels since 1991, but this has been optional for groups, and currently 52% of groups have at least one female youth member. Since 2000 new sections have been required to accept girls. The Scout Association has decided that all Scout groups and sections will become co-educational by January 2007, the year of Scouting's centenary.

In the United States, the Cub Scout and Boy Scout programs of the BSA are for boys only; however, for youths age 14 and older, Venturing is co-educational. The Girl Scouts of the USA (GSUSA) is an independent organization for girls and young women only. Adult leadership positions in the BSA and GSUSA are open to both men and women.

In 2006, of the 155 WOSM member National Scout Organizations (representing 155 countries), 122 belonged only to WOSM, and 34 belonged to both WOSM and WAGGGS. Of the 122 which belonged only to WOSM, 95 were open to boys and girls in some or all program sections, and 20 were only for boys. All 34 that belonged to both WOSM and WAGGGS were open to boys and girls.

WAGGGS had 144 Member Organizations in 2007 and 110 of them belonged only to WAGGGS. Of these 110, 17 were coeducational and 93 admitted only girls.

Membership

As of 2008, there are over 28 million registered Scouts and 10 million registered Guides around the world, from 216 countries and territories.

Top 20 countries with Scouting and Guiding, sorted by total male and female membership of all organisations

Country	Membership	Scouting introduced	Guiding introduced
United States	9,500,000	1910	1912
Indonesia	8,100,000	1912	1912
India	3,700,000	1909	1911
Philippines	2,550,000	1910	1918
Thailand	1,400,000	1911	1957
United Kingdom	1,000,000	1907	1909
Bangladesh	950,000	1920	1928
Pakistan	575,000	1909	1911
Kenya	420,000	1910	1920
Korea	280,000	1922	1946
Germany[n.b. 2]	260,000	1910	1912
Canada	260,000	1908	1910
Japan	240,000	1913	1919
Italy[n.b. 3]	220,000	1910	1912
Uganda	210,000	1915	1914
France[n.b. 4]	190,000	1910	1911
Nigeria	160,000	1915	1919
Poland[n.b. 5]	160,000	1910	1910
Belgium[n.b. 6]	160,000	1911	1915
Hong Kong	160,000	1914	1916

1. Full tables on List of World Organization of the Scout Movement members and List of World Association of Girl Guides and Girl Scouts members.
2. Including 90,000 non-aligned Scouts and Guides, see Scouting in Germany

3. Including 30,000 non-aligned Scouts and Guides, see Scouting in Italy
4. Including 60,000 non-aligned Scouts and Guides, see Scouting in France
5. Including 20,000 non-aligned Scouts and Guides, see Scouting in Poland
6. Including 5,000 non-aligned Scouts and Guides, see Scouting in Belgium

Nonaligned and Scout-like Organizations

Fifteen years passed between the first publication of Scouting for Boys and the creation of the current largest supranational Scout organization, WOSM, and millions of copies had been sold in dozens of languages. By that point, Scouting was the purview of the world's youth, and several Scout associations had already formed in many countries.

Alternative groups have formed since the original formation of the Scouting "Boy Patrols". They can be a result of groups or individuals who maintain that the WOSM and WAGGGS are currently more political and less youth-based than envisioned by Lord Baden-Powell. They believe that Scouting in general has moved away from its original intent because of political machinations that happen to longstanding organizations, and want to return to the earliest, simplest methods. Others do not want to follow all the original ideals of Scouting but still desire to participate in Scout-like activities.

In 2008, there were at least 539 independent Scouting organizations around the world, 367 of them were a member of either WAGGGS or WOSM. About half of the remaining 172 Scouting organizations are only local or national orientated. About 90 national or regional Scouting associations have felt the need to create alternative international Scouting organizations to set standards for Scouting and to coordinate activities among member associations. Those are served by four international Scouting organizations:

- Order of World Scouts – the first international Scouting organisation, founded in 1911.
- Confédération Européenne de Scoutisme, established in 1978.
- Union Internationale des Guides et Scouts d'Europe, an independent faith-based Scouting organization founded in 1956.
- World Federation of Independent Scouts, formed in Laubach, Germany, in 1996.

Some Scout-like organizations are also served by international organizations for example:

- Pathfinders
- Royal Rangers

Controversy and Conflict

Since the inception of Scouting in the early 1900s, the movement has sometimes been entangled in social controversies such as the civil rights struggle in the American South and in nationalist resistance movements in India. Scouting was introduced to Africa by British officials as a way to strengthen their rule, but turned to challenge the legitimacy of the British Empire, as African Scouts used the Scout Law's principle that a Scout is a brother to all other Scouts to collectively claim full imperial citizenship. More recently, Boy Scouts of America has been criticized for not allowing the participation of atheists, agnostics, or homosexuals.

In Film and the Arts

Scouting has been a facet of culture during most of the 20th century in many countries; numerous films and artwork focus on the subject. It is especially prevalent in the United States, where Scouting is tied closely to the ideal of Americana. Movie critic Roger Ebert mentioned the scene in which the young Boy Scout, Indiana Jones, discovers the Cross of

Coronado in the movie Indiana Jones and the Last Crusade, as "when he discovers his life mission."

The works of painters Norman Rockwell, Pierre Joubert and Joseph Csatari and the 1966 film Follow Me, Boys! are prime examples of this idealized American ethos. Scouting is often dealt with in a humorous manner, as in the 1989 film Troop Beverly Hills, the 2005 film Down and Derby, and the film Scout Camp and is often fictionalized so that the audience knows the topic is Scouting without any mention of Scouting by name. In 1980, Scottish singer and songwriter Gerry Rafferty recorded I was a Boy Scout as part of his Snakes and Ladders album.

The Boy Scouts of America are quite particular about how and when the Scout uniforms and insignia may be used in film and other portrayals, however, and for that reason, most films and television productions made in the U.S. utilize "ersatz" Scouting organizations. Examples of this include the "Order of the Straight Arrow," portrayed in the King of the Hill cartoon series, and the "Indian Guides" depicted in the 1995 Chevy Chase film Man of the House. A notable exception to this policy, is the final scene of The Sopranos television show, where Tony Soprano (apparently about to be murdered) sits down to dinner in a restaurant. At another table, several Webelos Cub Scouts, in full uniform, are seated.

Chapter 9

Hang Gliding

Hang gliding is an air sport in which a pilot flies a light and unmotorized foot-launchable aircraft called a hang glider (also known as Delta plane or Deltaplane). Most modern hang gliders are made of an aluminium alloy or composite-framed fabric wing. The pilot is ensconced in a harness suspended from the airframe, and exercises control by shifting body weight in opposition to a control frame, but other devices, including modern aircraft flight control systems, may be used. In the sport's early days, pilots were restricted to gliding down small hills on low-performance hang gliders. However, modern technology gives pilots the ability to soar for hours, gain thousands of feet of altitude in thermal updrafts, perform aerobatics, and glide cross-country for hundreds of miles. The Fédération Aéronautique Internationale and national airspace governing organizations control some aspects of hang gliding. Gaining the safety benefits from being instructed is highly recommended.

History of Hang Gliding

Hang gliding is an air sport employing foot-launchable aircraft known as a hang glider. Typically, a hang glider is constructed of an aluminium alloy or composite-framed fabric wing. The pilot is ensconced in a harness suspended from the airframe, and exercises control by shifting body weight in opposition to a control frame.

Early hang glider designs did not reliably achieve safe flight, their builders lacking a comprehensive understanding of the underlying principles of flight. The first recorded controlled flights were by German engineer Otto Lilienthal, whose research, published in 1889, strongly influenced later designers. The type of aircraft employed by Lilienthal is now referred to as a hang glider. Further hang glider research was undertaken during the 1920s in Europe, Australia and the U.S.A, where designers tested several wing concepts and the 'pendulum weight-shift control system'.

In 1957 the American space agency NASA began testing various formats of a new wing called the Rogallo wing with the intent of possibly implementing the design as a recovery system for the Gemini space capsules. The wing's simplicity of design and ease of construction, in combination with its slow flight characteristics, did not go unnoticed by hang glider enthusiasts; Rogallo's flexible wing airfoil was soon adapted to the purpose of recreational flight, launching a hang glider Renaissance.

Early History

The sleek high performance jets, sailplanes and hang gliders of today have a heritage that dates back to man's first attempts at flight.

According to historian Ahmed Mohammed al-Maqqari (1591–1632), several contemporary accounts report that the polymath Abbas Ibn Firnas (810-887) attempted an early glider flight near Cordoba, Spain which ended in heavy back injuries. It is considered the first attempt at heavier-than-air flight in aviation history. In either 1003 or 1008, Jauhari attempted flight by some apparatus from the roof of a mosque in Nishapur, Khorasan, Iran, and fell to his death as a result.

The monk Eilmer of Malmesbury is reported by William of Malmesbury (c. 1080-1143), a fellow monk and historian, to have flown off the roof of his Abbey in Malmesbury, England, sometime between 1000 and 1010, gliding about 200 metres

(220 yd) before crashing and breaking his legs. Going by the sketchy reports, both Ibn Firnas and Eilmer used a set of (feathery) wings, and both blamed their crash on the lack of a tail. There is one record of a Turk named Hezârfen Ahmed Çelebi who reportedly flew across the Bosphorus straight in the 17th century.

Starting in the 1880s advancements were made in aerodynamics and construction that led to the first truly practical gliders; this information was often shared and published by early aviators and inventors, building a long series of incremental achievements. Through the 1880s several aviation pioneers emerged in different countries around the world all perusing glider designs with varying degrees of success. Chief among these were Otto Lilienthal in Berlin, Germany, Lawrence Hargrave in Sydney, Australia, Percy Pilcher in the United Kingdom, John Joseph Montgomery at Otay Mesa near San Diego, California (1880s) as well as at Santa Clara, California (1905) Octave Chanute and his team in Gary, Indiana in the U.S.A., just to name a few.

Otto Lilienthal duplicated some of his contemporaries' work and greatly expanded on it from 1874, publishing all of his research in 1889. He also produced a series of gliders, and in 1891 was able to make flights of 25 metres (82 ft) or more routinely, as well as some soaring flights. He rigorously documented his work, influencing later designers; for this reason he is one of the best known and influential of the early aviation pioneers. His type of aircraft is now known as a hang glider. By 1896 he had made about 2000 flights on a number of his designs when he crashed from a height of roughly 17 metres (56 ft) fracturing his spine. Percy Pilcher took a growing interest in aviation and built a glider called The Bat which he flew for the first time in 1895. Later that year Pilcher met and consulted with Otto Lilienthal, who was the leading expert in gliding; these discussions led to Pilcher building two more hang gliders, The Beetle and The Gull. Based on the work of his mentor Otto Lilienthal, in 1897 Pilcher built a third hang glider called

The Hawk with which he broke the world distance record when he flew 250 metres (820 ft).

Wasserkuppe

The hang glider lost some importance through the introduction of wing warping in 1902 by the Wright brothers and subsequently of aileron control by the French. When the World War I ended in 1918, the Treaty of Versailles practically ended engine driven flights in Germany, thus, in the 1920s and 1930s, while aviators and aircraft makers in the rest of the world were working to improve the performance of powered aircraft, the Germans were designing, developing and flying ever more efficient gliders and discovering ways of using the natural forces in the atmosphere to make them fly farther and faster. These activities on Wasserkuppe promoted a renaissance of gliding aviation. Many of these gliders flown in 1920 were hang gliders in that they were controlled by the pilot's weight shift alone. The first Wasserkuppe glider competition was held in 1920 and from 1924 they were organised by Rhön-Rossitten Gesellschaft. Over the next decade, the contest grew in popularity. As many as 70 glider clubs from Europe sent their best gliders and pilots to compete for duration, altitude and distance prizes, the most coveted prize was that donated by President von Hindenburg. As many as 60,000 spectators dotted the mountain slopes to watch these events. Virtually every European aeronautical engineer of the time tested and modified their aircraft there and reports were generated. Some competing hang glider designers were Alfried Gymnich, Gottlob Espenlaub, Alexander Lippisch, Heinz Schneider, Francis Chardon, Willi Pelzner, Hans Richter and Segelflieger Peltzner, while engineer Henri Mignet was busy in France and Czes?aw Tan'ski was busy in Poland.

Invention of the Flexible Wing

In 1904 Jan Lavezzari at Berck-sur-Mer, France, a stiffened flexible-wing hang glider was demonstrated in flight; hence invention of the flexible-wing hang glider occurred at least by 1904. In 1908, a key cable-stayed [triangle control frame] (TCF) with pilot tethered behind the TCF was demonstrated for a hang glider in a gliding club in the territory of Breslau; such TCF is used even today on many kinds of hang gliders including flexible-wing hang gliders. On 1948, aeronautical engineer Francis Rogallo invented a self-inflating wing which he patented on March 20, 1951 as the Flexible Wing, also known as the flexwing and Rogallo wing. Francis Rogallo had first proposed his flexible wing concept to the Langley Research Center in the late 1940s as a simple, inexpensive approach to recreational flying, but the idea was not accepted as a project.

It was on October 4, 1957 when the Russian satellite Sputnik became a concern to the United States and marked the beginning of the 'space race' and the creation of NASA. Rogallo was in position to seize the opportunity and with his help at the wind tunnels, NASA began a series of experiments testing Rogallo's flexible wing, which got renamed Parawing, in order to evaluate it as a recovery system for the project Gemini space capsules. Rogallo designed his flexible wing to allow the astronauts to deploy it like a parachute at subsonic speeds during reentry, then glide their capsule to a specified touchdown point. F. Rogallo's team collaborated with at least two American aircraft companies, Ryan Aeronautical Company and North American Aviation, as there was potential for gliders, dirigible parachutes, and other new types of manned aircraft; this mainly involved stabilizing the leading edges with compressed air beams or rigid structures like aluminium tubes. By 1961 NASA had already made test flights of an experimental STOL 'aerial utility aircraft' called Ryan XV-8 (the Flying Jeep or Fleep) and by March 1962, of a weight-shift glider called Paresev.

Round parachutes were selected over the Rogallo wing to be used on the Gemini spacecraft and on 1965, funding on flexible wings stopped.

Flexible Wing Hang Gliders

The simplicity of the Rogallo wing, ease of construction, capability of slow flight and its gentle landing characteristics did not go unnoticed by some hang glider and ultralight glider enthusiasts. The publicity on the Fleep and the Paresev tests sparked interest in independent builders like Barry Palmer and John Dickenson, who separately explored distinct airframes and control systems to be adapted to a Rogallo wing and be flown as a hang glider.

On August 1961, American engineer Barry Palmer developed and flew the first foot-launched Rogallo wing hang glider. This took place near Latrobe, east of Sacramento, California. Palmer used aluminium tubing and no wires for construction, fearing kinking during assembly. Most flights were performed with just a set of inclined parallel bars that split his weight between his underarms and hands. The last of Palmer's foot-launched hang gliders flew in the summer of 1962 and it had a ski-lift type of seat mounted to the keel with a universal joint for pendulum weight-shift control; a single control stick was projected down from the wing. During the period from 1961 to 1963 Barry Palmer made tens of flights using this concept. His longest flight ranged in length up to 180 metres (590 ft), at altitudes up to 24 metres (79 ft), and had an overall glide ratio of 4.5 to 1.

Palmer's wing was heavy by today's standards and was not particularly portable. Palmer relates that he had a good aerospace job and was flying for fun. He did not attempt to modernize or market the flexible wing hang glider and shared all details with anybody interested.

In April 1963 Mike Burns first flew the Skiplane, a flexible wing glider on pontoons. In September 1963, Australian John Dickenson set out to build a water ski wing that could be released at altitude and glide to a safe landing. After seeing a Rogallo airfoil in a magazine, Dickenson designed the ski kite he called the Ski Wing. Dickenson fashioned an airframe that incorporated a triangle control frame and utilized wire bracing to distribute the load to the Rogallo airfoil; the pilot sat on a swinging seat. Dickenson's Ski Wing was stable and controllable, unlike the flat manned kites used at water ski shows at the time. The Ski Wing was first flown in public at the Grafton Jacaranda Festival, Australia, in September 1963 by Rod Fuller while towed behind a motorboat. The Ski Wing was light and portable so Dickenson decided to file for a patent; however, lacking resources, Dickenson procured a provisional patent - which would later lapse. By 1972, Australian builders Bill Bennett and Bill Moyes developed the Dickenson format of water ski kite into a foot-launched hang glider.

Rigid Wing Hang Gliders

There have been several rigid wing hang gliders flown since Otto Lilienthal took his first flights in the 1890s. Jack Lambie from California, designed in 1971 the popular Hang Loose Chanute hang glider, and the first two high performing modern hang gliders were the Mitchell Wing and the Icarus.

Jack Lambie was schoolteacher, as well as an innovative and experienced airman who had accompanied Captain Dick Merrill as copilot on the first commercial transatlantic flight on May 10, 1937. He helped build the first Human powered Aircraft, the Gossmer Condor, and many of his innovative design concepts have made their way into modern everyday life. He designed the first cab over Diesel Semi Truck fairing (the Fuel Saver) that is now used "stock" on practically all 18 wheelers. His teardrop/Dart Vader Bicycle helmet (the Lambie Lid) was first used by U.S.A. 84' Olympic Bike team to win Gold. Jack was singularly responsible for organizing the first modern era hang glider meet, the original Otto Meet, on the hills of Balboa in Sept., 1972.

Lambie organized the Otto Lilienthal Universal Hang Glider Championships held on a hilltop in Corona del Mar, California on May 23, 1971.

On 1971 and 1972 the Icarus I and Icarus II were built, respectively. These were rigid biplane flying wing designs by Taras Kiceniųk, Jr. The Icarus V was essentially a monoplane version of the previous Icarus designs. All of the hang gliders in the Icarus series had hand-controlled rudders and the pilot flew in a reclining position (rather than a prone position as with other hang gliders). Although many Icarus II and Icarus V gliders were built from plans sold by Kiceniuk, they were never commercially produced.

In the early 1940s Don Mitchell, an aeronautical engineer, first became involved with flying wing glider design and construction. WWII interrupted his research until 1974, with the advent of hang glider mania, adventurers were experimenting with design and exploring records worldwide. It was then that Mitchell's flying wing resurfaced. Dr. Howard Long took an interest and asked Don Mitchell to make him a refined 'flying wing' hang glider. The result was the foot-launched Mitchell Wing. When the foot-launched Mitchell Wing B-10 flew in the 1977 U.S.A. Nationals, the hang gliding world was completely astounded. The Mitchell Wing then went on to set and hold every world record in its class. In 1980, George Worthington soared to 17,000 feet (5,200 m) high and glided 105 miles (169 km), setting two new rigid wing records. The Mitchell Wing had a single "D" spar with aircraft birch plywood torsion proof leading edge and 3-axes control. Foam ribs placed every 4.5 inches (110 mm) hold the D shape. The built-up truss ribs aft of the spar are covered with fabric. This structural design is simple, extremely strong and light (under 80 Lbs).

The Exxtacy, designed by Felix Ruehle In the early 1990s, followed by the IXBO, became the first two rigid wing hang gliders on the market with a leading edge of carbon fiber. Ruehle then produced the ATOS in 1999. The nose angle and wing span of modern rigid wings are a little larger than flexible wings and the sail is rather stiff.

Popularity

The research by NASA as well as government reports and photographs of the flexible wing, were published and became available to the general public and soon, the Rogallo wing was turned into an easily constructed, inexpensive, foot-launchable glider. Barry Palmer corresponded Richard Miller, who in 1964 developed the Bamboo Butterfly, followed by Tara Kiceniuk's Batso. Dave Kilbourne published his plan for a Rogallo wing Kilbo Kite hang glider in the early 1970s. Jim Foreman produced the Bat-Glider plans for a Rogallo wing hang glider and sold copies for $5 USD throughout the world; later, Taras Kiceniuk, Tom Dickinson and two other team members made a similar hang glider called Batso and sold copies of its plans. The plans of these hang gliders circulated in some magazines in the mid 1960s.

Eventually, word of John Dickenson's success got out and more portable flexible wing gliders were built; the sudden commercial availability of his improved water ski hang gliders in 1969 by manufacturers like Bill Bennett (Delta Wing) and Bill Moyes (Moyes Gliders) added signinicantly to the flexible wing's popularity, which began to rise world wide as a full fledged sport.

The extreme nature of foot-launched hang gliding appealed to the freewheeling culture of the early 1970s across America more as an expression of freedom than an air sport. Popularity was further fueled by the distribution of specialized international publications such as the Low & Slow magazine founded in 1971, Hang Glider Weekly and Ground Skimmer in 1972 and Glider Rider in 1975. Hang gliding was simultaneously promoted by major international publications such as Popular Mechanics, Popular Science and the Life magazine, all three magazines distributed worldwide in 1971; the Sky Raiders hang gliding movie was released in 1976 with a powerful effect. The British SkyWings magazine has been published monthly since 1975 and Cross Country, the first truly international hang gliding magazine began publication in 1988.

Free hang gliding took longer to catch on in Australia, where hang gliding was a water skiing sport and part of the New South Wales Water Skiing Association. In fact, Dickenson's Ski Wing was competing in the NSWWSA kite-flying section against the polygonal Japanese style flat kites. The first recorded foot-launched flight in Australia occurred in 1972 and the Australian Self Soaring Association was formed by foot-launched pilots in 1974. The first foot-launched Australian Championships were held in 1976.

First flights in the early 1970s from Mt. Kilimanjaro by Moyes, and Caril Ridley's flights in India met with headlines. On 1973 the ZDF German Television produced a 30 min documentary on Mike Harker's world record hang glider flight from Mt. Zugspitze in Germany, this TV documentary helped promote the development of hang gliding in Europe. Harker also produced other hang gliding documentaries in the mid 1970s which were presented in TV by 16 countries.

Although by the early 1970s many rigid wings were developed, none sold terribly well, while dozens of flexible wing hang glider companies were springing up all over the world. The mid 1970s underwent significant improvements in hang glider design as manufacturers were bringing out new and improved models at a fast rate. From the simple structures of the early 1970s, the aspect ratio of the gliders increased dramatically, sails became tighter, battens became the rule, and the gliders became safer. In the late 1970s preformed aluminium battens became common and in 1980, the Comet took the industry by storm and popularized the free-floating internalized crossbar and double-surface sail construction that has since become the standard.

As usual, essentially parallel developments can be difficult to sort out and serialize, but in fact, the flexible wing hang glider popularity started with the publicized Paresev and Fleep concept, followed by John Dickenson's adaptation and the aggressive entrepreneurial energies of Bill Bennett, Bill Moyes, Joe Faust, Dick Eipper, Mike Riggs, the Wills brothers and the massive enthusiasm of thousands of people wanting to glide, and began what is now an estimated $50 million USD annual industry. Ironically, Dickenson never made any money and Francis Rogallo never claimed the rights to the patent he held, thus allowing his flexible wing airfoil to be used royalty free.

It is certain that many people from many countries, made contributions to the development of the flexible wing hang glider. In the aviation context of 'first flights' and recreational vs. commercial developments, it must be noted that new and old inventions often complement in synergy; it is in this evolutionary and social context that the crucial developments put together by Francis Rogallo and John Dickenson, were the ones that were most successful and influential on the evolution of hang gliders.

Timeline

- 1804 AD. Sir George Cayley built several gliders, distinguished between lift and drag and formulated the concepts of vertical tail surfaces, steering rudders and rear elevators.
- 1883 John Joseph Montgomery independently built several gliders in the United States and used wind and water tables to formulate thoughts on lifting surfaces.
- 1891 First controlled flights, Otto Lilienthal of Germany. His gliders have many features in common with modern hang gliders; they were foot-launched and controlled by displacing the center of gravity, referred to as 'weight-shift'.
- 1891–1896. First soaring flights. Germany, near Berlin at Gross Lichterfelde. Otto Lilienthal.
- 1904, February 15. Jan Lavezzari flew a double lateen sail hang glider off Berck beach, France.
- 1905 LIFE magazine shows a photograph of an early glider.
- 1905 Aeronaut Daniel Maloney pilots a balloon-launched tandem wing Montgomery glider from a release thousands

of feet above the ground to a landing at a predescribed location.

- 1908 in the territory of Breslau, the [triangle control frame] with hang glider pilot hung behind the triangle was evident at the gliding club. Such device continued to have uses in hang gliding up to today.
- 1920. Soaring becomes an organized sport at Wasserkuppe, Germany as the World War I Versailles treaty outlaws flying powered aircraft in Germany.
- 1921. Dr. Wolfgang Klemperer breaks the Wright Brothers 1911 soaring record with a 13-minute flight in Germany. Both flights used ridge lift.
- 1921. Gottlob Espenlaub demonstrates triangle control frame (TCF) for hang gliders in Rhon, Germany.
- 1923. Platz Glider. Not foot-launchable by the pilot alone. Controlled by the pilot directly deforming the front canard wings. It was not a weight-shift hang glider but it was simple enough to be folded into a single length to be carried by Platz while riding a bicycle.
- 1928. Austrian Robert Kronfeld proved that thermal lift could be used by a sailplane to gain altitude.
- 1929. Aero towing becomes popular, the three forms of lift are becoming well known.
- 1929. George A. Spratt demonstrated the use of the triangular control frame for hang glider pendulum weight-shift control, mechanically similar to that used in 1908 in a hang glider in Breslau. . Later in the 1930s he invented the Control Wing aircraft.
- 1933. Wave lift was discovered by Wolf Hirth and one of his students in Germany.
- 1948. Francis Rogallo invents the flexible wing (Rogallo wing).
- 1956. Aeronautical engineer Paul MacCready invents the MacCready Speed Ring, used by glider pilots the world over to select optimum flight speed.

- 1957, October. Francis Rogallo released the flexible wing patent to the U.S.A. government and NASA, producing the Parawing, to be used as a deployable space capsule parachute/glider.
- 1960. Paresev (Paraglider Research Vehicle) - This experimental spacecraft re-entry kite/glider made use of the Rogallo wing; flight tests made in early 1962 inspired manufacture of flexible wing hang gliders by hobbyists.
- 1960 The 13-yr old Tony Prentice built a framed hang glider with tether control system.
- 1961. Fleep. Powered flexible wing aircraft design & manufacture begins.
- 1961–1962. First documented foot-launch with a Rogallo flex wing hang glider: Barry Hill Palmer, California, U.S.A. Hang glider inspired from a photo of NASA's Fleep.
- 1961. Celebrity Jim Hobson (of Lawrence Welk Show fame) began experimenting with the Rogallo wing in model form, leading to the construction of a full size glider which he flew it at Dockweiler Beach on January 2, 1962. The glider frame was fabricated from aluminum and aircraft bolts supported by aircraft cable attached to hardware store eye bolts and turnbuckles. A second larger hang glider was taken to Dockweiler Beach; it featured a 4 mil polyester film reinforced with fiberglass tape. Movies of August, 1962 flights were made.
- 1961. Engineer Thomas Purcell builds a 4.9 metres (16 ft) wide Rogallo airfoil glider with an aluminium frame, wheels, a seat and basic control rods.
- 1962. Ryan Aeronautical Company publicizes images of the Fleep flexible wing aircraft.
- 1962. Mike Burns and Dick Swinbourne from Aerostructures, Sydney, Australia, design the Skiplane kite-glider based on the Rogallo wing. It used pendulum weight-shift control and floats.

- 1963. John Dickenson, Australia. Making of the Ski Wing, the most influential hang glider model, encompassing a control frame and weight-shift control.
- 1963, September. First flight of the Ski Wing, towed behind a motor boat. The kite/glider was piloted by Rod Fuller and then John Dickenson. Grafton, NSW, Australia.
- 1963. First release and land of a Ski Wing. Grafton, Australia. Pilot: John Dickenson.
- 1960s England. Tony Prentice designed and flew several non-Rogallo hang gliders.
- 1966. Mike Burns and Dick Swinbourne (Aerostructures) begin commercial production of Dickenson's Mark V model.
- 1966. Early flex wing hang glider, Vista Del Mar. California, U.S.A. by Richard Miller. His gliders, based on Barry Palmer's hang glider, were named Batso and Bamboo Butterfly. Their photos and plans were published in a few magazines during the 1960s. (See the Popularity section.)
- 1966. Irvin Industries start marketing a commercial version of the Rogallo Wing to sport parachuting enthusiasts.
- 1967, March. Bill Moyes and Bill Bennett taught to fly the Mark V hang glider by Mike Burns and John Dickenson.
- 1967. First Australian ski-launch of a flexible wing hang glider without auxiliary power (no towing). Launched from a snowed mountain with snow skis.- Bill Moyes. Mt. Crackenback, Australia. The hang glider was a Mark V purchased from Aerostructures.
- 1969. Initial tether into headwind then released onto ridge to soar (32 minutes). Bill Moyes. NSW, Australia.
- 1969. Tony Prentice. First flex wing hang glider foot-launch in the United Kingdom.
- 1971. Dave Kilbourne foot-launches and soars on ridge and thermal lift (1 hour) at Mission Peak, California, U.S.A.

This seems to be the first foot-launch of a flexible wing not using skis.

- 1971. Alfio Caronti, first flexible wing launched in Italy.
- 1972. Rick Poynter and Murray Sargeson introduce hang gliding to New Zealand at the 'Fly a Kite Day' in Auckland. The New Zealand Hang Gliding Association is formed as a result of this.
- 1973. Rock Poynter starts Pacific Sails in Auckland, New Zealand, manufacturing U.S. and Australian Hang Glider designs under license (Seagull III, Stinger), and developing competitive indigenous designs (Falcon, Lancer I, II, IV).
- 1974. Caril Ridley conducted high altitude flights soaring from a Maharaja's lookout tower near Sonar Hot Springs, India. The event got world wide coverage.
- 1976. Rudy Kishazy performs the first loop and series of loops at Grands Montets, France.
- 1977. Jerry Katz first to soar a distance of over 161 kilometres (100 mi), launching from Cerro Gordo Peak, in California's Owens Valley.
- 1978. Terry DeLore from New Zealand is crowned first World Hang Gliding Champion.
- 1983. Gérard Thévenot, the manufacturer of the Cosmos trike, introduced aerotowing, the use of weak links, parachute retrieval system of tow line and centre of thrust towing.
- 1992 The Exxtacy rigid wing hang glider, designed by Felix Ruehle.
- 1999 The ATOS rigid wing hang glider, designed by Felix Ruehle.

Production Era

The following generations follow the classification from the British Hang Gliding Museum's Hang Gliding History: Development in Britain of the Flexwing hang glider.

- 1971–1975. First Generation - Interest in the sport grew worldwide; development of hang gliders on a commercial scale.
- 1974–1976. Second Generation - Increased nose angle, deflexors.
- 1977–1979. Third Generation - Multiple deflexors.
- 1978–1980. Fourth Generation- Enclosed keel and tip rods.
- 1978. The Atlas (La Mouette) entered the market. The pilot flew in a prone position. The Atlas had all of the safety elements that can still be found today.
- 1980–1997. Fifth Generation - Preformed battens. Floating cross bar. Cross bar enclosed in double surface. Hang glider performance then increased rapidly. The first truly successful "double surface" hang gliders were Tom Peghiny's Kestrel and later the UP "Comet" designed by Roy Haggard (1980). Virtually all hang gliders over the next decade were refinements of the Comet. The first fifth-generation hang gliders to dispense with a raised keel pocket were the Wills Wing "HP" in the U.S.A. and Enterprise Wings "Foil" in Australia (1984). Bob Trampenau of Seedwings introduced the VG (variable geometry), which was copied on most other hang gliders.
- 1997–Present. Sixth Generation - Topless (without kingpost). While topless gliders had been experimented with in the past using struts or cantilever nose plates, in the late 1990s the use of strong carbon fiber crossbars allowed the kingpost on top of the wing to be more conveniently removed to further increase performance by reducing drag.

Training and Safety

Since its inception, hang gliding has traditionally been considered an unsafe sport. Modern hang gliders are very sturdy when constructed by HGMA, BHPA, DHV or other certified standards and using modern materials. Although they remain lightweight craft, they can be easily damaged, either through misuse or by continued operation in unsafe wind/weather conditions. All modern gliders have built-in dive recovery mechanisms such as luff lines in kingposted gliders. Nevertheless, the inherent danger of gliding at the mercy of thermal and wind currents, has resulted in numerous fatal accidents and many serious injuries over the years, even to experienced pilots, and the resultant adverse publicity has affected the popularity of hang gliding.

As a backup, pilots may carry a parachute in the harness. In case of serious problems the parachute is deployed and carries both pilot and glider down to earth. Pilots also wear helmets and generally carry other safety items such as hook knives (for cutting their parachute bridle after impact or cutting their harness lines and straps in case of a tree or water landing), light ropes (for lowering from trees to haul up tools or climbing ropes), radios (for calling for help) and first-aid equipment.

The accident rate from hang glider flying has been dramatically decreased by pilot training. Early hang glider pilots learned their sport through trial and error. Training programs have been developed for today's pilot, with emphasis on flight within safe limits, as well as the discipline to cease flying when weather conditions are unfavorable, for example: excess wind or risk cloud suck.

Launch

Launch techniques include foot-launching from a hill, tow-launching from a ground-based tow system, aerotowing (behind a powered aircraft), powered harnesses, and being towed up by a boat. Modern winch tows typically utilize hydraulic systems designed to regulate line tension, this reduces scenarios for lock out as strong winds result in additional length of rope spooling out rather than direct tension on the tow line. Other more exotic launch techniques have also been used successfully, such as hot air balloon drops for very high altitude. Flights in non-soarable conditions are referred to as "sled runs".

Soaring Flight and Cross-country Flying

A glider is continuously descending through nearby air, yet glider pilots can stay airborne for hours by flying in areas of rising air. Once this skill has been mastered, pilots can glide long distances to fly cross-country (XC). Rising air masses derive from the following sources:

Thermals

The most commonly used source of lift is created by the sun's energy heating the ground which in turn heats the air above it. This warm air rises in columns known as thermals. Soaring pilots quickly become aware of land features which can generate thermals; and of visual indications of thermals such as soaring birds, cumulus clouds, cloud streets, dust devils, and haze domes. Also, nearly every glider contains an instrument known as a variometer (a very sensitive vertical speed indicator) which shows visually (and often audibly) the presence of lift and sink. Having located a thermal, a glider pilot will circle within the area of rising air to gain height. In the case of a cloud street thermals can line up with the wind creating rows of thermals and sinking air. A pilot can use a cloud street to fly long straight-line distances by remaining in the row of rising air.

Ridge Lift

Ridge lift occurs when the wind meets a mountain, cliff or hill. The air is deflected up the windward face of the mountain, causing lift. Gliders can climb in this rising air by flying along the feature. Another name for flying with ridge lift is slope soaring.

Mountain Waves

The third main type of lift used by glider pilots is the lee waves that occur near mountains. The obstruction to the airflow can generate standing waves with alternating areas of lift and sink. The top of each wave peak is often marked by lenticular cloud formations.

Convergence

Another form of lift results from the convergence of air masses, as with a sea-breeze front. More exotic forms of lift are the polar vortexes which the Perlan Project hopes to use to soar to great altitudes. A rare phenomenon known as Morning Glory has also been used by glider pilots in Australia.

Performance

With each generation of materials and with the improvements in aerodynamics, the performance of hang gliders has increased. One measure of performance is the glide ratio. For example, a ratio of 12:1 means that in smooth air a glider can travel forward 12 meters while only losing 1 meter of altitude.

Some performance figures as of 2006:

- Topless gliders (no kingpost): glide ratio ~17:1, speed range ~30 to >145 km/h, best glide at ~45 to 60 km/h
- Rigid wings: glide ratio ~20:1, speed range ~ 35 to > 130 km/h, best glide at ~50 to 60 km/h.

Ballast

The extra weight provided by ballast is advantageous if the lift is likely to be strong. Although heavier gliders have a slight disadvantage when climbing in rising air, they achieve a higher speed at any given glide angle. This is an advantage in strong conditions when the gliders spend only little time climbing in thermals.

Stability and Equilibrium

Because hang gliders are most often used for recreational flying, a premium is placed on gentle behavior especially at the stall and natural pitch stability. The wing loading must be very low in order to allow the pilot to run fast enough to get above stall speed. Unlike a traditional aircraft with an extended fuselage and empennage for maintaining stability, hang gliders rely on the natural stability of their flexible wings to return to equilibrium in yaw and pitch. Roll stability is generally set up to be near neutral. In calm air, a properly designed wing will maintain balanced trimmed flight with little pilot input. The flex wing pilot is suspended beneath the wing by a strap attached to his harness. The pilot lies prone (sometimes supine) within a large, triangular, metal control frame. Controlled flight is achieved by the pilot pushing and pulling on this control frame thus shifting his weight fore or aft, and right or left in coordinated maneuvers.

Roll

Most flexible wings are set up with near neutral roll due to sideslip (anhedral effect). In the roll axis, the pilot shifts his body mass using the wing control bar, applying a rolling moment directly to the wing. The flexible wing is built to flex differentially across the span in response to the pilot applied roll moment. For example, if the pilot shifts his weight to the right, the right wing trailing edge flexes up more than the left, allowing the right wing to drop and slow down.

Yaw

The yaw axis is stabilized through the sweep back of the wings. The swept planform, when yawed out of the relative wind, creates more lift on the advancing wing and also more drag, stabilizing the wing in yaw. If one wing advances ahead of the other, it presents more area to the wind and causes more drag on that side. This causes the advancing wing to go slower and to fall back. The wing is at equilibrium when the aircraft is traveling straight and both wings present the same amount of area to the wind.

Pitch

The pitch control response is direct and very efficient. It is partially stabilized by the sweep of the wings. The wing center of gravity is close to the hang point and at the trim speed, the wing will fly "hands off" and return to trim after being disturbed. The weight-shift control system only works when the wing is positively loaded (right side up); To maintain a minimum safe amount of washout when the wing is unloaded or even negatively loaded (upside down), positive pitching devices such as reflex lines or washout rods are employed. Flying faster than trim speed is accomplished by moving the pilot's weight forward in the control frame; flying slower by shifting the pilot's weight aft (pushing out).

Furthermore, the fact that the wing is designed to bend and flex, provides favorable dynamics analogous to a spring suspension. This allows the wing to be less susceptible to turbulence and provides a gentler flying experience than a similarly sized rigid-winged aircraft.

Instruments

To maximize a pilot's understanding of how the hang glider is flying, most pilots carry instruments. The most basic being a variometer and altimeter—often combined. Some more advanced pilots also carry airspeed indicators and radios. When flying in competition or cross country, pilots often also carry maps and/or GPS units. Hang gliders do not have instrument panels as such, so all the instruments are mounted to the control frame of the glider or occasionally based on one's watch.

Variometer

Gliding pilots are able to sense the acceleration forces when they first hit a thermal, but have difficulty gauging constant motion. Thus it is difficult to detect the difference between constantly rising air and constantly sinking air. A variometer is a very sensitive vertical speed indicator. In other words, the variometer indicates climb rate or sink rate with audio signals (beeps) and/or a visual display. These units are generally electronic, vary in sophistication, and often include an altimeter and an airspeed indicator. More advanced units often incorporate a barograph for recording flight data and/or a built-in GPS. The main purpose of a variometer is in helping a pilot find and stay in the 'core' of a thermal to maximize height gain, and conversely indicating when he or she is in sinking air and needs to find rising air. Variometers are sometimes capable of electronic calculations based on the MacCready Speed Ring to indicate the optimal speed to fly for given conditions. The MacCready theory answers the question on how fast a pilot should cruise between thermals, given both the average lift the pilot expects in the next thermal climb, as well as the amount of lift or sink he encounters in cruise mode. Some electronic variometers make the calculations automatically, after allowing for factors such as the glider's theoretical performance (glide ratio), altitude, hook in weight and wind direction.

Radio

Pilots use radio for training purposes, and for communicating with other pilots in the air – particularly when traveling together on cross-country flights.

One type of radios used are PTT (push-to-talk) transceivers, operating in or around the FM VHF 2-meter band (144 MHz–148 MHz). Usually a microphone is incorporated in the helmet, and the PTT switch is either fixed to the outside of the helmet, or strapped to a finger. It should be emphasized that operating a 2-meter band radio without an appropriate Amateur Radio license is illegal in most countries (such as the United States) that have regulated airwaves.

As aircraft operating in airspace occupied by other aircraft, hang glider pilots also use the appropriate type of radio i.e. the aircraft transceiver. It can, of course, be fitted with a PTT switch to a finger and speakers inside the helmet. The use of aircraft transceivers is subject to regulations specific to the use in the air such as frequencies restrictions but has several advantages over FM (i.e. frequency modulated) Amateur Radios. One is the great range it has (without repeaters) because of its amplitude modulation (i.e. AM). Two is the ability to contact, inform and be informed directly by other aircraft pilots of their intentions thereby improving collision avoidance and increasing safety. Three is to allow greater liberty regarding distance flights in regulated airspaces, in which the aircraft radio is normally a legal requirement. Four is the universal emergency frequency monitored by all other users and satellites and used in case of emergency or impending emergency.

GPS

GPS (global positioning system) is a necessary accessory when flying competitions, where it has to be demonstrated that way-points have been correctly passed.

It can also be interesting to view a GPS track of a flight when back on the ground, to analyze flying technique. Computer software is available which allows various different analyses of GPS tracks (e.g. CompeGPS).

Other uses include being able to determine drift due to the prevailing wind when flying at altitude, providing position information to allow restricted airspace to be avoided, and identifying one's location for retrieval teams after landing-out in unfamiliar territory.

More recently, the use of GPS data, linked to a computer, has enabled pilots to share 3D tracks of their flights on Google Earth. This fascinating insight allows comparisons between competing pilots to be made in a detailed post-flight analysis.

Records

Records are sanctioned by the FAI. The world record(s) (as of 2005) for "free distance" is held by Manfred Ruhmer with 700.6 km (435.3 miles) in 2001 and Michael Barber flew a distance of 704 km (437 miles) on June 19, 2002 in Zapata Texas.

Other records include:

Out-and-Return distance - 332.5 km (206.6 mi), July 5, 2007 by George Stebbins, starting and ending just South of Lone Pine, California.

Largest triangle - 357.12 km (221.9 mi), December 16, 2000 by Tomáš Suchánek a Czech HG and sailplane pilot, starting and ending from Riverside Australia.

Competition

Competitions started with "flying as long as possible" and spot landings. With increasing performance, cross-country flying replaced them. Usually two to four waypoints have to be passed with a landing at a goal. In the late 1990s low-power GPS units were introduced and have completely replaced photographs of the goal. Every two years there is a world championship. The Rigid and Women's World Championship in 2006 was hosted by Quest Air in Florida. Big Spring, Texas hosted the 2007 World Championship. Hang gliding is also one of the competition categories in World Air Games organized by Fédération Aéronautique Internationale (World Air Sports Federation - FAI), which maintains a chronology of the FAI World Hang Gliding Championships.

Classes

For competitive purposes, there are three classes of hang glider:

- Class 1 The flexible wing hang glider, having flight controlled by a wing whose shape changes by virtue of the shifted weight of the pilot. This is not a paraglider.
- Class 5 The rigid wing hang glider, having flight controlled by spoilers, typically on top of the wing. In both flexible and rigid wings the pilot hangs below the wing without any additional fairing.
- Class 2 (designated by the FAI as Sub-Class O-2) where the pilot is integrated into the wing by means of a fairing.

These offer the best performance and are the most expensive.

In addition to typical launch configurations, a hang glider may be so constructed for alternative launching modes other than being foot launched; one practical avenue for this is for people who physically cannot foot-launch.

Chapter 10

Paragliding

Paragliding is a recreational and competitive flying sport. A paraglider is a free-flying, foot-launched aircraft. The pilot sits in a harness suspended below a fabric wing, whose shape is formed by its suspension lines and the pressure of air entering vents in the front of the wing.

History

In 1952 Domina Jalbert advanced governable gliding parachutes with multi-cells and controls for lateral glide.

In 1954, Walter Neumark predicted (in an article in Flight magazine) a time when a glider pilot would be "able to launch himself by running over the edge of a cliff or down a slope ... whether on a rock-climbing holiday in Skye or ski-ing in the Alps".

In 1961, the French engineer Pierre Lemoigne produced improved parachute designs which led to the Para-Commander. The 'PC', had cut-outs at the rear and sides that enabled it to be towed into the air and steered – leading to parasailing/ parascending.

Sometimes credited with the greatest development in parachutes since Leonardo da Vinci by whom, the American Domina Jalbert invented the Parafoil which had sectioned cells in an aerofoil shape; an open leading edge and a closed trailing edge, inflated by passage through the air – the ram-air design. He filed US Patent 3131894 on January 10, 1963.

Meanwhile, David Barish was developing the Sail Wing for recovery of NASA space capsules – "slope soaring was a way of testing out ... the Sail Wing". After tests on Hunter Mountain, New York in September 1965, he went on to promote 'slope soaring' as a summer activity for ski resorts (apparently without great success). NASA originated the term 'paraglider' in the early 1960s, and 'paragliding' was first used in the early 1970s to describe foot-launching of gliding parachutes.

In 1971, Steve Snyder marketing the first wing : Paraplane.

Author Walter Neumark wrote Operating Procedures for Ascending Parachutes, and he and a group of enthusiasts with a passion for tow-launching 'PCs' and ram-air parachutes eventually broke away from the British Parachute Association to form the British Association of Parascending Clubs (BAPC) in 1973. Authors Patrick Gilligan (Canada) and Betrand Dubuis (Switzerland) wrote the first flight manual "The Paragliding Manual" in 1985, officially coining the word Paragliding.

These threads were pulled together in June 1978 by three friends Jean-Claude Bétemps, André Bohn and Gérard Bosson from Mieussy Haute-Savoie, France. After inspiration from an article on 'slope soaring' in the Parachute Manual magazine by parachutist & publisher Dan Poynter, they calculated that on a suitable slope, a 'square' ram-air parachute could be inflated by running down the slope; Bétemps launched from Pointe du Pertuiset, Mieussy, and flew 100 m. Bohn followed him and glided down to the football pitch in the valley 1000 metres below. 'Parapente' (pente being French for slope) was born.

From the 1980s equipment has continued to improve and the number of paragliding pilots has continued to increase. The first World Championship was held in Kössen, Austria in 1989.

Equipment

Wing

The paraglider wing or canopy is known in aeronautical engineering as a ram-air airfoil, or parafoil. Such wings comprise two layers of fabric which are connected to internal supporting material in such a way as to form a row of cells. By leaving most of the cells open only at the leading edge, incoming air (ram-air pressure) keeps the wing inflated, thus maintaining its shape. When inflated, the wing's cross-section has the typical teardrop aerofoil shape.

In some modern paragliders (from the 1990s onwards), especially higher performance wings, some of the cells of the leading edge are closed to form a cleaner aerodynamic airfoil. Like the wingtips, these cells are kept inflated by the internal pressure of the wing Wings Infos.

The pilot is supported underneath the wing by a network of lines. The lines are gathered into two sets as left and right risers. The risers collect the lines in rows from front to back in either 3 or 4 rows, distributing load as in a whippletree. The risers are connected to the pilot's harness by two carabiners.

Paraglider wings typically have an area of 20–35 square metres (220–380 sq ft) with a span of 8–12 metres (26 39 ft), and weigh 3–7 kilograms (6.6–15 lb). Combined weight of wing, harness, reserve, instruments, helmet, etc. is around 12–18 kilograms (26–40 lb).

The glide ratio of paragliders ranges from 8:1 for recreational wings, to about 11:1 for modern competition models. For comparison, a typical skydiving parachute will achieve about 3:1 glide. A hang glider will achieve about 15:1 glide. An idling (gliding) Cessna 152 will achieve 9:1. Some sailplanes can achieve a glide ratio of up to 72:1.

The speed range of paragliders is typically 20–60 kilometres per hour (12–37 mph), from stall speed to maximum speed. Beginner wings will be in the lower part of this range, high-performance wings in the upper part of the range. The range for safe flying will be somewhat smaller.

Modern paraglider wings are made of high-performance non-porous fabricș such as OLKS from Gelvenor, with Dyneema/ Spectra or Kevlar/Aramid lines.

For storage and carrying, the wing is usually folded into a stuffsack (bag), which can then be stowed in a large backpack along with the harness. For pilots who may not want the added weight or fuss of a backpack, some modern harnesses include the ability to turn the harness inside out such that it becomes a backpack.

Tandem paragliders, designed to carry the pilot and one passenger, are larger but otherwise similar. They usually fly faster with higher trim speeds, are more resistant to collapse, and have a slightly higher sink rate compared to solo paragliders.

Since 2000 Juan Salvadori in Argentina has been exploring a variant wing termed Paramontante that involves some firm beams. In April 2009 Pere Casellas has joined in a collaboration with Juan Salvadori for polishing the paramontante. Laboratori d'envol Paramontante

Harness

The pilot is loosely and comfortably buckled into a harness which offers support in both the standing and sitting positions. Modern harnesses are designed to be as comfortable as a lounge chair in the sitting position. Many harnesses even have an adjustable 'lumbar support'. A reserve parachute is also typically connected to a paragliding harness.

The primary purpose of parachutes (including skydiving canopies) is for descending, as when jumping out of an aircraft or dropping cargo. In contrast, the primary purpose of paragliders is for ascending. Paragliders are categorized as "ascending parachutes" by canopy manufacturers worldwide, and are designed for "free flying" meaning flight without a tether (for an example of tethered flight, see parasailing). However, in areas without high launch points, paragliders may be towed aloft by a ground vehicle or a stationary winch, after which they are released, creating much the same effect as a mountain launch. Such tethered launches can give a paraglider pilot a higher starting point than many mountains do, offering similar opportunities to catch thermals and to remain airborne by "thermaling" and other forms of lift. As with other forms of free flight, paragliding requires the significant skill and training required for aircraft control, including aeronautical theory, meteorological knowledge and forecasting, personal/emotional safety considerations, adherence to applicable Federal Aviation Regulations (US), and knowledge of equipment care and maintenance.

Instruments

Most pilots use variometers, radios, and, increasingly, GPS units when flying.

Variometer

Birds are highly sensitive to atmospheric pressure, and can tell when they are in rising or sinking air. People can sense the acceleration when they first hit a thermal, but cannot detect the difference between constant rising air and constant sinking air, so turn to technology to help. Modern variometers are capable of detecting rates of climb or sink of 1 cm per second, such is the case of the Flymaster B1 which uses extremely low noise electronics and complex algorithms to detect such minute changes in air pressure.

A variometer indicates climb-rate (or sink-rate) with short audio signals (beeps, which increase in pitch and tempo during ascent, and a droning sound, which gets deeper as the rate of descent increases) and/or a visual display. It also shows altitude: either above takeoff, above sea level, or (at higher altitudes) "flight level".

The main purpose of a variometer is in helping a pilot find and stay in the "core" of a thermal to maximise height gain and, conversely, to indicate when a pilot is in sinking air and needs to find rising air.

The more advanced variometers have an integrated GPS. This is not only more convenient, but also allows one to record the flight in three dimensions. The track of the flight is digitally signed and stored and can be downloaded after the landing. Digitally signed tracks can be used as proof for record claims, replacing the 'old' method of photo documentation.

Radio

Pilots use radio for training purposes, for communicating with other pilots in the air, particularly when travelling together on cross-country flights, and for reporting the location of landing.

Radios used are PTT (push-to-talk) transceivers, normally operating in or around the FM VHF 2-metre band (144–148 MHz). The "2 Meter" band is an amateur radio band, sometimes used for interpersonal communications, and Aviation Frequencies are usually 108 MHz to 136 MHz. Usually a microphone is incorporated in the helmet, and the PTT switch is either fixed to the outside of the helmet, or strapped to a finger.

Use of an Amateur Radio without a Federal Amateur Radio License is HIGHLY ILLEGAL!!!! Modifying said radio is also ILLEGAL! Fines will be issued WHEN you are caught. At least $15,000, but higher have also been issued upto $70,000, plus federal prison time. Radios are type accepted by the federal government according to the intended service. 150 Mhz to 170 Mhz is NOT for use on an Amateur Radio. A number of pilots use FRS/GMRS radios for pilot to pilot communications. There are other parts of the country where VHF radio contact is preferred, especially when flying out of local airports where regulations permit. Also, many pilots carry a cell phone so they can call for pickup should they land away from their point of destination.

VHF Aviation Band radios such as the Icom IC-A5, A6 or A23 are recommended. No license is required for their use. It is always good to be able to communicate with airports and other flyers, especially in the more populated parts of the country. In some areas, the ability to communicate with the control tower is required.

Use of radios made for the amateur 2 meter band is NOT legal unless you are a licensed amateur radio operator. Hams are very protective of their frequencies and do not like interference generated by unlicensed flyers. Many hams own direction finding equipment and will enjoy the sport of finding you and reporting you to the FCC. Recently, a major fly-in was issued a warning by the FCC not to use the 2 meter band for communciations. Also one California interferer was just sentenced to 7 years in jail and fined $25,000 for unlicensed use of 2 meters.

Unlicensed flyers are relatively easy to spot as they are not aware of the 2 meter band plan and will just "pick a frequency" for use. They stick out like a sore thumb and are easy to track.

Your best bet is to stick with FRS and aviation band radios.

GPS

GPS (global positioning system) is a necessary accessory when flying competitions, where it has to be demonstrated that way-points have been correctly passed.

It can also be interesting to view a GPS track of a flight when back on the ground, to analyze flying technique. Computer software is available which allows various different analyses of GPS tracks (e.g. CompeGPS, See You).

Other uses include being able to determine drift due to the prevailing wind when flying at altitude, providing position information to allow restricted airspace to be avoided, and identifying one's location for retrieval teams after landing-out in unfamiliar territory.

More recently, the use of GPS data, linked to a computer, has enabled pilots to share 3D tracks of their flights on Google

Earth. This fascinating insight allows comparisons between competing pilots to be made in a detailed 'post-flight' analysis.

Control

Brakes: Controls held in each of the pilot's hands connect to the trailing edge of the left and right sides of the wing. These controls are called 'brakes' and provide the primary and most general means of control in a paraglider. The brakes are used to adjust speed, to steer (in addition to weight-shift), and flare (during landing).

Weight Shift: In addition to manipulating the brakes, a paraglider pilot must also lean in order to steer properly. Such 'weight-shifting' can also be used for more limited steering when brake use is unavailable, such as when under 'big ears' (see below). More advanced control techniques may also involve weight-shifting.

Speed Bar: A kind of foot control called the 'speed bar' (also 'accelerator') attaches to the paragliding harness and connects to the leading edge of the paraglider wing, usually through a system of at least two pulleys (see animation in margin). This control is used to increase speed, and does so by decreasing the wing's angle of attack. This control is necessary because the brakes can only slow the wing from what is called 'trim speed' (no brakes applied). The accelerator is needed to go faster than this.

More advanced means of control can be obtained by manipulating the paraglider's risers or lines directly:

- Most commonly, the lines connecting to the outermost points of the wing's leading edge can be used to induce the wingtips to fold under. The technique, known as 'big ears', is used to increase rate of descent (see picture and therefore description below).
- The risers connecting to the rear of the wing can also be manipulated for steering if the brakes have been severed or are otherwise unavailable.

- In a 'B-line stall'

Fast Descents

Problems with "getting down" can occur when the lift situation is very good or when the weather changes unexpectedly. There are three possibilities of rapidly reducing altitude in such situations, each of which has benefits and issues to be aware of:

- Big ears induces descent rates of 2m/s or so. It is the most controllable of the techniques, and the easiest for beginners to learn.
- A B-line stall induces descent rates of 5m/s or so. It increases loading on parts of the wing (the pilot's weight is mostly on the B-lines, instead of spread across all the lines). There is not a risk of the pilot becoming disoriented as a result of using this technique.
- A spiral dive offers the fastest rate of descent, at 10-15m/sec. It places greater loads on the wing than other techniques do, and requires the highest level of skill from the pilot to execute safely.

Big Ears

By pulling on the outer A-lines the wing tips of the glider can be folded in. This method drastically deteriorates the glide angle with only a small decrease in forward speed. The effectiveness of this technique can be increased by using the speed system at the same time.

To reinflate on a low performance glider (e.g. DHV1 rated) it is simply necessary to release the lines. On higher performance gliders (e.g. DHV1/2 and above) it may be necessary to help the reinflation with brief, deep pumps of the brakes.

Whilst big ears are in use, the loading on the remaining flying surface of the glider is increased and it is therefore more stable and less prone to collapse. However there is an increased risk of stalling because 'pulling the ears' increases the angle of attack and reduces the speed of the wing. So while 'ears' and speed bar is a good combination, 'ears' and brake is not - it is best not to use the brakes when the ears are 'in'.

B-Line Stall

In a 'B-line stall', the second set of risers from the leading-edge/front (the B-lines) are pulled down independently of the other risers; with the specific lines used to initiate the condition being responsible for its name. This puts a crease in the upper surface of the wing, thereby destroying the laminar flow of air over the aerofoil. This dramatically reduces the lift produced by the canopy and thus induces a higher rate of descent.

The B-line stall should be initiated with the wing in normal flight (no speed bar; not accelerated). Grasp the B-lines on both sides above the line links and pull them down. There is no need to release the brake toggles while B-stalling. DHV 1/2 wings are very resistant to creasing; the pilot may have to pull on the B-lines with sufficient force to almost lift themselves out of the seat to get the wing to crease. Once the crease is in, it requires less effort to keep it in that it does to initiate it.

The sensation for the pilot when the B-line stall is induced is that the breeze is upwards rather than in your face. Pulling the B-lines even further down will not enhance the sink rate, but can lead to a more unstable flight position.

To recover from the B-line stall, release the B-risers so that the aerofoil shape of the wing is resumed. This will normally be sufficient to resume normal flight, but if the canopy remains in a stall push forward gently on the A-risers to lower the leading edge of the wing and reattach the laminar airflow to the upper surface of the wing.

Spiral Dive

The spiral dive is the most rapid form of controlled fast descent. With a little bit of practice you will achieve a sink rate of 15 m/s and more.

However, spiral dives put strong G-forces on the wing and glider and must be done carefully and skilfully. The G-forces involved can induce blackouts, and the rotation can produce disorientation. Spiral dives, as with all paragliding techniques, are best learned under expert supervision. Paragliding 'SIV' courses offer a chance to practice spiral dives over water with a rescue boat standing by.

The spiral dive is initiated by pulling the brake on one side and holding it down. Constant pulling on one brake narrows the radius of the turn and forms a spiral rotation in which high sink rates can be reached. As soon as the glider is in a spiral dive (clear increase of sink rate and turn bank), the outside wing should always be stabilised with the outside brake and the desired sink rate should be controlled with great delicacy.

Flying

Launching

As with all aircraft, launching and landing are done into wind (though in mountain flying, it is possible to launch in nil wind and glide out to the first thermal).

Forward Launch

In low winds, the wing is inflated with a 'forward launch', where the pilot runs forward so that the air pressure generated by the forward movement inflates the wing.

Reverse Launch

In higher winds, particularly ridge soaring, a 'reverse launch' is used, with the pilot facing the wing to bring it up into a flying position, then turning under the wing to complete the launch.

Reverse launches have a number of advantages over a forward launch. It is more straight forward to inspect the wing and check the lines are free as it leaves the ground. In the presence of wind, the pilot can be tugged toward the wing and facing the wing makes it easier to resist this force, and safer in case the pilot slips (as opposed to being dragged backwards). These launches are normally attempted with a reasonable wind speed making the ground speed required to pressurise the wing much lower - the pilot is initially launching while walking forwards as opposed to running backward.

Towed Launch

In flatter countryside pilots can also be launched with a tow. Once at full height, the pilot pulls a release cord and the towline falls away. This requires separate training, as flying on a winch has quite different characteristics from free flying. There are two major ways to tow: Pay-in and pay-out towing. Pay-in towing involves a stationary winch that pays in the towline and thereby pulls the pilot in the air. The distance between winch and pilot at the start is around 500 meters or more. Pay-out towing involves a moving object, like a car or a boat, that pays out line slower than the speed of the object thereby pulling the pilot up in the air. In both cases it is very important to have a gauge indicating daN to avoid pulling the pilot out of the air. There is one other form of towing; 'static' towing. This involves a moving object, like a car or a boat, attached to a paraglider or hanglider with a fixed length line. This is very dangerous because now the forces on the line have to be controlled by the moving object itself, which is almost impossible to do. With static line towing a lockout is bound to happen sooner or later. Static line towing is forbidden in most countries and if not, should be avoided at all cost.

Landing

Landing involves lining up for an approach into wind, and just before touching down, 'flaring' the wing to minimise horizontal speed. In light winds, some minor running is common. In moderate to medium headwinds, the landings can be without forward speed.

Slope Soaring

The slope can be a Dune or Ridge. In slope soaring, pilots fly along the length of a slope feature in the landscape, relying on the lift provided by the air which is forced up as it passes over the slope. Slope soaring is highly dependent on a steady wind within a defined range (the suitable range depends on the performance of the wing and the skill of the pilot). Too little wind, and insufficient lift is available to stay airborne (pilots end up 'scratching' along the slope). With more wind, gliders can fly well above and forward of the slope, but too much wind, and there is a risk of being 'blown back' over the slope.

Thermal Flying

When the sun warms the ground, it will warm some features more than others (such as rock-faces or large buildings), and these set off thermals which rise through the air. Sometimes these may be a simple rising column of air; more often, they are blown sideways in the wind, and will break off from the source, with a new thermal forming later.

Once a pilot finds a thermal, he or she begins to fly in a circle, trying to center the circle on the strongest part of the thermal (the "core"), where the air is rising the fastest. Most pilots use a 'vario' (vario-altimeter), which indicates climb rate with beeps and/or a visual display, to help 'core-in' on a thermal.

Coring: The technique to "core" a thermal is simple: turn tighter as lift decreases, and turn less as lift increases. This ensures you are always flying around the core.

Often there is strong sink surrounding thermals, and there is often also strong turbulence resulting in wing collapses as a pilot tries to enter a strong thermal. Once inside a thermal, shear forces reduce somewhat and the lift tends to become smoother.

Good thermal flying is a skill which takes time to learn, but a good pilot can often "core" a thermal all the way to cloud base.

Cross-country Flying

Once the skills of using thermals to gain altitude have been mastered, pilots can glide from one thermal to the next to go 'cross-country' ('XC'). Having gained altitude in a thermal, a pilot glides down to the next available thermal. Potential thermals can be identified by land features which typically generate thermals, or by cumulus clouds which mark the top of a rising column of warm, humid air as it reaches the dew point and condenses to form a cloud. In many flying areas, cross-country pilots also need an intimate familiarity with air law, flying regulations, aviation maps indicating restricted airspace, etc.

In-flight Wing Deflation (Collapse)

Since the shape of the wing (airfoil) is formed by the moving air entering and inflating the wing, in turbulent air, part or all of the wing (airfoil) can deflate (collapse). Piloting techniques referred to as "active flying" will greatly reduce the frequency and severity of deflations or collapses. On modern recreational wings, such deflations will normally recover without pilot intervention. In the event of a severe deflation, correct pilot input will speed recovery from a deflation, but incorrect pilot input may slow the return of the glider to normal flight, so pilot training and practice in correct response to deflations is necessary. For the rare occasions when it is not possible to recover from a deflation (or from other threatening situations such as a spin), most pilots carry a reserve (rescue, emergency) parachute. Most pilots never have cause to 'throw' their reserve. Should a wing deflation occur at low altitude, i.e. shortly after takeoff or just before landing, the wing (paraglider) may not recover its correct structure rapidly enough to prevent an accident, with the pilot often not having enough altitude remaining to successfully deploy a reserve parachute (with the minimum altitude for this being approximately 200 ft, but typical deployment to stabilization periods using up 400 – 600 ft of altitude). Different packing methods of the reserve parachute affect its deploying time. It is also important to note that, should the wing collapse have been due to turbulence, this 'bad air' can cause the reserve parachute to take significantly longer to inflate and stabilise. In this example, it may be of greater benefit to the paraglider to purposefully lose altitude to 'clear' this turbulent air before deploying their reserve; should they have spare altitude to use on this process. Low altitude wing failure can result in serious injury or death due to the subsequent velocity of a ground impact where, ironically, a higher altitude failure may allow more time to regain some degree of control in the descent rate and, critically, deploy the reserve if needed. In-flight wing deflation and other hazards are minimized by flying a suitable glider and choosing appropriate weather conditions and locations for the pilot's skill and experience level.

Sports/competitive Flying

Some pilots like to stretch themselves beyond recreational flying. For such pilots, there are multiple disciplines available:

- Cross-country leagues – annual leagues of the greatest distance 'XC' flying.
- "Comps" – competitive flying based on completing a number of tasks such as flying around set waypoints.
- Accuracy – spot landing competitions where pilots land on targets with a 3 cm centre spot out to a full 10 meter circle.
- "Acro" – aero-acrobatic manoeuvres and stunt flying; heart stopping tricks such as helicopters, wing-overs, synchro spirals, infinity tumbles, and so on.
- National/international records – despite continually improving gliders, these become ever more difficult to achieve; aside from longest distance and highest altitude, examples include distance to declared goal, distance over triangular course, speed over 100 km triangular course, etc.

Competitive flying is done on high performance wings which demand far more skill to fly than their recreational counterparts, but which are far more responsive and offer greater feedback to the pilot, as well as flying faster with better glide ratios.

The current world champion is Andy Aebi of Switzerland; he won the title in February 2009 at Valle de Bravo in Mexico. His predecessor was Bruce Goldsmith.

Safety

There is great potential for injury for the unlucky, the reckless or ill-prepared. Safety is directly influenced by the pilot's mental attitude, experience, skill, reaction time, active nature of the air and whether or not the paraglider is flying at an altitude where the emergency reserve parachute might possibly have time to open in the event of an unrecoverable collapse or spiral dive. Incidents of any nature that happen in an altitude that does not allow to recover or deploy the reserve parachute (as while start and landing) are the most likely situtations to cause severe or fatal injuries.

Given that equipment failure of properly certified paragliding equipment can be considered a non-issue, it is accurate to say that paragliding can be a very safe sport. The individual pilot is the ultimate indicator of his or her personal safety level.

In general:

- The safe pilot will not fly at sites that pose an unreasonable challenge to his/her flying skills.
- The safe pilot will not be influenced by the possibly negative examples set by others.
- The safe pilot will only fly on days in which the weather is conducive to safe flight. Turbulence in all its forms is enemy #1 for a flying paraglider wing. Because paragliders have no solid support, their shape (and ability to fly) can be ruined by an errant down draft or the like. Therefore, turbulence or conditions conducive to turbulence generation is a primary factor in determining whether the weather is safe.

The following weather is to be avoided:

- Excessive wind speed or gustiness. 15 mph (24 km/h) wind is fairly windy for a paraglider, and most pilots won't take off in much more wind than that. High winds will also increase the effect of mechanical turbulence. Gusty conditions will make take-offs and landings more dangerous and will make collapses more likely while in flight. The limit of 15 mph is fairly arbitrary, and also depends on local parameters. At some sites people fly safely at 20 mph winds, at other sites 10 mph may be too much.
- A wind direction that will not allow a take-off (or landing) into the wind, or at least generally so. Tail-wind take-offs are to be avoided at all cost. Assurance that an [apparent] headwind is not actually a 'rotor' is also critical (rotors comprise a form of mechanical turbulence).
- Excessively high atmospheric instability, indicated in part by overdeveloped cumulus clouds, or in worse situations by cumulo-nimbus cloud formation. Such conditions will contribute to turbulence. If cumulo-nimbus (thunderstorm) clouds are anywhere in sight, the effect of severe atmospheric instability may exist where you are.
- Rain or snow. Because a paraglider wing is made from fabric, it has the ability to absorb moisture. Moreover, the weight (or lack thereof) of a paraglider wing is critical to its performance. Flying into heavy rain or snow will weigh the wing down and may terminate a flight quickly. A wet wing is also less controllable, less stable and will exhibit less tendency to recover into normal flight.

General safety precautions include pre-flight checks, helmets, harnesses with back protection (foam or air-bag), reserve parachutes, and careful pre-launch observation of other pilots in the air to evaluate conditions.

For pilots who want to stretch themselves into more challenging conditions, advanced 'SIV' (simulation d'incidents en vol, or simulation of flying incidents) courses are available to teach pilots how to cope with hazardous situations which can arise in flight. Through instruction over radio (above a lake), pilots deliberately induce major collapses, stalls, spins, etc, in order to learn procedures for recovering from them. (As mentioned above, modern recreational wings will recover from minor collapses without intervention).

As always, fatalities and freak accidents can occur, but most properly-trained, responsible pilots risk only minor injuries, such as twisted ankles.

Learning to Fly

Most popular paragliding regions have a number of schools, generally registered with and/or organized by national associations. Certification systems vary widely between countries, though around 10 days instruction to basic certification is standard.

There are several key components to a paragliding pilot certification instruction program. Initial training for beginning pilots usually begins with some amount of ground school to discuss the basics, including elementary theories of flight as well as basic structure and operation of the paraglider.

Students then learn how to control the glider on the ground, practicing take-offs and controlling the wing 'overhead'. Low, gentle hills are next where students get their first short flights, flying at very low altitudes, to get used to the handling of the wing over varied terrain. Special winches can be used to tow the glider to low altitude in areas that have no hills readily available.

As their skills progress, students move on to steeper/higher hills (or higher winch tows), making longer flights, and learning to turn the glider, control the glider's speed, then moving on to 360° turns, spot landings, 'big ears' (used to increase the rate of descent for the paraglider), and other more advanced techniques. Training instructions are often provided to the student via radio, particularly during the first flights.

A third key component to a complete paragliding instructional program provides substantial background in the key areas of meteorology, aviation law, and general flight area etiquette.

To give prospective pilots a chance to determine if they would like to proceed with a full pilot training program, most schools offer tandem flights, in which an experienced instructor pilots the paraglider with the prospective pilot as a passenger. Schools often offer pilot's families and friends the opportunity to fly tandem, and sometimes sell tandem pleasure flights at holiday resorts.

Most recognised courses lead to a national licence and an internationally recognised International Pilot Proficiency Information/Identification card. The IPPI specifies five stages of paragliding proficiency, from the entry level ParaPro 1 to the most advance stage 5.

World Records

FAI (Fédération Aéronautique Internationale) world records:

- Straight distance – 502.9 km: Nevil Hulett (South Africa); Copperton - Lesotho, South Africa; 14 December 2008.
- Previous Straight distance – 461.6 km: Frank Brown, Marcelo Prieto, Rafael Monteiro Saladini (Brazil); Quixada – Duque, Brazil; 14 November 2007.
- Straight distance – 411.3 km: Nevil Hulett (South Africa); Copperton - Lesotho, South Africa; 14 December 2008.
- Previous Straight distance to declared goal – 368.9 km: Aljaž Valic(, Urban Valic((Slovenia); Vosburg – Jamestown (South Africa); 7 December 2006.
- Gain of height – 4526 m: Robbie Whittall (UK); Brandvlei (South Africa); 6 January 1993.

Other records (distance/speed for out-and-return and triangular course) can be seen on the FAI site

Recently a flight of over 500 km was made by Nevil Hulett in excellent conditions in South Africa; Flight record

Pilot Numbers

Numbers of actively flying pilots can only be a rough estimate, but France is believed to have the largest number, at around 25,000. Next most active flying countries are Germany, Austria, Switzerland, Japan, and Korea, at around 10,000 – 20,000, followed by Italy, the UK, and Spain with around 5,000 – 10,000. The USA has around 4,500.

Chapter 11

Mountain Biking

Mountain biking is a sport which consists of riding bicycles off-road, often over rough terrain, using specially adapted mountain bikes. Mountain bikes share similarities with other bikes, but incorporate features designed to enhance durability and performance in rough terrain.

Mountain biking can generally be broken down into multiple categories: cross country, trail riding, all mountain, downhill, freeride, street riding, dirt jumping and trials. The vast majority of mountain biking falls into the recreational XC and Trail Riding categories.

This individual sport requires endurance, core strength and balance, bike handling skills and self-reliance. XC type mountain biking generally requires a smaller range of skills but a higher level of fitness than other types of mountain biking. Advanced riders pursue steep technical descents and, in the case of freeriding, downhilling, and dirt jumping, aerial maneuvers off of specially constructed jumps and ramps.

Mountain biking can be performed almost anywhere from a back yard to a gravel road, but the majority of mountain bikers ride off-road trails, whether country back roads, fire roads, or singletrack (narrow trails that wind through forests, mountains, deserts, or fields). There are aspects of mountain biking that are more similar to trail running than regular bicycling. Because riders are often far from civilization, there is a strong ethic of self-reliance in the sport. Riders learn to repair their broken bikes or flat tires to avoid being stranded miles from help. This reliance on survival skills accounts for the group dynamics of the sport. Club rides and other forms of group rides are common, especially on longer treks. A combination sport named mountain bike orienteering adds the skill of map navigation to mountain biking.

History of The Mountain Bike and Mountain Biking

The history of the mountain bike and mountain biking is nearly as long and varied as that of the bicycle itself. Originally known as Klunkerz, these bicycles have been ridden off-road since their invention. In 1988, the Mountain Bike Hall of Fame was founded to chronicle the history of the mountain bike and mountain biking, and to recognize the individuals and groups that have contributed significantly to this sport.

1800s

One of the first examples of bicycles modified specifically for off-road use is the expedition of Buffalo Soldiers from Missoula, Montana, to Yellowstone and back in August 1896.

1900s–1960s

Another early example of riding bicycles off-road is when road racing cyclists used cyclo-cross as a means of keeping fit during the winter. Cyclo-cross eventually becoming a sport in its own right in the 1940s, with the first world championship in 1950. The French Velo Cross Club Parisien (VCCP) comprised about twenty-one young cyclists from the outskirts of Paris, who between 1951 and 1956 developed a sport that was remarkably akin to present-day mountain biking.

The Roughstuff Fellowship was established in 1955 by off-road cyclists in the UK. In Oregon, one Chemeketan club member, D.Gwynn, built a rough terrain trail bicycle in 1966. He named it a "mountain bicycle" for its intended place of use. This may be the first use of that name.

In England in 1968, Geoff Apps, a motorbike trials rider, began experimenting with off-road bicycle designs. By 1979 he had developed a custom built lightweight bicycle which was uniquely suited to the wet and muddy off-road conditions found in the south-east of England. They were designed around 2inch x 650b Nokiā snow tyres though a 700c (29er) version was also produced. These were sold under the Cleland Cycles brand until late 1984. Bikes based on the Cleland design were also sold by English Cycles and Highpath Engineering until the early 1990s.

1970s–1980s

There were several groups of riders in different areas of the U.S.A. who can make valid claims to playing a part in the birth of the sport. Riders in Crested Butte, Colorado and Cupertino, California tinkered with bikes and adapted them to the rigors of off-road riding. Modified heavy cruiser bicycles, old 1930s and '40s Schwinn bicycles retrofitted with better brakes and fat tires, were used for freewheeling down mountain trails in Marin County, California in the mid-to-late 1970s. At the time, there were no mountain bikes. The earliest ancestors of modern mountain bikes were based around frames from cruiser bicycles such as those made by Schwinn. The Schwinn Excelsior was the frame of choice due to its geometry. Riders used balloon-tired cruisers and modified them with gears and motocross or BMX-style handlebars, creating "klunkers". The term would also be used as a verb since the term "mountain biking" was not yet in use. Riders would race down mountain fireroads, causing the hub brake to burn the grease inside, requiring the riders to repack the bearings. These were called "Repack Races" and triggered the first innovations in mountain bike technology as well as the initial interest of the public. The sport originated in California on Marin County's Mount Tamalpais.

It was not until the late 1970s and early 1980s that road bicycle companies started to manufacture mountain bicycles using high-tech lightweight materials. Joe Breeze is normally credited with introducing the first purpose-built mountain bike in 1978. Tom Ritchey then went on to make frames for a company called MountainBikes, a partnership between Gary Fisher, Charlie Kelly and Tom Ritchey. Tom Ritchey, a welder with skills in frame building, also built the original bikes. The company's three partners eventually dissolved their partnership, and the company became Fisher Mountain Bikes, while Tom Ritchey started his own frame shop. The first mountain bikes were basically road bicycle frames (with heavier tubing and different geometry) with a wider frame and fork to allow for a wider tire. The handlebars were also different in that they were a straight, transverse-mounted handlebar, rather than the dropped, curved handlebars that are typically installed on road racing bicycles. Also, some of the parts on early production mountain bicycles were taken from the BMX bicycle. Other contributors were Otis Guy and Keith Bontrager.

Tom Ritchey built the first regularly available mountain bike frame, which was accessorized by Gary Fisher and Charlie Kelly and sold by their company called MountainBikes (later changed to Fisher Mountain Bikes then bought by Trek, still under the name Gary Fisher, currently sold as Trek's "Gary Fisher Collection"). The first two mass produced mountain bikes were sold in 1982: the Specialized Stumpjumper and Univega Alpina Pro. In 2007 the documentary film Klunkerz: A Film About Mountain Bikes was released. The film documents the subject of mountain bike history during this formative period in Northern California.

At the time, the bicycle industry was not impressed with the mountain bike, which many regarded as a short-term fad. In particular, large manufacturers such as Schwinn and Fuji failed to see the significance of an all-terrain bicycle and the coming boom in 'adventure sports'. Instead, the first mass-produced mountain bikes were pioneered by new companies such as

MountainBikes (later, Fisher Mountain Bikes), Ritchey, and Specialized. Specialized was an American startup company that arranged for production of mountain bike frames from factories in Japan and Taiwan. First marketed in 1981, Specialized's mountain bike largely followed Tom Ritchey's frame geometry, but used TiG welding to join the frame tubes instead of fillet-brazing, a process better suited to mass production and which helped to reduce labor and manufacturing cost. The bikes were configured with 15 gears using derailleur shifting, triple chainrings, and five rear cogs.

1990s–2000s

Throughout the 1990s and 2000s, mountain biking moved from a little-known sport to a mainstream activity. Mountain bikes and mountain bike gear that was once only available at specialty shops or via mail order became available at standard bike stores. By the mid-2000s, even department stores such as Wal-Mart began selling inexpensive mountain bikes with full-suspension and disc brakes. In the 2000s, the trends in mountain bikes include the "all mountain bike", the 29er and the singlespeed. The "all mountain bike" is characterized by 4–6 inches (100–150mm) of travel, the ability to descend and handle very rough conditions and still pedal efficiently for climbing. 29er bikes are those using 700c sized rims (as do most road bikes), but wider and suited for tires of two inches (50mm) width or more; the increased diameter wheel is able to roll over obstacles better and offers a greater tire contact patch, but also results in a longer wheelbase, making the bike less agile, and in less travel space for the suspension; thus the 29er is not suited for small riders and small winding trails. The single-speed is considered a return to simplicity with no drivetrain components or shifters, but thus requires a stronger rider.

Following the growing trend in 29-inch bikes (29ers as stated above), there have been other trends in the mountain biking community involving tire size. One of the more prevalent is the new, somewhat esoteric and exotic 650B (27.5 inch) wheelsize, based on the obscure wheel size for touring road bikes. Another interesting trend in mountain bikes is outfitting dirt jump or urban bikes with rigid forks. These bikes normally use 4–5" travel suspension forks. The resulting product is used for the same purposes as the original bike. A commonly cited reason for making the change to a rigid fork is the enhancement of the rider's ability to transmit force to the ground, which is important for performing tricks. In the mid-2000s, an increasing number of mountain bike-oriented resorts opened. Often, they are similar to or in the same complex as a ski resort or they retrofit the concrete steps and platforms of an abandoned factory as an obstacle course, as with Ray's MTB Indoor Park. Mountain bike parks which are operated as summer season activities at ski hills usually include chairlifts which are adapted to bikes, a number of trails of varying difficulty, and bicycle rental facilities.

Equipment

Bike

Mountain bikes differ from other bikes primarily in that they incorporate features aimed at increasing durability and improving performance in rough terrain. Most modern mountain bikes have front fork or dual suspension, 26 inch and also 29 or 27.5(650b) inch diameter tires, usually from 1.7 to 2.5 inches in width, and a wider, flat or upwardly-rising handlebar that allows a more upright riding position. They have a smaller, reinforced frame, usually made of wide tubing. Tires usually have a pronounced lugged tread, and mounted on rims which are stronger than those used on most non-mountain bicycles. Compared to other bikes, mountain bikes also tend to more frequently use disc brakes and indexed gears. They also tend to have a lower gears to facilitate climbing steep hills and traversing obstacles. Generally speaking, enhanced durability and off-road capabilities also result in a heavier bicycle weight to rider ratio than road touring bicycles.. Recent trends include the use of fixed gear systems, single speed systems and internal gear systems.

Accessories

- Gloves differ from road touring gloves, are made of heavier construction, and often have covered thumbs or all fingers covered for hand protection. They are sometimes made with padding for the knuckles.
- Glasses with little or no difference from those used in other cycling sports, help protect against debris while on the trail. Filtered lenses, whether yellow for cloudy days or shaded for sunny days, protect the eyes from strain. Downhill and freeride mountain bikers often use goggles similar to motorcross or snowboard goggles in unison with their fullface helmets.
- Shoes generally have gripping soles similar to those of hiking boots for scrambling over un-ridable obstacles, unlike the smooth-bottomed shoes used in road cycling. The shank of mountain bike shoes is generally more flexible than road cycling shoes. Shoes compatible with clipless pedal systems are also frequently used.
- Clothing is chosen for comfort during physical exertion in the backcountry, and its ability to withstand falls. Road touring clothes are often inappropriate due to their delicate fabrics and construction.
- Hydration systems are important for mountain bikers in the backcountry, ranging from simple water bottles to water bags with drinking tubes in lightweight backpacks (e.g., Camelbaks).
- GPS navigation device is sometimes added to the handlebars and is used to display and monitor progress on trails downloaded from the internet or pre-made mapping systems, record trails on the fly, and keep track of trip times and other data. The GPS system is often a handheld GPS device with color screen and rugged, waterproof (IPX7) design.

- Pump to inflate flat tires.
- Bike tools and extra bike tubes are important, as mountain bikers frequently find themselves miles from help, with flat tires or other mechanical problems that must be handled by the rider.
- Pedals vary from simple platform pedals, where the rider simply places the shoes on top of the pedals, to clipless, where the rider uses a specially equipped shoe with a sole that engages mechanically into the pedal. Pedals with toe cages (clips) are rarely used anymore as they take longer to get out of than clipless or platform if one takes a fall on the rough terrain.
- High-power lights based on LED technology, especially for mountain biking at night.

Protective Gear

The style and level of protection worn by individual riders varies greatly and is affected by many factors including terrain, environment, weather, potential obstacles on the trail, experience, technical skill, fitness, perceived risk, desired style and others too numerous to mention. A cross-country helmet and simple long fingered gloves are a good minimum for the majority of riding.

Limb protection becomes important when speeds rise, surfaces become loose and sketchy, terrain technical and crashes more common and more severe. Full-face helmets and armored suits or jackets are more suited to "gravity" and "air"-orientated disciplines which use jumps and drops, where their extra bulk and weight is outweighed by the bigger and more frequent crashes with worse consequences. Still, within XC community, the typical road-racing attire is what most riders use. Whatever protection is used it should fit well, be comfortable (or it won't be worn) on the bike as well as in the shop and suited for the particular type of riding. Gloves can offer increased comfort while riding, by alleviating compression and friction, and protection in the event of strikes to the back or palm of the hand or when putting the hand out in a fall. Gloves also protect the hand, fingers, and knuckles from abrasion on rough surfaces such as concrete. Many different styles of gloves exist, with various fits, sizes, finger lengths, palm padding and armor options available. Armoring knuckles and the backs of hands with plastic panels is common in more extreme types of mountainbiking.

Helmets provide important head protection. The use of helmets, in one form or another, is almost universal amongst all mountain bikers. The main three types are cross-country, rounded skateboarder style (nicknamed "half shells" or "skate style") and full face. Cross-country helmets tend to be light and well ventilated, and more comfortable to wear for long periods, especially while perspiring in hot weather. In XC competitions, most bikers use the usual road racing style helmets, for their lightweight and aerodynamic qualities. Skateboard helmets are simpler and cheaper than other helmet types; provide greater coverage of the head and resist minor scrapes and knocks. Unlike road biking helmets, skateboard helmets typically have a thicker, hard plastic shell which can take multiple impact before it needs to be replaced. The trade-off for this is that they tend to be much heavier and less ventilated (sweatier), therefore not suitable for endurance-based riding.Full-face helmets (BMX-style) provide the highest level of protection, being stronger again than skateboard style and including a jaw guard to protect the face. The weight is the main issue with this type but nowadays they are often relatively well ventilated and made of high-tech materials, such as carbon fiber. As all helmets should meet minimum standards, SNELL B.95 (American Standard) BS EN 1078:1997 (European Standard), DOT or "motorized ratings" are making their way into the market. The choice of helmet often comes down to rider preference, likelihood of crashing and on what features or properties of a helmet they place emphasis. Helmets are mandatory at competitive events and almost without exception at bike parks, most organisations also stipulate when and where full-face helmets must be used.

Body armor and pads, often referred to simply as "armor", protect limbs and trunk in the event of a crash. While initially made for and marketed at downhillers, freeriders and jump/ street riders, body armor has trickled into other areas of mountain biking as trails have become faster and more technical. Armor ranges from simple neoprene sleeves for knees and elbows to complex, articulated combinations of hard plastic shells and padding that cover a whole limb or the entire body. Some companies market body armor jackets and even full body suits designed to provide greater protection through greater coverage of the body and more secure pad retention. Most upper body protectors also include a spine protector that comprises plastic or metal reinforced plastic plates, over foam padding, which are joined together so that they articulate and move with the back. Some mountain bikers also use BMX-style body armor, such as chest plates, abdomen protectors, and spine plates. New technology has seen an influx of integrated neck protectors that fit securely with full face helmets. There is a general correlation between increased protection and increased weight/decreased mobility, although different styles balance these factors differently. Different levels of protection are deemed necessary/desirable by different riders in different circumstances. Backpack hydration systems such as Camelbaks where a water filled bladder is held close to the spine used by some riders for their perceived protective value. However, there is only anecdotal evidence of protection and with the exception of one specific product by the company Deuter, they are never sold as spine protection.

First aid kits are often carried by mountain bikers, so that they are able to clean and dress cuts and abrasions and splint broken limbs. Experienced mountain bike guides may be trained in dealing with suspected spinal injuries (e.g., immobilizing the victim and keeping the neck straight). Seriously injured people may have to be removed by stretcher, by a motor vehicle suitable for the terrain, or by helicopter.

Types

Mountain biking is dominated by these major categories:

Cross-Country (XC) is the most popular form of mountain biking, and the standard for most riders. It generally means riding point-to-point or in a loop including climbs and descents on a variety of terrain. A typical XC bike weighs around 9-13 kilos (20-30 lbs), and has 0-125 millimeters (0-5 inches) of suspension travel front and sometimes rear.

All-mountain (AM) bike category typically provides 125-180 millimeters (5-7 inches) of rear and front suspension travel and stronger components than XC models, while still providing overall weight suitable for climbing and descending on a variety of terrain.

Downhill (DH) is, in the most general sense, riding mountain bikes downhill. The rider usually travels to the point of descent by other means than cycling, such as a ski lift or automobile, as the weight of the downhill mountain bike often precludes any serious climbing. While cross country riding inevitably has a downhill component, Downhill (or DH for short) usually refers to racing-oriented downhill riding. Downhill-specific bikes are universally equipped with front and rear suspension, large disc brakes, and use heavier frame tubing than other mountain bikes. Because of their extremely steep terrain (often located in summer at ski resorts), downhill courses are one of the most extreme and dangerous venues for mountain biking. They include large jumps (up to and including 12 meters (40 feet)), drops of 3+ meters (10+ feet), and are generally rough and steep top to bottom. To negotiate these obstacles at race speed, racers must possess a unique combination of total body strength, aerobic and anaerobic fitness, and mental control. Minimum body protection in a true downhill setting is knee pads and a full face helmet with goggles, although riders and racers commonly sport full body suits to protect themselves. Downhill bikes now weigh around 16-20 kilos (35-45 lbs), while professional downhill mountain bikes can weigh as little as 15 kilos (33 lbs), fully equipped with custom carbon fibre parts, air suspension, tubeless tires and more. Downhill frames get anywhere from 170-250 millimeters (7 to 10 inches) of travel and are usually mounted with an 200 millimeter (8 inch) travel dual-crown fork.

Four Cross/Dual Slalom (4X) is a sport in which riders compete either on separate tracks, as in Dual Slalom, or on a short slalom track, as in 4X. Most bikes used are light hard-tails, although the last World Cup was actually won on a full suspension bike. The tracks have dirt jumps, berms, and gaps. Professionals in gravity mountain biking tend to concentrate either on downhill mountain biking or 4X/dual slalom because they are very different. However, some riders, such as Cedric Gracia, still do 4X and DH, although that is becoming more rare as 4X takes on its own identity.

Freeride / Big Hit / Hucking. Freeride, as the name suggests is a 'do anything' discipline that encompasses everything from downhill racing without the clock to jumping, riding 'North Shore' style (elevated trails made of interconnecting bridges and logs), and generally riding trails and/or stunts that require more skill and aggressive techniques than XC. Freeride bikes are generally heavier and more amply suspended than their XC counterparts, but usually retain much of their climbing ability. It is up to the rider to build his or her bike to lean more toward a preferred level of aggressiveness. "Slopestyle" type riding is an increasingly popular genre that combines big-air, stunt-ridden freeride with BMX style tricks. Slopestyle courses are usually constructed at already established mountain bike parks and include jumps, large drops, quarter-pipes, and other wooden obstacles. There are always multiple lines through a course and riders compete for judges' points by choosing lines that highlight their particular skills. A "typical" freeride bike is hard to define, but 13-18 kilos (30-40) lbs with 150-250 millimeters (6-10 inches) of suspension front and rear.

Dirt Jumping (DJ) is one of the names given to the practice of riding bikes over shaped mounds of dirt or soil and becoming airborne. The idea is that after riding over the 'take off' the rider will become airborne, and aim to land on the 'landing'. Dirt jumping can be done on almost anything but the bikes are generally smaller and more maneuverable hardtails so that tricks e.g. backflips, are easier to complete. The bikes are simpler so that when a crash occurs there are fewer components to break or cause the rider injury.

Trials riding consists of hopping and jumping bikes over obstacles, without touching a foot onto the ground. It can be performed either off-road or in an urban environment. It requires an excellent sense of balance. The emphasis is placed on techniques of effectively overcoming the obstacles, although street-trials (as opposed to competition-oriented trials) is much like Street and DJ, where doing tricks with style is the essence. Trials bikes look almost nothing like mountain bikes. They use either 20", 24" or 26" wheels and have very small, low frames, some types without a saddle.

Urban/Street is essentially the same as urban BMX (or Freestyle BMX), in which riders perform tricks by riding on/ over man made objects. The bikes are the same as those used for Dirt Jumping, having 24" or 26" wheels. Also, they are very light, many in the range of 25-30 lbs, and are typically hardtails with between 0-100 millimeters of front suspension. As with Dirt Jumping and Trials, style and execution are emphasized.

Mountain Bike Touring is long distance touring on dirt roads and single track with a mountain bike. With the popularity of the Great Divide Trail, the Colorado Trail and other long distance off road biking trails specially fitted mountain bikes are increasingly being used for touring. Bike manufacturers like Salsa have even developed MTB touring bikes like the Fargo model. Mixed Terrain Cycle-Touring or rough riding is a form of mountain bike touring but involves cycling over a variety of surfaces and topography on a single route, with a single bicycle. The recent popularity of mixed terrain touring is in part a reaction against the increasing specialization of the bike industry.

Focusing on freedom of travel and efficiency over varied surfaces, mixed terrain bicycle travel has a storied past.

Risks

The risk of injury is inherent in the sport of mountain biking, especially in the more extreme disciplines such as downhill biking. Injuries range from relatively minor wounds, such as cuts and abrasions from falls on gravel to serious injuries such as striking the head or spine on a boulder or tree.

Protective equipment can protect against minor injuries, and reduce the extent or seriousness of major impacts, but it cannot protect a rider against the most serious impacts or accidents. To truly reduce the risk of injury, a rider needs to take steps to make injuries less likely, such as picking trails that they can handle given their experience level, ensuring that they are fit enough to deal with the trail they have chosen, and keeping their bike in top mechanical shape. If a mountain biker wishes to explore more dangerous trails or disciplines (types of mountain biking) such as downhill riding, they will need to learn new skills, such as jumping and avoiding obstacles.

Fitness is another issue; if a rider is not in good enough shape to ride a certain class of trail, they will become fatigued, which puts them at a higher risk of having an accident.

Lastly, maintenance of one's bike needs to be done more frequently for mountain biking than for casual commuter biking in the city. Mountain biking places much higher demands on every part of the bike. Jumps and impacts can crack the frame or damage the derailleurs or the tire rims, and steep, fast descents can quickly wear out brake pads. Thus, whereas a casual in-the-city rider may only check over and maintain their bike every few months, a mountain biker should check and properly maintain the bike before every ride.

Advocacy

Mountain bikers have faced land access issues from the beginnings of the sport. Areas where the first mountain bikers have ridden have faced serious restrictions or elimination of riding.

Opposition to the sport has led to the development of local, regional, and international mountain bike groups. The different groups that formed generally work to create new trails, maintain existing trails, and help existing trails that may have issues. Groups work with private and public entities from the individual landowner to city parks departments, on up through the state level at the DNR, and into the federal level. Different groups will work individually or together to achieve results.

Advocacy organizations work through a variety of means including education, trail work days, and trail patrols. Examples of the education an advocacy group can provide include: Educate local bicycle riders, property managers, and other user groups on the proper development of trails, and on the International Mountain Bicycling Association's rules of the Trail. Examples of trail work days can include: Flagging, cutting, and signing a new trail, or removing downed trees after a storm. A trail patrol is a bike rider who has had some training to help assist other (including non cyclists) trail users.

The International Mountain Bicycling Association (IMBA), is a non-profit advocacy group whose mission is to create, enhance and preserve trail opportunities for mountain bikers worldwide. IMBA serves as an umbrella organization for mountain biking advocacy worldwide, and represents more than 700 affiliated mountain biking groups. In 1988, five California mountain bike clubs linked to form IMBA. The founding clubs were: Concerned Off Road Bicyclists Association, Bicycle Trails Council East Bay, Bicycle Trails Council Marin, Sacramento Rough Riders, and Responsible Organized Mountain Pedalers.

IMBA developed "Rules of the Trail" to promote responsible and courteous conduct on shared-use trails.

IMBA Rules of the Trail

1. Ride On Open Trails Only

2. Leave No Trace
3. Control Your Bicycle
4. Yield to Others
5. Never Scare Animals
6. Plan Ahead

Environmental Impact

Studies reported in the IMBA (International Mountain Bike Association) Trail Solutions manual found that a mountain bike's impact on a given length of trail surface is comparable to that of a hiker and substantially less than that of an equestrian.

A critical literature review by Jason Lathrop on the ecological impacts of mountain biking notes that few studies take mountain biking into account. He quotes the BLM: "An estimated 13.5 million mountain bicyclists visit public lands each year to enjoy the variety of trails. What was once a low use activity that was easy to manage has become more complex".

The environmental impacts of mountain biking can be greatly reduced by not riding on wet or sensitive trails, not skidding, and by staying on the trail.

CHAPTER 12

MOUNTAINEERING

Mountaineering or mountain climbing is the sport, hobby or profession of hiking, skiing, and climbing mountains. While mountaineering began as attempts to reach the highest point of unclimbed mountains, it has branched into specialisations that address different aspects of the mountain and consists of three areas: rock-craft, snow-craft and skiing, depending on whether the route chosen is over rock, snow or ice. All require experience, athletic ability, and technical knowledge to maintain safety. The UIAA or Union Internationale des Associations d'Alpinisme is the world governing body in mountaineering and climbing, addressing issues like Access, Medical, Mountain Protection, Safety, Youth and Ice Climbing.

Technique

Snow

Compacted snow conditions allow mountaineers to progress on foot. Frequently crampons are required to travel efficiently over snow and ice. Crampons have 8-14 spikes and are attached to a mountaineer's boots. They are used on hard snow (neve) and ice to provide additional traction and allow very steep ascents and descents. Varieties range from lightweight aluminium models intended for walking on snow covered glaciers, to aggressive steel models intended for vertical and overhanging ice and rock. Snowshoes can be used to walk through deep snow. Skis can be used everywhere snowshoes can and also in steeper, more alpine landscapes, although it takes considerable practice to develop strong skills for difficult terrain. Combining the techniques of alpine skiing and mountaineering to ascend and descend a mountain is a form of the sport by itself, called Ski Mountaineering. Ascending and descending a snow slope safely requires the use of an ice axe and many different footwork techniques that have been developed over the past century, mainly in Europe. The progression of footwork from the lowest angle slopes to the steepest terrain is first to splay the feet to a rising traverse, to kicking steps, to front pointing the crampons. The progression of ice axe technique from the lowest angle slopes to the steepest terrain is to use the ice axe first as a walking stick, then a stake, then to use the front pick as a dagger below the shoulders or above, and finally to swing the pick into the slope over the head. These various techniques may involve questions of differing ice-axe design depending on terrain, and even whether a mountaineer uses one or two ice axes. Anchors for the rope in snow are sometimes unreliable, and include snow stakes, called pickets, deadman devices called flukes which are fashioned from aluminium, or devised from buried objects that might include an ice axe, skis, rocks or other objects. Bollards, which are simply carved out of consolidated snow or ice, also sometimes serve as anchors.

Glaciers

When travelling over glaciers, crevasses pose a grave danger. These giant cracks in the ice are not always visible as snow can be blown and freeze over the top to make a snowbridge. At times snowbridges can be as thin as a few inches. Climbers use a system of ropes to protect themselves from such hazards. Basic gear for glacier travel includes crampons and ice axes. Teams of two to five climbers tie into a rope equally spaced. If a climber begins to fall the other members of the team perform a self-arrest to stop the fall. The other members of the team enact a crevasse rescue to pull the fallen climber from the crevasse.

Ice

Multiple methods are used to safely travel over ice. If the terrain is steep but not vertical, then the lead climber can place ice screws in the ice and attach the rope for protection. Each climber on the team must clip past the anchor, and the last climber picks up the anchor itself. Occasionally, slinged icicles or bollards are also used. This allows for safety should the entire team be taken off their feet. This technique is known as Simul-climbing and is sometimes also used on steep snow and easy rock.

If the terrain becomes too steep, standard ice climbing techniques are used in which each climber is belayed, moving one at a time.

Shelter

Climbers use a few different forms of shelter depending on the situation and conditions. Shelter is a very important aspect of safety for the climber as the weather in the mountains may be very unpredictable. Tall mountains may require many days of camping on the mountain.

Base Camp

The "Base Camp" of a mountain is an area used for staging an attempt at the summit. Base camps are positioned to be safe from the harsher conditions above. There are base camps on many popular or dangerous mountains. Where the summit cannot be reached from base camp in a single day, a mountain will have additional camps above base camp. For example, the southeast ridge route on Mount Everest has Base Camp plus (normally) camps I through IV.

Hut

The European alpine regions, in particular, have a network of mountain huts (called "refuges" in France, "rifugi" in Italy, "cabanes" in Switzerland, "refugios" in Spain and "hytte" in Norway). Such huts exist at many different heights, including in the high mountains themselves – in extremely remote areas, more rudimentary shelters may exist. The mountain huts are of varying size and quality, but each is typically centred on a communal dining room and have dormitories equipped with mattresses, blankets or duvets, and pillows; guests are expected to bring and to use their own sleeping bag liner. The facilities are usually rudimentary but, given their locations, huts offer vital shelter, make routes more widely accessible (by allowing journeys to be broken and reducing the weight of equipment needing to be carried), and offer good value. In Europe, all huts are staffed during the summer (mid-June to mid-September) and some are staffed in the spring (mid-March to mid-May). Elsewhere, huts may also be open in the fall. Huts also may have a part that is always open, but unmanned, a so-called winter hut. When open and manned, the huts are generally run by full-time employees, but some are staffed on a voluntary basis by members of Alpine clubs (such as Swiss Alpine Club and Club alpin français). The manager of the hut, termed a guardian or warden in Europe, will usually also sell refreshments and meals; both to those visiting only for the day and to those staying overnight. The offering is surprisingly wide; given that most supplies, often including fresh water, must be flown in by helicopter, and may include glucose-based snacks (such as Mars and Snickers bars) on which climbers and walkers wish to stock up, cakes and pastries made at the hut, a variety of hot and cold drinks (including beer and wine), and high carbohydrate dinners in the evenings. Not all huts offer a catered service, though, and visitors may need to provide for themselves. Some huts offer facilities for both, enabling visitors wishing to keep costs down to bring their own food and cooking equipment and to cater using the facilities provided. Booking for overnight stays at huts is deemed obligatory, and in many cases is essential as some popular huts; even with more than 100 bed spaces may be full during good weather and at weekends. Once made, the cancellation of a reservation is advised as a matter of courtesy – and, indeed, potentially of safety, as many huts keep a record of where climbers and walkers state they planned to walk to next. Most huts may be contacted by telephone and most take credit cards as a means of payment.

Bivouac (Bivy)

In the mountaineering context, a bivouac or "bivy" is a makeshift resting or sleeping arrangement in which the climber has less than the full complement of shelter, food and equipment that would normally be present at a conventional campsite. This may involve simply getting a sleeping bag and Bivouac sack and lying down to sleep. Many times small partially sheltered areas such as a bergschrund, cracks in rocks or a trench dug in the snow are used to provide additional shelter from wind. These techniques were originally used only in emergency; however some climbers steadfastly committed to alpine style climbing specifically plan for bivouacs in order to save the weight of a tent when suitable snow conditions or time is unavailable for construction of a snow cave. The principal hazard associated with bivouacs is the greater level of exposure to cold and the elements.

Tent

Tents are the most common form of shelter used on the mountain. These may vary from simple tarps to much heavier designs intended to withstand harsh mountain conditions. In exposed positions, windbreaks of snow or rock may be required to shelter the tent. One of the downsides to tenting is that high winds and snow loads can be dangerous and may ultimately lead to the tent's failure and collapse. In addition, the constant flapping of the tent fabric can hinder sleep and raise doubts about the security of the shelter. When choosing a tent, alpinists tend to rely on specialised mountaineering tents that are specifically designed for high winds and moderate to heavy snow loads. Tent stakes can be buried in the snow ("deadman") for extra security.

Snow cave

Where conditions permit snow caves are another way to shelter high on the mountain. Some climbers do not use tents at high altitudes unless the snow conditions do not allow for snow caving, since snow caves are silent and much warmer than tents. They can be built relatively easily, given sufficient time, using a snow shovel. A correctly made snow cave will hover around freezing, which relative to outside temperatures can be very warm. They can be dug anywhere where there is at least four feet of snow. Another shelter that works well is a quinzee, which is excavated from a pile of snow that has been work hardened or sintered (typically by stomping). Igloos are used by some climbers, but are deceptively difficult to build and require specific snow conditions.

Hazards

Dangers in mountaineering are sometimes divided into two categories: objective hazards that exist without regard to the climber's presence, like rockfall, avalanches and inclement weather, and subjective hazards that relate only to factors introduced by the climber. Equipment failure and falls due to inattention, fatigue or inadequate technique are examples of subjective hazard. A route continually swept by avalanches and storms is said to have a high level of objective danger, whereas a technically far more difficult route that is relatively safe from these dangers may be regarded as objectively safer.

In all, mountaineers must concern themselves with dangers: falling rocks, falling ice, snow-avalanches, the climber falling, falls from ice slopes, falls down snow slopes, falls into crevasses and the dangers from altitude and weather. To select and follow a route using one's skills and experience to mitigate these dangers is to exercise the climber's craft.

Falling rocks

Every rock mountain is slowly disintegrating due to erosion, the process being especially rapid above the snow-line. Rock faces are constantly swept by falling stones, which may be possible to dodge. Falling rocks tend to form furrows in a mountain face, and these furrows (couloirs) have to be ascended with caution, their sides often being safe when the middle is stoneswept. Rocks fall more frequently on some days than on others, according to the recent weather. Ice formed during the night may temporarily bind rocks to the face but warmth of the day or lubricating water from melting snow or rain may easily dislodge these rocks. Local experience is a valuable help on determining typical rock fall on such routes.

The direction of the dip of rock strata sometimes determines the degree of danger on a particular face; the character of the rock must also be considered. Where stones fall frequently debris will be found below, whilst on snow slopes falling stones cut furrows visible from a great distance. In planning an ascent of a new peak or an unfamiliar route, mountaineers must look for such traces. When falling stones get mixed in considerable quantity with slushy snow or water a mud avalanche is formed (common in the Himalayas). It is vital to avoid camping in their possible line of fall.

Falling Ice

The places where ice may fall can always be determined beforehand. It falls in the broken parts of glaciers (seracs) and from overhanging cornices formed on the crests of narrow ridges. Large icicles are often formed on steep rock faces, and these fall frequently in fine weather following cold and stormy days. They have to be avoided like falling stones. Seracs are slow in formation, and slow in arriving (by glacier motion) at a condition of unstable equilibrium. They generally fall in or just after the hottest part of the day. A skilful and experienced ice-man will usually devise a safe route through a most intricate ice-fall, but such places should be avoided in the afternoon of a hot day. Hanging glaciers (i.e. glaciers perched on steep slopes) often discharge themselves over steep rock-faces, the snout breaking off at intervals. They can always be detected by their debris below. Their track should be avoided.

Falls from Rocks

A rock climber's skill is shown by their choice of handhold and foothold, and their adhesion to the holds once chosen. Much depends on the ability to estimate the ability of the rock to support the weight placed on it. Many loose rocks are quite firm enough to bear a person's weight, but experience is needed to know which can be trusted, and skill is required in transferring the weight to them without jerking. On rotten rocks the rope must be handled with special care, lest it should dislodge loose stones on to those below. Similar care must be given to handholds and footholds, for the same reason. When a horizontal traverse has to be made across very difficult rocks, a dangerous situation may arise unless at both ends of the traverse there are firm positions. Mutual assistance on hard rocks takes all manner of forms: two, or even three, people climbing on one another's shoulders, or using an ice axe propped up by others for a foothold. The great principle is that of co-operation, all the members of the party climbing with reference to the others, and not as independent units; each when moving must know what the climber in front and the one behind are doing. After bad weather steep rocks are often found covered with a veneer of ice (verglas), which may even render them inaccessible. Crampons are useful on such occasions.

Avalanches

The avalanche is the most underestimated danger in the mountains. People generally think that they will be able to recognise the hazards and survive being caught. The truth is a somewhat different story. Every year, 120 to 150 people die in small avalanches in the Alps alone. The vast majority are reasonably experienced male skiers aged 20–35 but also include ski instructors and guides.There is always a lot of pressure to risk a snow crossing. Turning back takes a lot of extra time and effort, supreme leadership, and most importantly there is seldom an avalanche that proves the right decision was made. Making the decision to turn around is especially hard if others are crossing the slope, but any next person could become the trigger.

There are many types of avalanche, but two types are of the most concern:

1. Slab avalanche

This type of avalanche occurs when a plate of snow breaks loose and starts sliding downhill; these are the largest and most dangerous.

1. Hard slab avalanche

This type of avalanche is formed by hard-packed snow in a cohesive slab. The slab will not break up easily as it slides down the hill, resulting in large blocks tumbling down the mountain.

1. Soft slab avalanche

This type of avalanche is formed again by a cohesive layer of snow bonded together, the slab tends to break up more easily.

2. Loose snow avalanche

This type of avalanche is triggered by a small amount of moving snow that accumulates into a big slide. Also known as a "wet slide or point release" avalanche. This type of avalanche is deceptively dangerous as it can still knock a climber or skier off their feet and bury them, or sweep them over a cliff into a terrain trap.

Dangerous slides are most likely to occur on the same slopes preferred by many skiers: long and wide open, few trees or large rocks, 30 to 45 degrees of angle, large load of fresh snow, soon after a big storm, on a slope "lee to the storm". Solar radiation can trigger slides as well. These will typically be a point release or wet slough type of avalanche. The added weight of the wet slide can trigger a slab avalanche. Ninety percent of reported victims are caught in avalanches triggered by themselves or others in their group.

When going off-piste or travelling in alpine terrain, parties are advised to always carry:

1. avalanche beacon
2. probe
3. shovel (retrieving victims with a shovel instead of hands is five times faster)

They are also advised to have had avalanche training. Ironically, expert skiers who have avalanche training make up a large percentage of avalanche fatalities; perhaps because they are the ones more likely to ski in areas prone to avalanches, and certainly because most people do not practice enough with their equipment to be truly fast and efficient rescuers.

Even with proper rescue equipment and training, there is a one-in-five chance of dying if caught in a significant avalanche, and only a 50/50 chance of being found alive if buried more than a few minutes. The best solution is to learn how to avoid risky conditions.

Ice Slopes

For travel on slopes consisting of ice or hard snow, crampons are a standard part of a mountaineer's equipment. While step-cutting can sometimes be used on snow slopes of moderate angle, this can be a slow and tiring process, which does not provide the higher security of crampons. However, in soft snow or powder, crampons are easily hampered by balling of snow, which reduces their effectiveness. In either case, an ice axe not only assists with balance but provides the climber with the possibility of self-arrest in case of a slip or fall. On a true ice slope however, an ice axe is rarely able to effect a self-arrest. As an additional safety precaution on steep ice slopes, the climbing rope is attached to ice screws buried into the ice.

True ice slopes are rare in Europe, though common in mountains in the tropics, where newly-fallen snow quickly thaws on the surface and becomes sodden below, so that the next night's frost turns the whole mass into a sheet of semi-solid ice.

Snow Slopes

Snow slopes are very common, and usually easy to ascend. At the foot of a snow or ice slope is generally a big crevasse, called a bergschrund, where the final slope of the mountain rises from a snow-field or glacier. Such bergschrunds are generally too wide to be stepped across, and must be crossed by a snow bridge, which needs careful testing and a painstaking use of the rope. A steep snow slope in bad condition may be dangerous, as the whole body of snow may start as an avalanche. Such slopes are less dangerous if ascended directly, rather than obliquely, for an oblique or horizontal track cuts them across and facilitates movement of the mass. New snow lying on ice is especially dangerous. Experience is needed for deciding on the advisability of advancing over snow in doubtful condition. Snow on rocks is usually rotten unless it is thick; snow on snow is likely to be sound. A day or two of fine weather will usually bring new snow into sound condition. Snow cannot lie at a very steep angle, though it often deceives the eye as to its slope. Snow slopes seldom exceed 40°. Ice slopes may be much steeper. Snow slopes in early morning are usually hard and safe, but the same in the afternoon are quite soft and possibly dangerous; hence the advantage of an early start.

Crevasses

Crevasses are the slits or deep chasms formed in the substance of a glacier as it passes over an uneven bed. They may be open or hidden. In the lower part of a glacier the crevasses are open. Above the snow-line they are frequently hidden by arched-over accumulations of winter snow. The detection of hidden crevasses requires care and experience. After a fresh fall of snow they can only be detected by sounding with the pole of the ice axe, or by looking to right and left where the open extension of a partially hidden crevasse may be obvious. The safeguard against accident is the rope, and no one should ever cross a snow-covered glacier unless roped to one, or even better to two companions. Anyone venturing onto crevasses should be trained in crevasse rescue.

Weather

The primary dangers caused by bad weather centre around the changes it causes in snow and rock conditions, making movement suddenly much more arduous and hazardous than under normal circumstances.

Whiteouts make it difficult to retrace a route while rain may prevent taking the easiest line only determined as such under dry conditions. In a storm the mountaineer who uses a compass for guidance has a great advantage over a merely empirical observer. In large snow-fields it is, of course, easier to go wrong than on rocks, but intelligence and experience are the best guides in safely navigating objective hazards.

Summer thunderstorms may produce intense lightning. If a climber happens to be standing on or near the summit, they risk being struck. There are many cases where people have been struck by lightning while climbing mountains. In most mountainous regions, local storms develop by late morning and early afternoon. Many climbers will get an "alpine start"; that is before or by first light so as to be on the way down when storms are intensifying in activity and lightning and other weather hazards are a distinct threat to safety. High winds can speed the onset of hypothermia, as well as damage equipment such as tents used for shelter. Under certain conditions, storms can also create waterfalls which can slow or stop climbing progress. A notable example is the Fohn wind acting upon the Eiger.

Altitude

Rapid ascent can lead to altitude sickness. The best treatment is to descend immediately. The climber's motto at high altitude is "climb high, sleep low", referring to the regimen of climbing higher to acclimatise but returning to lower elevation to sleep. In the South American Andes, the chewing of coca leaves has been traditionally used to treat altitude sickness symptoms.

Common symptoms of altitude sickness include severe headache, sleep problems, nausea, lack of appetite, lethargy and body ache. Mountain sickness may progress to HACE (High Altitude Cerebral Edema) and HAPE (High Altitude Pulmonary Edema), both of which can be fatal within 24 hours.

In high mountains, atmospheric pressure is lower and this means that less oxygen is available to breathe. This is the underlying cause of altitude sickness. Everyone needs to acclimatise, even exceptional mountaineers that have been to high altitude before. Generally speaking, mountaineers start using bottled oxygen when they climb above 7,000 m. Exceptional mountaineers have climbed 8000-metre peaks (including Everest) without oxygen, almost always with a carefully planned program of acclimatisation.

Solar Radiation

Solar radiation increases significantly as the atmosphere gets thinner with increasing altitude thereby absorbing less ultraviolet radiation. Snow cover reflecting the radiation can amplify the effects up to 75% increasing the risks and damage from sunburn and snow blindness.

In 2005, researcher and mountaineer John Semple established that above-average ozone concentrations on the Tibetan plateau may pose an additional risk to climbers.

Volcanic Activity

Some mountains are active volcanoes as in the case of the many stratovolcanoes that form the highest peaks in island arcs and in parts of the Andes. Some of these volcanic mountains may cause several hazards if they erupt, such as lahars, pyroclasitc flows, rockfalls, lava flows, heavy tephra fall, volcanic bomb ejections and toxic gases.

Styles of Climbing: Expedition Climbing vs. Alpinism

There are two main styles of climbing: expedition climbing and alpinism. In Europe mountain climbing is referred to as alpinism. In the Americas this term refers to a particular style of mountain climbing that involves a mixture of ice climbing, rock climbing, and mixed climbing where climbers carry all their loads with them at all times. The term alpinism as used in the Americas contrasts with expedition style climbing (as commonly undertaken in the Himalayan region) where climbers use porters, pack animals, cooks, etc. to carry their loads and cook meals. The prevelance of expedition style climbing in the Himalaya is largely a function of the nature of the mountains in the region. Due to the fact that Himalayan base camps can take days or weeks to trek to, and Himalayan mountains can take weeks or perhaps even months to climb, a large number of personnel and amount of supplies are necessary. This is why expedition style climbing is frequently used on large and isolated peaks in the Himalaya. In Europe and North America there is less of a need for the expedition style as mountains can often be accessed from roads, are at a lower altitude and can be climbed in a day or two.

According to "Mountaineering: The Freedom of the Hills" the differences between, and advantages and disadvantages of the two kinds of climbing are as follows:

Expedition Style

- uses multiple trips between camps to carry supplies up to higher camps
- group sizes are larger than alpine style climbs because more supplies are carried between camps
- fixed lines are often used to minimize the danger involved in continually moving between camps
- more time is spent on the mountain and this means climbers are exposed to objective hazards for a longer period of time

Alpinism

- climbers only climb the route once because they do not continually climb up and down between camps with supplies
- fewer supplies are used on the climb therefore fewer personnel are needed
- alpinism does not leave the climber exposed to objective hazards as long as an expedition style climb does; however, because of the speed of the ascent relative to an expedition style climb there is less time for acclimitization

Locations

Mountaineering has become a popular sport throughout the world. In Europe the sport largely originated in the Alps, and is still immensely popular there. Other notable mountain ranges frequented by climbers include the Caucasus, the Pyrenees, Rila mountains, the Tatra mountains and Carpathian Mountains. In North America climbers frequent the Rocky Mountains, the Sierra Nevada of California, the Cascades of the Pacific Northwest and the high peaks of Alaska. There has been a long tradition of climbers going on expeditions to the Greater Ranges, a term generally used for the Andes and the high peaks of Asia including the Himalaya, Pamirs and Tien Shan. In the past this was often on exploratory trips or to make first ascents. With the advent of cheaper, long-haul air travel, mountaineering holidays in the Greater Ranges are now undertaken much more frequently and ascents of even Everest and Vinson Massif (the highest mountain in Antarctica) are offered as a "package holiday". Other mountaineering areas of interest include the Southern Alps of New Zealand, the Japanese Alps, the South Korean mountains, the Coast Mountains of British Columbia, the Scottish Highlands, and the mountains of Scandinavia, especially Norway.

History

Though it is unknown whether his intention was to reach a summit, "Ötzi" ascended at least 3,000 m in the Alps about

5,300 years ago. His remains were found at that altitude, preserved in a glacier.

The first recorded mountain ascent in the Common Era is Roman Emperor Hadrian's ascent of Etna (3,350 m) to see the sun rise in 121.

Peter III of Aragon climbed Canigou in the Pyrenees in the last quarter of the 13th century.

The first ascent of the Popocatépetl (5,426 m in Mexico) was reported in 1289 by members of a local tribe (Tecanuapas)

Jean Buridan climbed Mont Ventoux around 1316.

The Italian poet Petrarch wrote that on April 26, 1336 he, together with his brother and two servants, climbed to the top of Mont Ventoux (1,909 m). His account of the trip was composed later as a letter to his friend Dionigi di Borgo San Sepolcro.

The Rochemelon (3,538 m) in the Italian Alps was climbed in 1358.

In the late 15th and early 16th centuries, ascents were made of numerous high peaks in the Andes, for religious purposes by the citizens of the Inca Empire and their subjects. They constructed platforms, houses and altars on many summits and carried out sacrifices, including human sacrifices. The highest peak they are known for certain to have climbed is Llullaillaco (6,739 m). They may also have ascended the highest peak in the Andes, Aconcagua (6,962 m) as a sacrifice victim has been found at over 5,000 m on this peak.

In 1492 the ascent of Mont Aiguille was made by order of Charles VIII of France. The Humanists of the 16th century adopted a new attitude towards mountains, but the disturbed state of Europe nipped in the bud the nascent mountaineering of the Zurich school.

Leonardo da Vinci climbed to a snow-field in the neighborhood of Monte Rosa and made scientific observations.

in 1573, Francesco De Marchi reached the summit of Gran Sasso (2912m) in central Italy.

In 1642 Darby Field made the first recorded ascent of Mount Washington, then known as Agiocochook, in New Hampshire.

Konrad Gesner and Josias Simler of Zurich visited and described mountains, and made regular ascents. The use of ice axe and rope were locally invented at this time. No mountain expeditions of note are recorded in the 17th century.

Richard Pococke and William Windham's historic visit to Chamonix was made in 1741, and set the trend for visiting glaciers.

In 1744 the Titus was climbed, the first true ascent of a snow-mountain.

The first attempt to ascend Mont Blanc was made in 1775 by a party of natives. In 1786 Dr Michel Paccard and Jacques Balmat gained the summit for the first time. Horace-Bénédict de Saussure, the initiator of the first ascent followed next year.

The Norwegian mountain climber, Jens Esmark was the first person to ascend Snøhetta in 1798, part of the Dovrefjell range in Southern Norway. The same year he lead the first expedition to Bitihorn, a small mountain in the southernmost outskirts of Jotunheimen, Norway. In 1810 he was the first person to ascend Mount Gaustatoppen in Telemark, Norway.

The Grossglockner was climbed in 1800, the Ortler in 1804, the Jungfrau in 1811, the Finsteraarhorn in 1812, and the Breithorn in 1813. Thereafter, tourists showed a tendency to climb, and the body of Alpine guides began to come into existence as a consequence.

Aconcagua (22,831 feet), the highest peak of the Andes was first climbed in 1897 and the Grand Teton (13,747 feet)in North America's Rocky Mountains was ascended in 1898.

The Italian Duke of the Abruzzi in 1897 made the first ascent on Mount St.Elias (18,009 feet) which stands at the boundary of Alaska and Canada and in 1906 successfully climbed

Margherita in the Ruwenzori group (16,795 feet) in East Africa. In 1913, an American,Hudson Stuck ascended Mount Mckinley (20,320 feet) in Alaska, the highest peak in North America.

Citlaltépetl (5720 m in Mexico) was first climbed in 1848 by F. Maynard & G. Reynolds.

Systematic mountaineering, as a sport, is usually dated from Sir Alfred Wills's ascent of the Wetterhorn in 1854. The first ascent of Monte Rosa was made in 1855.

The Alpine Club was founded in London in 1857, and was soon imitated in most European countries. Edward Whymper's ascent of the Matterhorn in 1865 marked the close of the main period of Alpine conquest, the Golden age of alpinism, during which the craft of climbing was invented and "perfected", the body of professional guides formed and their traditions fixed.

Passing to other ranges, the exploration of the Pyrenees was concurrent with that of the Alps. The Caucasus followed, mainly owing to the initiative of D. W. Freshfield; it was first visited by exploring climbers in 1868, and most of its great peaks were climbed by 1888.

The Edelweiss Club Salzburg was founded in Salzburg in 1881, and had 3 members make the first ascent on two Eight-thousanders, Broad Peak (1957) and Dhaulagiri (1960).

Trained climbers turned their attention to the mountains of North America in 1888, when the Rev. W. S. Green made an expedition to the Selkirk Mountains. From that time exploration has gone on apace, and many English and American climbing parties have surveyed most of the highest peaks; Pikes Peak (14,110 ft) having been climbed by Mr. E. James and party in 1820, and Mt. Saint Elias (18,008 ft) by the Duke of the Abruzzi and party in 1897. The exploration of the highest Andes was begun in 1879-1880, when Whymper climbed Chimborazo and explored the mountains of Ecuador. The Cordillera between Chile and Argentina was visited by Dr. Gussfeldt in 1883, who ascended Maipo (17,270 ft) and attempted Aconcagua (22,841 ft). That peak was first climbed by the Fitzgerald expedition in 1897.

The Andes of Bolivia were first explored by Sir William Martin Conway in 1898. Chilean and Argentine expeditions revealed the structure of the southern Cordillera in the years 1885-1898. Conway visited the mountains of Tierra del Fuego.

New Zealand's Southern Alps were first visited in 1882 by the Rev. W. S. Green, and shortly afterwards a New Zealand Alpine Club was founded, and by their activities the exploration of the range was pushed forward. In 1895, Major Edward Arthur Fitzgerald, made an important journey in this range. Tom Fyfe and party climbed Aoraki/Mount Cook on Christmas Day 1894, denying Fitzgerald the first ascent. Fitzgerald was en route from Britain with Swiss guide Matthias Zurbriggen to claim the peak. So piqued at being beaten to the top of Mount Cook, he refused to climb it and concentrated on other peaks in the area. Later in the trip Zubriggen soloed Mount Cook up a ridge that now bears his name.

The first mountains of the arctic region explored were those of Spitsbergen by Sir W. M. Conway's expeditions in 1896 and 1897.

Of the high African peaks, Kilimanjaro was climbed in 1889 by Dr. Hans Meyer, Mt. Kenya in 1899 by Halford John Mackinder, and a peak of Ruwenzori by H. J. Moore in 1900.

The Asiatic mountains were initially surveyed on orders of the British Empire. In 1892 Sir William Martin Conway explored the Karakoram Himalaya, and climbed a peak of 23,000 ft (7,000 m) In 1895 Albert F. Mummery died while attempting Nanga Parbat, while in 1899 D. W. Freshfield took an expedition to the snowy regions of Sikkim. In 1899, 1903, 1906 and 1908 Mrs Fannie Bullock Workman made ascents in the Himalayas, including one of the Nun Kun peaks (23,300 ft). A number of Gurkha sepoys were trained as expert mountaineers by Major the Hon. C. G. Bruce, and a good deal of exploration was accomplished by them.

The Sierra Club was founded by John Muir in San Francisco, California in 1892.

The Rucksack Club was founded in Manchester, England in 1902.

The American Alpine Club was founded in 1902.

In 1902, the Eckenstein-Crowley Expedition, led by mountaineer Oscar Eckenstein and author and occultist Aleister Crowley, was the first to attempt to scale Chogo Ri (now known as K2 in the west). They reached 22,000 feet (6,700 m) before turning back due to weather and other mishaps.

In 1905, Aleister Crowley led the first expedition to Kangchenjunga, the third highest mountain in the world. Four members of that party were killed in an avalanche. Some claims say they reached around 21,300 feet (6,500 m) before turning back, however Crowley's autobiography claims they reached about 25,000 feet (7,600 m).

A few Olympics in the 1920s included prizes for alpinism, but these were discontinued after World War II.

The British made several attempts in the 1920s to climb Mount Everest. The first in 1921 was more of an exploratory expedition but the 1922 expedition reached 8,320 metres (27,300 ft) before being aborted on the third summit attempt after seven porters were killed in an avalanche. The 1924 expedition saw another height record achieved but still failed to reach the summit when George Mallory and Andrew Irvine disappeared on the final attempt.

1938 saw the first ascent of the North Face of the Eiger by Andreas Heckmair, Wiggerl Vorg, Fritz Kasparek and Heinrich Harrer. This route was feted as the "last great problem of the Alps" (one of several).

The 1950s saw the first ascents of all the eight-thousanders but two, starting with Annapurna in 1950 by Maurice Herzog and Louis Lachenal. The world's highest mountain (above mean sea level), Mount Everest (8,848 m) was first climbed on May 29, 1953 by Sir Edmund Hillary and Tenzing Norgay from the south side in Nepal. Just a few months later, Hermann Buhl made the first ascent of Nanga Parbat (8,125 m), a siege style expedition culminating in a remarkable solo push for the summit, it's the only eight-thousander to be summited solo on the first ascent. K2 (8,611 m), the second highest peak in the world was first scaled in 1954. In 1964, the final eight-thousander to be climbed was Shishapangma (8,013 m), the lowest of all the 8,000 metre peaks.

BIBLIOGRAPHY

- The Development of Social Network Analysis Vancouver: Empirical Press.
- Cox, Steven M. and Kris Fulsaas, ed., ed (2003-09). Mountaineering: The Freedom of the Hills (7 ed.). Seattle: The Mountaineers. ISBN 0898868289.
- Cymerman, A; Rock, PB. Medical Problems in High Mountain Environments. A Handbook for Medical Officers. USARIEM-TN94-2. US Army Research Inst. of Environmental Medicine Thermal and Mountain Medicine Division Technical Report.
- Hamilton, AJ. Biomedical Aspects of Military Operations at High Altitude. USARIEM-M-30/88. US Army Research Inst. of Environmental Medicine Thermal and Mountain Medicine Division Technical Report.
- Roach, Robert; Stepanek, Jan; and Hackett, Peter. (2002). "24". Acute Mountain Sickness and High-Altitude Cerebral Edema. In: Medical Aspects of Harsh Environments.
- Roach, James M. and Schoene, Robert B. (2002). "25". High-Altitude Pulmonary Edema. In: Medical Aspects of Harsh Environments. 2. Washington, DC.
- Muza, SR; Fulco, CS; Cymerman, A (2004). "Altitude Acclimatization Guide.". US Army Research Inst. of

Environmental Medicine Thermal and Mountain Medicine Division Technical Report (USARIEM-TN-04-05).

- Mountainous plateau creates ozone "halo" around Tibet

- Lynn Thorndike, Renaissance or Prenaissance, Journal of the History of Ideas, Vol. 4, No. 1. (Jan., 1943), pp. 69-74.

- The Ascent of Mount Ventoux http://www.idehist.uu.se/distans/ilmh/Ren/ren-pet-ventoux.htm http://www.fordham.edu/halsall/source/petrarch-ventoux.html http://petrarch.petersadlon.com/read_letters.html?s=pet17.html

- Cameron, Ian (1990). Kingdom of the Sun God: a history of the Andes and their people. New York: Facts on File. pp. 174-175. ISBN 0-8160-2581-9.

- Mackinder, Halford John (May 1900). "A Journey to the Summit of Mount Kenya, British East Africa". The Geographical Journal 15 (5): 453-476. doi:10.2307/1774261.

- Cohen, Michael P., The History of the Sierra Club 1892-1970 (Sierra Club Books, San Francisco, 1988) ISBN 0-87156-732-6

- Which Events are Olympic? Olympics at Sports Reference.com, 2008

- Pagen, Dennis (January 1992). Understanding the Sky - A Sport Pilot's Guide to Flying Conditions. Mingoville, Pennsylvania, USA: Dennis Pagen. pp. 280. ISBN 13: 978-0936310107.

- Mike Barber needed to fly 1% further than Ruhmer's 435 miles (700 km) in order to break the official FAI record; Barber needed to fly only 3 more miles for a total of 440 miles (710 km). Barber's flight remains the longest hang glider flight ever.

- Chronology of the FAI World Hang Gliding Championships

- The Equity: "Esprit rafting to be featured in commercial". Wednesday, May 14th, 2008, print edition

• AJ Hackett (2008). Welcome to Cairns. Retrieved on 17 October 2008.

• Jungle Bungy Jump (2008). Phuket Thailand.

• Kockelman JW, Hubbard M. Bungee jumping cord design using a simple model. Sports Engineering 2004; 7(2):89-96.

• AJ Hackett (2008). History. Retrieved on 17 October 2008.

• Eric Larson, 2003 p135, The Devil in the White City; Murder, Magic, and Madness at the Fair that Changed America. Citing Chicago Tribune, Nov. 9, 1889.

• Aerial Extreme Sports (2008). History of Bungee.

• "Can you Hackett?". Unlimited - Inspiring Business. 23 August 2004.

• "AJ Hackett Bungy". Bungy.co.nz.

• "Guinness World Record - the Highest Commercial Decelerator Descent". Macautower.com.mo. 2005-08-17. http://www.macautower.com.mo/eng/press/award02.asp.

• CRUZ FILHO, F. Murillo, Bartolomeu Lourenço de Gusmão: Sua Obra e o Significado Fáustico de Sua Vida, Rio de Janeiro, Biblioteca Reprográfica Xerox, 1985

• SILVA, Inocencio da, ARANHA, Brito, Diccionario Bibliographico Portuguez, Lisboa, Imprensa Nacional, T. I, pp. 332-334

• TAUNAY, Affonso d'Escragnolle, Bartolomeu de Gusmão: inventor do aerostato: a vida e a obra do primeiro inventor americano, S. Paulo, Leia, 1942

• TAUNAY, Affonso d'Escragnolle, Bartholomeu de Gusmão e a sua prioridade aerostatica, S. Paulo: Escolas Profissionaes Salesianas, 1935, Sep. do Annuario da Escola Polytechnica da Univ. de São Paulo, 1935

- "FAI Ballooning Commission Achievements". Fédération Aéronautique Internationale. http://www.fai.org/ballooning/achieve.asp. Retrieved 2010-04-11. "A list of notable balloon and airship flights has been assembled by Hans Åkerstedt from Sweden. The list has been compiled with much help from Troy Bradley, USA and Norman Pritchard, UK. Information from many other sources have also been used - FAI record files, personal log books and commercially available literature."

- "CIA Notable flights and performances: Part 01, 0000-1785". Svenska Ballong Federationen. http://www.ballong.org/notable/rpt00.php?num=01&period=0000-1785.

- "Date 1709-08-08 Pilot: Bartholomeu Lourenço de Gusmão, Earliest recorded model balloon flight."

- "CIA Notable flights and performances: Part 01, 0000-1785". Svenska Ballong Federationen. http://www.ballong.org/notable/rpt00.php?num=01&period=0000-1785. Retrieved 2010-04-11. "Date 1783-11-21 Pilot: Jean-François Pilâtre de Rozier, First recorded manned flight."

- Bruce, Eric Stuart (1914). Aircraft in war. London: Hodder and Stoughton. pp. 8. http://www.archive.org/stream/aircraftinwar00brucuoft#page/8/mode/1up.

Index